THE PARTHENON MARBLES DISPUTE

Why are we still arguing over the Parthenon Marbles? This book provides a new take on the history of those famous pieces of ancient sculpture removed from the Acropolis in Athens by Lord Elgin's men in the early 19th century, explaining how they became the cause célèbre of the larger debate around cultural heritage and restitution now taking place. The subject is one that is currently embroiling museums, governments, universities, and the public at large.

The book offers a balanced and thorough account of the history of the Marbles from a critical perspective, while considering the legalities of their initial removal and the ethics of their retention by the British Museum. It incorporates the views of curators, museum directors, lawyers, archaeologists, politicians and others in both London and Athens. It explains why this particular dispute has not been satisfactorily resolved, and suggests new ways of seeking resolution – for the Parthenon Marbles, as well as for the many other cultural treasures held in museum collections outside their countries of origin. Importantly, the book offers a way forward for these disputes based on evidence of past practice, legal rules around the transfer of cultural objects and the role of museums in negotiating outcomes on the basis of international exchanges.

Volume 1 in the Art Law Library series

T0281866

The Art Law Library

The Art Law Library includes books on all aspects of the law relating to art in its widest sense, including antiquities, museums, intangible cultural heritage, archives, intellectual property and human remains. Titles in the series are invaluable to those working and studying in the fields of law, museums, galleries, libraries, planning, archaeology and law enforcement. The series continues the imprint of the Institute of Art and Law.

Series Editor: Ruth Redmond-Cooper, Editor of Art Antiquity and Law, *and founder of the Institute of Art and Law*

The Parthenon Marbles Dispute

Heritage, Law, Politics

Alexander Herman

·HART·

OXFORD · LONDON · NEW YORK · NEW DELHI · SYDNEY

HART PUBLISHING

Bloomsbury Publishing Plc

Kemp House, Chawley Park, Cumnor Hill, Oxford, OX2 9PH, UK

1385 Broadway, New York, NY 10018, USA

29 Earlsfort Terrace, Dublin 2, Ireland

HART PUBLISHING, the Hart/Stag logo, BLOOMSBURY and the Diana logo are
trademarks of Bloomsbury Publishing Plc

First published in Great Britain 2023

Reprinted 2024

A catalogue record for this book is available from the British Library.

A catalogue record for this book is available from the Library of Congress.

Library of Congress Control Number: 2023941768

ISBN:	PB:	978-1-50996-717-9
	ePDF:	978-1-50996-720-9
	ePub:	978-1-50996-719-3

Typeset by Compuscript Ltd, Shannon
Printed and bound in Great Britain by CPI Group (UK) Ltd, Croydon CR0 4YY

To find out more about our authors and books visit www.hartpublishing.co.uk.
Here you will find extracts, author information, details of forthcoming events
and the option to sign up for our newsletters.

Dedicated to the memory of four men who laboured and delighted in the shadow of the Parthenon –

Norman Palmer, Dimitrios Pandermalis, Ian Jenkins and William St Clair

ACKNOWLEDGEMENTS

I am most grateful to all those who offered insight and helping hands as I worked through the text that became this book: above all Ruth Redmond-Cooper, as well as Emily Gould, Geoffrey Bennett, Katerina Vagia, Stratos Lampousis, Elena Lampousis, Lilian Palmer, Debbie De Girolamo, Chiara Gallo, Thomas Harrison, Lesley Fitton, Dominic Spenser Underhill and Ana-Maria Herman. Thanks are also due to Changyue Yin, Artemis Papathanassiou, Matthew Taylor, Anna Bonini, Frances Halahan, Hugh Johnson-Gilbert and the Melina Mercouri Foundation. Finally, I am indebted to Roberta Bassi and the great team at Hart / Bloomsbury for bringing everything together so seamlessly.

The author and publisher gratefully acknowledge the permissions granted to reproduce the copyright material in this book.

Every effort has been made to trace copyright holders and to obtain their permission for the use of copyright material. The publisher apologises for any errors or omissions in the above list and would be grateful if notified of any corrections that should be incorporated in future reprints or editions of this book.

TABLE OF CONTENTS

LIST OF FIGURES

Introduction: A Matter Still Unresolved

Why do we still argue over the Parthenon Marbles? Why do they still capture our attention after all these years? They are, after all, discoloured carvings of figures that few would be able to identify without the help of a label. Many show mythological stories and gods that no one believes in anymore. Most are severely damaged and fragmentary: a disjointed procession; the legs of riderless horses; an incomplete pantheon; the remnants of a foot; a pair of handless arms raised to the sky. At times they have been called 'mutilated objects', 'misshapen monuments' and a 'mass of ruins'.[1] Yet every few years, a door opens wide enough for commentators of all stripes to express their views on the topic, only for it to then close again within months, without much of anything having been settled.

Practically everything about the Parthenon Marbles is contentious. Even the term itself. While it remains imperfect, it is at least marginally better than its competitors: the 'Elgin Marbles' and the 'Parthenon Sculptures', each of which has significant shortcomings.[2] And while not all the pieces at issue came from the Parthenon itself, the great majority – and the most symbolically prized – certainly did. The term is therefore a useful shorthand, a recognisable and effective way of denoting the artefacts fought over between Greece and the UK – or more precisely, between Greece and the British Museum – in what has become the world's longest-running high-profile cultural dispute.

The 'Parthenon Marbles' consist of about 90 large pieces of ancient sculpted marble (and several smaller fragments) originating from the Parthenon in Athens and now held at the British Museum.[3] These are separate from, though related to, those pieces from other classical buildings on the Acropolis also held at the British Museum.[4] The Marbles were, as many know, removed by men working in Athens under a British diplomat, the Earl of Elgin, in the first years of the nineteenth century. The legitimacy of that removal has always been a matter of dispute. Even during the Parliamentary debate of 1816, the one that led to the acquisition of the Marbles by the British Museum, accusations were made that the Marbles should never have left Athens in the first place. The arguments used on both sides of that debate – and indeed the strong feelings it elicited – have hardly progressed in the intervening two hundred years. Only the mouthpieces have changed.

But why such a fuss over dismembered sculptures of the ancient past? One apparent answer might be that they mean a great deal to Greece and yet Greece does not possess them. In that vein they have been called 'the essence of Greekness', 'the noblest symbol of excellence' and (for Greeks) 'our flag, our identity, our language'.[5] They come from a monument, the Parthenon, that stands tall in the Greek capital (if imperfectly) and is very much at the centre of the country's heritage and identity today. As specimens of architectural sculpture, they were originally made to be part of that monument. And yet they have remained for over 200 years in another country, held in a museum that has not once manifested an intention to permanently relinquish them. As such, this might resemble a straightforward property dispute: one party has something that the other party feels entitled to own. Such disputes are commonly dealt with by courts of law around the world. And yet this dispute is different. It has never been capable of resolution, judicial or otherwise. More importantly, it does not seem to *go away*: it has persisted for years – stretching back all the way to 1816 – with few signs of ever abating. It continues to serve as a point of contention in the cultural discourse, far more deep-seated than any fight over family heirlooms or a plot of farmland. As one Keeper from the British Museum wrote in a private report back in 1991: "The problem has not gone away, it is merely in hibernation; and when it wakes up, our successors will find that it is fiercer than before."[6] Judging by what has transpired over the past 30 years, his premonition has proven uncannily accurate.

Recently, the most noteworthy advocate for return has been the Greek Prime Minister. Kyriakos Mitsotakis is a vigorous and reforming figure in Greek politics, a member of the centre-right New Democracy party who has taken staunchly conservative stances on public spending and the migrant crisis. And yet he is also committed to the cause of recovering the Marbles. During a state visit to the UK in November 2021, he made an appearance on British television. 'I think the general approach that these Marbles belong to the British Museum because they have been there so long is anachronistic,' he said. 'We want the sculptures back for good – and we will not accept a loan.'[7] While passionate and patriotic statements will inevitably flow from the mouths of politicians, in Greece an overwhelming majority does appear to care deeply about the issue and to desire the Marbles' return. In 2014, for example, a survey of 1000 Greeks found that 96 per cent knew at least something about the Parthenon Marbles dispute, while 93 per cent said reunification of the Marbles was of extreme importance to the country.[8] Remarkably, this poll was conducted in the midst of the Greek financial crisis, and yet the strength of feeling on the issue nevertheless persisted.

Part of the reason for this attachment stems from the cultural identity of modern Greece. For many Greeks, the Parthenon and its sculptures represent a link with the ancient past, and more specifically with that quintessential epoch of classical Athens. The period remains important because of the developments it brought forth in art, architecture, philosophy, theatre, politics, poetry and mathematics. It is reflected in the respect shown today for archaeological sites, in the museums, in the dramas and comedies still performed, on postage stamps and the old banknotes, in school textbooks – and in the reproduction of the Marbles on display at the Akropoli station of the Athens Metro.[9] The fifth century BCE still elicits pride for Greeks, and Athenians in particular, despite (or perhaps because of) some of the darker episodes of the country's more recent past. 'When we walk around the sites from that period', someone explained to me in Greece, 'we are in awe of our own history'.[10] The Parthenon and its sculptures are a vital part of that history – like a time capsule containing everything worth keeping from a particular moment in the past – and the existence of many of the dismembered pieces in a foreign land seems inexplicable, if not repugnant, to many Greeks.[11]

But if cultural identity helps to explain the importance of the Marbles in Greece, it might say something about the position in Britain as well. The resistance to returning the Marbles has much to do with the twin sentiments of conservatism and irritation, often heard in the telling phrase, 'leave well enough alone'.[12] But these sentiments may have their own causes linked to the particular culture of Britain. The British Museum is an important part of that culture and has, since it opened to the public in 1759, been at the heart of the country's cultural evolution, from the first acquisitions to the golden age of collecting to the opening of the Great Court at the turn of the Millennium. The collections acquired over this period have come to mean a great deal to curators, directors, managers and trustees of the Museum, not to mention the researchers who delve into the holdings and the visitors who frequent the galleries; equally meaningful are the traditions and procedures that allowed the institution to grow as it did, and to thrive. The Parthenon Marbles have come to form part of this history as well. Those with the power to decide the issue are unlikely to want to simply give them all away, no matter what moral or legal foundation might form the basis of the handover. An alternative footing would need to be found.

The Deepening Chasm

If the Marbles today unite the Greeks, they divide the British. One reason why the dispute continues is that a significant portion of the British population does indeed support the principle of returning the Marbles. Opinion polls conducted in the UK have continually shown a majority in this camp, while only a minority believes the Marbles should remain at the British Museum: between 2017 and 2021, for instance, support for return hovered just below 60 per cent while support for retaining stayed around 20 per cent; a 3-to-1 ratio favouring return.[13] Added to this are the very vocal proponents of return and reunification from within the UK itself.

It could be said that the progenitor of many latter-day campaigns was the poet Lord Byron. Byron, who had been in Athens in 1809 and seen some of the Marbles crated up and shipped off, lambasted Elgin for removing the sculptures from the great monument, referring to his fellow aristocrat in the poem *Childe Harold's Pilgrimage* as 'the last, the worst, dull spoiler', wishing instead for the Marbles to remain on the Parthenon and to melt into the landscape. Many have taken their cue from Byron, in word if not in deed (as is well known, Byron died during the

War of Greek Independence in 1824). Lawyer Frederic Harrison wrote a celebrated article in the British press in 1890 entitled 'Return the Elgin Marbles', in which he argued that the Marbles were 'to the Greek nation a thousand times more dear and more important than they can ever be to the English nation, which simply bought them.'[14] And later, during World War II, Britain came as close as ever to handing the Marbles to Greece as a reward for the little country's heroic stand against the Fascists.[15]

Then, in 1983, inspired by Greece's diplomatic claim for return, an organisation called the British Committee for the Restitution of the Parthenon Marbles was founded and began recruiting prominent figures to the cause, including professors, actors, broadcasters and writers. They were joined by journalist and gadfly Christopher Hitchens. Hitchens wrote a book in 1987 entitled *The Elgin Marbles: Should They Be Returned to Greece?* in which he neatly set out the case for return (later editions of the book appeared in 1997 and 2008). After he died in 2011, the torch passed to his friend, the actor and writer Stephen Fry, who for many years has served as the public face of the campaign. More recently, an organisation called the Parthenon Project has entered the fray, seeking the return of the Marbles on the basis of a 'win-win' arrangement with the British Museum. The organisation, funded by a Greek-Canadian businessman, has an advisory board that consists of impressive figures from the British establishment, including Parliamentarians such as former Arts Minister Ed Vaizey and former Culture Secretary Ben Bradshaw, as well as Fry himself.

Despite the arguments, the impressive list of luminaries and the consistently high level of public support, no attempt has yet succeeded. The UK Government has remained staunch in its support of the status quo, claiming repeatedly that the Marbles were legitimately acquired by Lord Elgin, that they belong at the British Museum and that the existing law in the UK (the British Museum Act 1963) prevents the Trustees from returning the collection in any event. This has been the response whether the government of the day has been Conservative or Labour. The latest iterations have come from the mouths of successive Prime Ministers: Boris Johnson in 2021, Liz Truss in 2022 and Rishi Sunak in 2023.[16] Incredibly, the official position has barely changed since 1984, the year of the formal rejection of Greece's diplomatic claim. Similarly, the Trustees of the British Museum have maintained a firm stance over time, adducing the legal acquisition, the world-class institution, the importance of seeing the Marbles in the context of other great civilisations and the legal restrictions imposed upon them.[17]

And so, for many years, the battle lines have been drawn. They divide the sides into two distinct camps. One argues that the Marbles were wrongfully taken and should be returned; the other views the initial removal as legitimate and applauds the British Museum's retention of the pieces in the collection.[18] But both camps, in their extreme variations, are problematic. The side that paints Elgin as a despoiler of sweetness and light often falls prey to naïveté when considering the situation that prevailed in Athens in 1801. And while the appeal to 'send them home' might have a pleasing ring, it tends to overlook the vital role played by institutions such as the British Museum in managing, curating and caring for valuable and sensitive artefacts. On the other hand, many on the retentionist side have no moral qualms with a removal that occurred while the Greeks were subjected to a brutal Ottoman rule, that involved significant damage to the pieces themselves and that was facilitated by bribery. They often claim that artefacts are better managed and serve a more utilitarian purpose in large universal museums today than they would in their countries of origin.

All of which has proven classicist Mary Beard correct in her diagnosis of the dispute more than 20 years ago that 'there have been bad arguments on both sides'.[19] And yet, despite the often unappetising nature of the positions, a surprising number of supporters still seems to congregate around each camp. At times it has felt as though the chasm dividing the two has only continued to grow.

On the cover of this book is a metope originally from the Parthenon's south entablature and now at the British Museum. Here we see a duel between a lapith and a centaur. The lapith is crouched on the ground as the centaur careens over him, his fist landing squarely on the centaur's exposed abdomen. Who in this scene is stronger? Who is about to deliver the final blow? Who will ultimately win the fight? The figures are hardened into place: for centuries they have been engaged in a battle frozen in time, without forward movement and lacking any finality. We see a raised arm, a fist, a rock ready to be flung at an adversary: each a sign of hope, of resilience, but also one of violent intent, a poised threat, an indication that the situation is in a state of arrested development. This image neatly evokes the status of the dispute over the Parthenon Marbles. Is there a way to somehow shift the ground beneath the parties? Will it ever be possible to break the persisting deadlock? Is there a way forward?

A New Turn

Change may well be at hand. Very recently the sound of the usual refrains has begun to subside. Part of this is due to the wider changes affecting society. The 'restitution' of cultural artefacts – their return as a way of doing justice for past wrongs – has become one of the central cultural issues of our time.[20] Now museums everywhere are addressing contentious artefacts in their collections and, in many instances, are returning pieces to their homelands. This is especially true in the context of returns to countries in Africa, a movement prompted by French President Emmanuel Macron and taken up in Germany, Belgium and the Netherlands. Certain institutions in the UK have also followed suit, with returns to Nigeria from institutions in Cambridge, Glasgow, Aberdeen and London.[21] But the change goes further, revealing a growing recognition in the museum sector that some of the traditional arguments against restitution are beginning to wear thin. Even the Pope has returned three Parthenon fragments from the Vatican collection to Athens, couching it as an ecumenical 'donation' to the Archbishop of Athens.[22]

Added to this is the general shift in mentality brought about by the COVID-19 pandemic. As can often happen after times of great societal upheaval, there appears to be a greater urgency to make right some of the lingering injustices of the past, especially in the context of slavery, racism and colonialism. The lockdowns that saw museums close for months have also allowed many to question some of the inherited assumptions about the continuity and consistency of cultural collections. When museums shifted to an entirely online presence, it began to make the unconditional attachment to physical property look increasingly out-of-step with society's general move towards all things digital. Taken together, many museums can now be seen to have entered a 'restitution paradigm'.[23]

Against this backdrop, we have perhaps seen the most surprising move of all coming from the British Museum itself. This was triggered by the former Chancellor of the Exchequer, George Osborne, who was appointed Chair of Trustees in 2021. Osborne surprised many when he said during a televised interview that there was 'a deal to be done' on the Parthenon Marbles.[24] This was the first time a senior representative of the institution had publicly expressed a real willingness to seek out a negotiated solution with Greek officials. It has even led the Museum to refer now to a 'Parthenon Partnership' and to refrain from some of the usual defensiveness of the past.[25] In the meantime it has transpired that Osborne and his colleagues have been holding a series of secret meetings with Greek representatives, sparked by Mitsotakis's state visit in November 2021.

But will this lead to a resolution of the dispute? Neither Osborne nor the Museum appears to have any intention of transferring title in the Marbles to Greece. In the first instance, this would be precluded by the terms of the British Museum Act 1963, which imposes severe restrictions on the Trustees' ability to dispose of objects from the collection. Secondly, it has been made clear in Osborne's public statements that the Marbles would still remain a fundamental part of the Museum's collection. As he said in his annual speech to the Trustees in November 2022, 'creating this global British Museum was the dedicated work of many generations. Dismantling it must not become the careless act of a single generation.'[26] Whatever the outcome of the negotiations, any deal with Greece would almost certainly need to be predicated around a series of long-term loans, potentially substantial ones, but with title remaining vested in the Trustees.

In the context of the longer dispute, the Museum's change of tack represents a watershed. But it is by no means guaranteed that it will lead to a satisfactory result. To begin, Mitsotakis has already made clear that a 'loan' of the Marbles would not suffice, so there would need to be some way of bridging the obvious divide. Next, a 'deal' might contradict the frequently reiterated position of the UK Government, so any financial support from public sources and changes to laws and regulations to facilitate the arrangement would be difficult for the Museum to secure. Lastly, the dispute has persisted for so long, and the relationships between the parties are now so damaged, that any solution may need to address matters that go beyond the 'mere' sharing of physical artefacts.

And yet, despite all this, there remains a very real possibility for change. This might in fact offer a unique opportunity for the British Museum to seek out a reasonable solution and resolve the dispute once and for all. Such a solution would not fall entirely on one side or the other of the traditional divide, but would take root in the considerable space between: a territory so often ignored that might prove fruitful. This could be good for Greece, good for the UK and good for the British Museum. A solution to this problem would demonstrate what can happen when parties locked in a dispute, their viewpoints entrenched, decide to change the tenor of the conversation. If they come together in a way that allows them to mend a frayed relationship this might offer a model for what can be achieved elsewhere. It would show that even the most longstanding disputes can be resolved in a way that, even if not entirely optimal to each party, is at least broadly acceptable to them both.

The Present Structure

In my attempt to consider the possible pathways forward, I will address a great number of factors relating to the Marbles, each of which has a bearing on the dispute itself. This will begin in chapter one with an overview of the eventful history of the Marbles from the construction of the Parthenon to the end of the eighteenth century and the eve of the arrival of Elgin's men in Athens. I will also take account of how the symbolic value of the Parthenon has developed over the centuries. Next, in chapter two, I will turn to the story of the removal of the Marbles from the Acropolis, with an attempt to highlight the contextual factors that allowed the deed to be done. Part of my intention is to downplay the role of Elgin himself. The debate over the Marbles has long been marred by unhelpful attacks on the character of Lord Elgin – and by equally unhelpful attempts at his vindication. In truth, as we shall see, his role was quite limited in the overall undertaking. Perhaps a recognition of this fact can allow the parties in the dispute to move 'beyond Elgin'.

Chapter three will consider the overall legality of the removal, as well as assessing it on ethical terms (two perspectives that do not necessarily align). In this investigation, new insights will be offered into the relevant legal documents of the time, several of which have only recently come to light through archival research. Chapter four will then recount the history of the Marbles from their arrival in Britain and their eventual acquisition by the British Museum, which followed a detailed report by a select committee and a fulsome debate in Parliament. This will provide an opportunity to assess the arguments from both sides of the debate, arguments which have remained largely unchanged over the intervening centuries.

In chapter five, I will look at the impact in Greece of the Marbles' departure, beginning at the point of Greek independence in 1832. This will prompt reflections on the importance to the newly-established country of the ancient past, as well as the controversy over the Marbles that simmered throughout the nineteenth and most of the twentieth century before erupting in the early 1980s. I will explore why matters developed in this way and whether there were moments when resolution could conceivably have been achieved. The account will then bring us to the present, to those recent suggestions of a potential deal between the British Museum and Greece.

The legal analysis will resume in chapter six, which concerns the Trustees' title to the Marbles, seeing this in relation to the inherent volatility of title. Following this, I will investigate whether an arrangement short of transferring title could succeed along the lines of recent suggestions. The chapter will end with an assessment of the legal vehicles that might serve to achieve such aims, including the availability of immunity from seizure if the Marbles do travel to Greece.

In chapter seven, I will consider matters relating to international law and whether they could have an impact on the dispute. It will begin with a consideration of an episode that broadly paralleled the acquisition of the Marbles: the return in 1815 of hundreds of works of art from Paris taken by Napoleon from across Europe, a policy championed by Great Britain. This will then spur an examination of the nineteenth century law of nations and the views on looted art at the time. The analysis will shift to contemporary international law, asking whether a case could be made (as some have suggested) that the retention of the Marbles constitutes a violation of a custom of international law.

Chapter eight then takes us to Athens. While there, I consider the current Greek view and ask why the Marbles continue to mean so much to the Greek political classes and, broadly speaking, the population as a whole. This will be compared to the British approach on cultural matters. I will query whether there is room for compromise. In chapter nine, I will look to the other side of the debate, locating it squarely within the walls of the British Museum. This will involve asking questions about the position of the Museum and seeing what ulterior reasons may exist to explain the longstanding conservatism of the institution and the Museum's champions in the political arena.

Finally, in chapter ten, I will bring all this together to see whether, despite the longevity of the dispute, the entrenchment of the positions and the damage done to the parties' relationship, there may be a way forward. The assessment will involve measuring this particular conflict against some of the leading theories on dispute resolution. If lingering problems can be addressed, the parties may be able to move forward in a sensible way. But much work still needs to be done.

Each chapter has a critical role to play in the book. Only by fully investigating the meaning of the Marbles, their removal and acquisition, their legal and ethical status, their position within international law and the opinions held about them both in Greece and in Britain can we hope to advance the discussion. Until then, it will be difficult – if not impossible – to move forward in any meaningful way.

If it is an attempt at facilitating a resolution, this book is not an advocacy piece. It does not promote the wholesale return nor the wholesale retention of the Marbles. Many such books and articles have been written in the past. But it is not an exercise in feeble neutrality either. While I will draw on existing literature – and the many compelling stories within the long saga of the Parthenon Marbles – I hope to provide much that is new as well, allowing readers to draw their own conclusions on many of the central themes at issue. This can hopefully bring the dispute one step closer to resolution. Or it may, at the very least, open up a new and exciting episode for all involved.

1

From the Slopes of Mount Pentelikos

I begin my journey on a hill in Greece, but it is not the Acropolis. It is an enormous mountain range to the northeast of Athens with many peaks. On one side is a vast quarry and at the mountain's tallest point (1,100 m) stands a modern radio tower. It is called Πεντελικό όρος ('Pentelikos Mountain') by the Greeks, an obvious link to its ancient name familiar to scholars, Mount Pentelicus.

The mountain is unique by reason of the pristine white marble found within. It was from these slopes that the Athenians of the fifth century BCE quarried the raw material that would be carved into blocks, steps, columns, capitals, architraves, frieze panels, metopes and figures for the Parthenon and other temples on the Acropolis. One can still see today the glistening white specks on the mountainside amidst the pines and patches of red earth, like scatterings of ivory across the landscape.

I have been brought here by a friend who has hired a local driver for us.[1] Apparently only a local can navigate the backroads that lead up the mountain. There are no tour buses here; and we even seem to be beyond the realm of GPS functionality. From the moment we take our seats in the car, the driver begins a monologue in Greek at lightning speed, with my friend doing her best to interpret for me. The driver talks of forest fires plaguing the mountain over the past 20 years, a series of underground tunnels that supposedly connect Penteli to the Hotel Grande Bretagne in downtown Athens, and the German rock band Scorpions who recently performed at the Kallimarmaro Stadium, itself built from Pentelic marble for the first modern Olympic Games of 1896. I barely have time to catch my breath before we arrive at the mountain's upper reaches.

When we come to a plateau, the car stops. I get out. I leave my friend and the driver to continue their conversation and I slowly begin the hike over rocks and past patches of dry shrubbery. The sweet fragrance from the yellow *sparti* flower surrounds me. I soon find what I am looking for: a series of mounds protruding here and there from the ground: Pentelic marble (see Figure 1). It is tempting to imagine these pieces being selected by ancient surveyors, dug out by labourers and loaded onto wooden carts ahead of that momentous descent.[2] But of course the choice pieces were all taken away. What remains are those deemed unworthy, these imperfect rocks that history has left behind.

Figure 1 The rock face atop Pentelikos Mountain, north of Athens, reveals part of the white Pentelic marble found within
Source: © Alexander Herman, 2018.

From my perch, I can survey the shimmering Athenian sprawl, which starts in the distance, but has made its way to the foot of the mountain and has even begun, following a spate of recent forest fires, to creep up the far side. In the distance I first make out the pyramid-shaped Lykavittos Hill and then, squinting, the flat top of the Acropolis to the right of it. One marvels at the distance. It beggars belief that ancient engineers were capable of designing and laying a road that stretched the full 15 km to the centre of Athens. Along this road each of the blocks would have been pulled: more than 2,000 in total.[3] Ten years ago, parts of the road were discovered just behind a row of shops in the nearby suburb of Halandri, and one must pity the poor shopkeeper upon whose land great archaeological works are now to be done.[4] Still, when compared with other sourcing routes of the period, the distance is not particularly long. Many temples and sculptures in Athens and elsewhere were made of marble from the island of Paros, over 200 km away.[5] But what is interesting here is that, despite having access to the most developed trade routes of the ancient world, Athens chose to use *Attic* material. From the very beginning, the project of building the Parthenon and its sister structures would be an intensely local one. Whatever its causes, the choice was telling.

The Periclean Project

The plan to beautify Athens and its environs with new temples and public monuments was undertaken at a high point of Athenian pride, what we might even call chauvinism. As the leader of the Delian League, a confederation of Greek city-states founded in 478 BCE, Athens had effectively seen off the threat of invasion from the Persians through the dominance of its navy. With Athenian ships now patrolling the Aegean, and with a peace treaty concluded with the Persian Empire in 449, the duties paid by other Greek city-states were soon diverted to Athens. Indicative of this is the fact that from 454 onwards, the tributes were no longer stored in the treasury of the remote and inoffensive island of Delos, but on the Acropolis itself.[6] This was starting to look like an empire – a particularly Athenian empire.

So what was to be done with the city's newfound glory and the money that came with it? More virtuous polities may have conserved it; lesser ones would have wasted it: but the proud city chose to anoint itself with new structures that celebrated its great achievements and its mythological history. This would consist of five new temples, spread across Attica. The intention was to commemorate the gods that held a special place for the Athenians: a temple dedicated to Hephaestus in the Agora, one to Poseidon on the cape of Sounion to the south, one to Nemesis near the battle site of Marathon and one to Ares on the outskirts of the city.[7] But the most important of these would be the great tribute to the patron goddess from whom the city took its name, Athena. For her would be reserved the most important place atop the Acropolis, in a temple that would form the architectural culmination of all the others, and indeed of the city itself.

The choice of this particular site for a monument to Athena was no surprise. The hill had long been associated with her ancient cult. An olive tree, said to be a gift from the goddess to the good people of Athens, providing them with sustenance through trade, grew near the northern slope. An early cult statue made of olivewood, the 'xoanon', had been worshipped at an altar here for at least two centuries.[8] In the sixth century BCE, an archaic temple dedicated to Athena had been built on the Acropolis, one which featured in its pediment a fearsome-looking goddess attacking the giant Engelados, whom she famously hurled into the Mediterranean Sea and covered with the island of Sicily.

This early temple, and all other structures on the hill, had been left as smouldering ruins by the Persians after they had sacked the city in 480. For over a generation thereafter, the Athenians were said to have kept an oath not to build upon the rubble, keeping it instead as 'a memorial of the Barbarian's impiety'.[9] It was only once the Persian threat had been kept safely at bay that Athenian confidence returned. New structures would be erected on the site, including two large statues of Athena: the first in bronze and facing the city; the other was the chryselephantine 'virgin' (Παρθένος or 'Parthenos') made of wood but covered in plaques of gold and ivory.[10] It was this second Athena that would warrant her own edifice: the Parthenon, which would double as a storage house for the tributes paid by the other city-states of the (now nominal) Greek confederacy.

According to the Roman historian Plutarch (46–120 CE), writing many centuries later, the most impressive feat was the speed at which the Parthenon was built.[11] And this was no hasty building project either, but instead comprised that rare combination of scale, quality and punctuality. Begun in 447 BCE, the overall structure was completed in less than 10 years with some of the sculptures (notably the pediment pieces) needing a further five to be finished and hoisted into place. So it took barely a decade to quarry, transport, fashion, assemble and refine the many pieces of marble, and a little longer to add the finishing touches.[12] Sources indicate that Ictinus was the architect, that Callicrates was the designer, and that Phidias, the greatest sculptor of antiquity, created the statue of Athena Parthenos inside – and was quite possibly also in charge of the sculptural designs for the entire building, though this role has been frustratingly unconfirmed by the archaeological evidence.[13] None of it would have been possible without political leadership, which came in the form of the most brilliant Athenian statesman of all, Pericles.

Pericles was, by all accounts, a great orator.[14] He rose to prominence following success as a soldier during the first Peloponnesian War between Athens and Sparta (460–445), and for over 20 years dominated the political scene of an increasingly radical democracy in Athens. Between 450 and 429, he won almost every election in which he stood and served in this period as one of the 10 'strategoi', men given the privilege of first addressing the assembly of Athenian citizens.[15] Having a silver tongue is undoubtedly a great advantage in a society where public debate and persuasion are held dear, but for Pericles it was especially valuable. While he succeeded in passing a number of legislative proposals, the most important – in terms of the present discussion – was the civic plan to beautify the city and to celebrate its greatness.

This was a costly project. Reports show that many in Athens were initially unimpressed with the idea of building anew on what had effectively become a war memorial.[16] It would be hugely expensive, with much of the money to be taken directly from the tributes paid by the city's allies for the purposes of defending Greece against the Persians. But Pericles was convincing. He spoke to the assembly: since the city had already equipped itself for war, it was only right that the abundance be used on projects that would 'bring her everlasting glory' and that would, in fact, be a unique employment opportunity for the citizenry.[17] It would require carpenters, modellers, metalworkers, stonemasons, dyers, gilders, painters and more; every male in the city who was not fighting in the army could therefore be employed on the project.[18] The assembled citizens, it seems, could not help but agree. And so the great temple, along with an impressive gateway and two smaller structures, would be built. As a public works project, it would serve as the most enduring of gifts.

The Sculptures Explained

The famous sculptures that formed part of the Parthenon can be divided into three principal categories – pediment sculptures, metopes and the frieze – in addition to other architectural pieces. The pediment sculptures featured larger-than-life figures that came from the triangular pediments under the roof at both the west and east ends of the building. They represented gods and their attendants in two distinct scenes from a particularly Athenian mythology. The west pediment would have been the first one visible upon entering the Acropolis: Athena establishing her supremacy against Poseidon for Athenian allegiance, her fecund olive tree outdoing his mighty trident and its offer of maritime glory. Surrounding the two combatants were the gods Hermes and Iris, both on horse-drawn chariots, local river gods and figures from the royal houses of King Kekrops and Eleusis.[19] Fittingly this scene faced west over the Bay of Salamis, the location of Greece's great naval victory against the Persians in 480 BCE, and evoked the olive tree growing on the same part of the hill since ancient times.[20]

The east pediment would have come into view only after walking past the building. It featured the birth of Athena, a remarkable moment even by mythological standards, since she appeared fully formed, in all her armour, from the head of Zeus, having been hacked free by her half-brother Hephaestus with his axe. Present at the birth were a variety of other gods (Poseidon, Demeter, Persephone, Aphrodite), displaying varying degrees of interest in the scene taking place. The pediment faced east and the morning sun, a fitting position since Athena's birth was said to have occurred at sunrise. The main gods were buttressed by two charioteers, also apt for a morning scene, Helios ascending with the rising sun and Selene descending with the moon, their sets of horses displaying the respective signs of exuberance and fatigue.[21]

The metopes were 92 square vignettes forming part of the entablature along the exterior sides of the Parthenon, above the columns and the architrave and below the overhanging cornice. They were interspersed with lined architectural features or triglyphs, which may have inspired the name 'metope' (μετόπη in Greek translates as 'between the eyes'). The set on each side represented a particular mythical conflict in high relief: immediately beneath the west pediment were scenes of Athenians fighting Amazonians; beneath the east pediment scenes of Gods and Giants; the north side featured Greeks and Trojans; while the south featured the great battle between lapiths and centaurs which had broken out after too much drink during the wedding feast of King Pirithous. There were also striking thematic parallels between the metopes on the east and west ends and the respective pediment scenes above them: the east featured the Gods in both instances atop Mount Olympos, while the west showed two contests over the city of Athens.[22]

Though it is now celebrated as the highlight of the Parthenon's sculptural decoration, the frieze was very unusual in its time, forming a 160 metre-long banner stretching across the top of the inner cella, which would have made it very difficult for anyone to see clearly at the time. Normally friezes were placed on the exterior of buildings or they faced inwards. The scene here was sculpted in low relief with all of the action, sometimes as many as six figures deep, carved into a depth of only six centimetres.[23] It almost certainly presents an idealised version of the Panathenaia, the famous festival that took place every year in honour of Athena, which included a procession up the slopes of the Acropolis to the goddess's effigy, which was covered in a purple cloak known as the *peplos*.[24]

On the frieze, the procession was shown with cavalry and charioteers (and no fewer than 200 horses),[25] parade marshals, elders, sacrificial animals, musicians, maidens with incense, libation bearers and ancient heroes, all leading towards a colloquy of the gods – many of whom also appeared in large format within the pediments, such as Zeus, Hermes, Hephaestus, Poseidon, Apollo, Aphrodite, Demeter, Persephone and of course Athena. The gods sit on either side of a stylised and seemingly unspectacular scene involving a man, a woman, three young children and what appears to be the peplos robe woven for the goddess's effigy. An enormous amount of literature exists on the exact meaning of the peplos scene.[26] Regardless of the differing academic interpretations, all are agreed that the frieze, in its entirety, is among the most stunning examples of art from antiquity, with one classicist calling it 'one of the wonders of the world'.[27]

It is important to note that each sculptural element of the Parthenon – pediment, metopes and frieze – was part of the building's overall design. While some of the pediment figures may have been put into place after the building's initial completion in 438 they were purpose-made to fit within the structure of the gable, exemplified by the river gods at either end of the west pediment lying snugly within the diminishing angle of the roof, or the charioteers of the east pediment appearing to rise out of, or fall into, the sea. The metopes were carved on blocks that formed the entablature of the external façade, while the 107 frieze pieces did the same for the cella and would have been chiselled in situ by artists working high up on the scaffolding. And, as we have seen, many of the figures were carved such that they appeared to directly respond to the geography (Athena's birth, Poseidon facing the sea, and so on). The sense of connection between the sculptures and place, and between the sculptures themselves, is integral to the scheme of the Parthenon.

Three other celebrated buildings of the classical age stood on the Acropolis, each completed only slightly after the Parthenon. The great gateway, the Propylaia (completed circa 432), with its massive Doric columns and impressive central hall, was the means by which all visitors would have entered the sanctuary on the Acropolis, including during the Panathenaiac festival which was depicted on the Parthenon's frieze. The nearby Erechtheion (completed circa 430) had its famous porch of Caryatids, six elegantly robed female figures holding up the roof with their heads, and its colonnade of finely carved Ionic columns. And the small Temple of Athena Nike near the westernmost precipice of the hill (completed circa 420) had an important frieze featuring battle scenes both real and mythological, and an assembly of gods echoing that of the Parthenon, as well as scenes sculpted into the parapet. There were thus echoes in the sculptural motif across the classical buildings of the Acropolis, underlying again the importance of the themes and positioning of each.

The Centrality of the Parthenon

The Parthenon was not the biggest of ancient temples. One must look to Samos or Ephesus for those. Nor was it the first of the Doric order. Such temples had been constructed across the Greek world for at least the previous 100 years. The inclusion of sculpted scenes was not in itself unique either. Images of centaurs fighting lapiths and giants fighting gods, as well as scenes from the Trojan War, had been depicted on other monumental buildings.[28] The ancient travel writer Pausanias, writing in the second century CE, in his account of a visit to Athens made only the briefest mention of the Parthenon as a building, focusing instead on the various tributes around the Acropolis and the sculpture of Athena Parthenos inside.[29] So what makes this monument so important today?

There are perhaps several reasons why the Parthenon has become, more than any other building, the iconic monument of ancient Greece. The first is the result of the context in which it was built, and the meaning of that context today. This was the high point of Athenian democracy, when Pericles was at the peak of his powers and the mechanisms for citizen control of the *polis* were strong (though not, of course, for women or slaves – nor indeed for the non-Athenian Greeks). In a way, the Parthenon was a democratic structure: as noted above, it needed citizen approval to be built and the subject-matter of its frieze included the people of Athens, stylised though they may have been, a true first in Greek monumental sculpture, which until then had featured only scenes of the mythical past.[30] Because today we live in democratic times, we tend to have a predilection for remnants that connect us to the Athenian prototype from two-and-a-half millennia ago.[31] For this reason, the Parthenon as a symbol continues to dominate.

Another explanation of the continuing importance of the Parthenon is that, although no individual architectural feature can be said to be first of its kind or entirely unique, the accumulated whole works perfectly in an overall harmonious scheme.[32] The structure was built according to a consistent 4:9 ratio (the height of the columns to the width of the façade, the diameter of each column to the distance between them, etc). Its designers took pains to offset inevitable optical illusions by subtly piecing it together with sloping lines throughout: the outside columns tilt inwards and the base slopes up towards the middle to ensure that the Parthenon *looks* right.[33] And while examples of pediment sculptures, metopes and a sculpted frieze can be found elsewhere, only on the Parthenon did the three elements come together in such a fulsome display. As classicist RE Wycherley explains, it 'surpassed all other temples in the richness and variety of its sculpture, and in the way in which each element formed part of a single coherent scheme, produced, one likes to think, by the mastermind of Pheidias and carefully worked out by his pupils and subordinates.'[34] No expense had been spared. Deep Athenian pockets, combined with the convincing oratory of Pericles, meant that the building could comprise the very best of everything.

A third reason to explain the Parthenon's primacy today is its symbolic position within the modern Greek State. This is the way one sees it from the vantage point of Mount Pentelikos, looking down at the vast metropolis, as the twinkling speck at its very centre. Athens loomed large in the minds of early modern visitors and so the Parthenon remained for them the architectural embodiment of that ideal. When Greece gained formal independence from the Ottoman Empire in 1832, Athens was chosen as the capital, not because it had been an important population or commercial centre (at the time it was a town of no more than 1300 houses[35]) but because of the past glory it represented. As modern Greece developed, the city of Athens grew with it. Today, a third of the country's population is Athenian, and the city remains the arrival gate for visitors coming to Greece from all over the world.[36] The Greek Parliament, the ministerial buildings and most embassies are a stone's throw from the Parthenon. It can be seen throughout the city, even from up on Pentelikos.[37]

And so, by a combination of factors – a close relationship to the origins of democracy, the structural harmony of the building and its position in the modern capital – the Parthenon is presented to us as the quintessential icon of the ancients. And it has transcended even this. Not only does it represent Ancient Greece to the world, but it has come to serve as one of the lasting symbols of world heritage, along with perhaps the Pyramids of Giza, the Colosseum in Rome, the Great Wall of China and several others. The site as a whole is registered for its 'outstanding universal value' on UNESCO's World Heritage List, for which the Acropolis and its monuments are described as 'universal symbols of the classical spirit and civilization', forming 'the greatest architectural and artistic complex bequeathed by Greek Antiquity to the world'.[38] It has been replicated globally, including recently in Kassel, Germany for the Documenta contemporary art festival, where, to celebrate free speech on the site of an infamous Nazi book burning of the 1930s, an artist reconstructed the monument entirely out of formerly-banned books.[39] The choice of *this* monument to make *that* statement was particularly telling.

Every day, a multitude of tourists flock to what is known in Greece as the 'Sacred Rock' (Ιερός Βράχος). The public is free to choose the sites it visits. But it is the state – in this case the Greek state – that chooses which sites to support, through funding and research, creating transport links and accentuating promotion – even building dedicated museums like the Acropolis Museum. By showing preference to some, others are inevitably excluded. In the race to become the emblem of modern Greece the Parthenon certainly triumphed, and for good reason. But this only happened at the expense of other sites: the Temple of Hephaestus in the Agora, that of Sounion, to say nothing of the remote temples of the Peloponnese, or even Mount Pentelikos, the true source of all that Acropolean beauty. Under our feet lie veins of marble that could, in theory, still be mined to construct a new Parthenon. In fact, this has been done as part of the ongoing attempt to restore and rebuild the structure: a way to replace those parts that had been lost or destroyed.[40]

I lean down and pick up a small piece of marble. I dust off the red earth and consider its own modest history. The famous Parthenon Marbles seem to go back much further than most of us realise: they are not two-and-a-half thousand years old; they are in fact millions of years old. To a certain extent, Pericles, Ictinus and the others of the fifth century had sought in their own time to exploit a natural resource, that of Pentelicus, and to arrest its development, moulding it into the columns, architraves and sculptures that would reflect *their* reality and tell *their* stories. This is perhaps what civilisations have always done: take raw material and harden it into culture, into production, into time capsules that can be passed on for posterity.

At times the raw material refuses to conform. Could we ever know how many pieces of Pentelic marble, transported over that great distance, were found to be impure, or chipped under a chisel, and were discarded?[41] And while Pericles may have hoped the monuments would remain a testament to Athenian glory, they of course would change with time. Pentelic marble does not remain white: due to the amount of iron on its surface, it undergoes a process of oxidisation. Its components, mixed with atmospheric elements, create a patina along the surface: in London, at the British Museum in the 1930s, Lord Duveen would try to scrape this away; in Athens it would eventually transform the buildings into a golden brown.[42] It is almost as if the monuments were, to use Lord Byron's famous phrase, melting into the landscape – or rather, as we might say, in less romantic times, blending with the chemical properties of the surroundings. Artefacts do change with time – physically, symbolically – sometimes despite our best efforts to preserve them. And this volatility needs to be appreciated, especially when it comes to the Parthenon. Nothing, in truth, is written in stone.[43]

On the way back down the mountain, I ask the taxi driver if he has heard of the 'Elgin Marbles'. My friend translates the question for him. He listens and nods resolutely, without saying anything. I ask him what he thinks of the way in which they were taken from the Acropolis over 200 years ago. He scoffs and gives a one-word answer, his eyes flashing towards me in the rearview mirror. My friend's translation follows a slow chuckle. 'Theft,' she explains. 'He says they were stolen.'

It is unclear if he learned this in the same way he learned about the underground tunnels that connect Penteli to the Hotel Grande Bretagne or if this knowledge was somehow inherited from the Greek landscape itself, almost like the preternatural knowledge of these obscure backroads. Whatever the reason, I promptly end this line of questioning. The driver goes back to the road and, for the time being at least, we ride on in silence.

The Venetian Bombardment

On the next day of my visit, I turn my attention to a different hill, this one much closer to the Acropolis. This is the Hill of Muses (*Λόφος Μουσών* or 'Museion Hill'), where the bards used to come for inspiration. The name also forms the root, rather fittingly, of the word 'museum'. Today it is known as Philopappos Hill, named after a half-collapsed monument to a Roman general at its peak. To the north can be seen the Aeropagos, the location of the early courts of Athens and the place from which St Paul preached to the inhabitants ('Men of Athens, I see you are in all things superstitious …'), and to the west of that is the Pnyx, where the assemblies took place in which several thousand citizens packed themselves in to pass the democratic laws from the sixth century BCE onwards (*Πνύκα* or 'pnyka' in Greek derives from the term 'dense', as in a densely-packed crowd). It was from the Pnyx too that Pericles would have inspired the crowds with his elocution. But the history we must now consider from the Hill of Muses is a far more tragic one, detailing the near-total destruction of one of the world's great treasures.

The year was 1687. Tensions between the Ottoman Turks and the Christian powers were at their height. The Ottomans had an empire that extended from the Persian Gulf to Hungary and across North Africa, including in its realm the present-day territory of Greece. But four years earlier, the grounds had begun to shift. The siege by the Ottomans at Vienna, the great Hapsburg capital, had been miraculously lifted in 1683 and now the Pope had conscripted a number of western powers, including Austria, Poland and the Republic of Venice, into a 'Holy Alliance' to remove the Turkish threat from Europe once and for all.

Those who took up the Papal call most earnestly were the Venetians. Venice had been an independent city-state since the seventh century (the 'Most Serene Republic') and, with trade routes throughout the eastern Mediterranean, was perhaps the commercial power with the most to lose (and gain) vis-à-vis the Ottomans. Venetian sights were set on Turkish-controlled Greece due to its strategic position between east and west and the Venetians promptly 'liberated' the Peloponnese. The next strategic point on the map would be Athens.

The Venetian fleet landed at Piraeus, the port about eight km to the southwest of the city, in early September 1687. A deputation of Greek worthies went out to welcome the newcomers, whom they saw as saviours. The few Turkish defenders abandoned the lower town and moved into position atop the Acropolis, as it was a citadel, offering a commanding position over the city and surrounding areas. The troops were put in position. The Parthenon, by now a functioning mosque, was seen by the Turks to occupy a safe enough position to shelter their women and children, numbering roughly 300, and to store the army's supply of gunpowder. It was this last decision that would prove fatal.[44]

The identity of the Parthenon had already changed several times over the intervening centuries. The first such change had occurred in the sixth century when Athena's temple was turned into a church dedicated to the Virgin Mary. By then the Christianity of St Paul had replaced the pagan religion of Athens and the great chryselephantine sculpture of Athena had long before disappeared (probably destroyed in a third-century fire).[45] It was during this period that the floorplan was enlarged, parts of the frieze were removed and many of the metope figures had their heads lopped off – by early Christians who were uncomfortable having pagan figures leering down at them as they made their way to mass. Later, the church was upgraded to cathedral status, though interestingly its focus remained, as in antiquity, on the feminine: it became known as the 'God-Bearing Mother of Athens'. Then in 1204, the city had been conquered by Crusaders and the cathedral was transformed from an orthodox place of worship to a Catholic one, this time anointed Notre Dame d'Athènes. The next major identity crisis happened in 1458 after the ruling Florentines had been ousted by the great ascendant power of the region, the Ottoman Empire. Notre Dame d'Athènes was again transformed, this time to a mosque, with a minaret added at its west end.[46]

The bombardment of the Acropolis by the Venetians began on 24 September 1687 and lasted three full days. The attack was orchestrated by a Swedish general, Count Koenigsmark, an aristocratic mercenary fighting for the Venetians under the command of General Francesco Morosini. Fifteen Venetian cannons were set up on Museion Hill, along with supporting artillery on the Aeropagus and Pnyx,[47] and no fewer than 700 cannonballs were hurled at the site. There was no reprieve. The Venetian forces had learnt from the Greek deputation about the powder magazine and where to find it, and it was clear that the Parthenon itself had become the target of the attack.[48] The results would be disastrous.

On the third day, the target was hit and the gunpowder ignited. The ensuing explosion rocked the building and, together with the fire that followed, killed the women and children, and others sheltering inside. The inner walls of the building were blown apart, the terracotta roof destroyed and 28 columns spanning the sides and entranceways, almost half the total number, were knocked to the ground.[49] The majority of sculptures – metopes, pediment pieces and large stretches of frieze – went down as well. The building was turned from a place of worship to a shattered shell. The structure that had stood for over 2,000 years, as temple, church, cathedral and then mosque, became a ruin.

It is difficult to overstate the effect this event had on the Parthenon. The year 1687 is an example (one amongst many, sadly) of the desecrations of war. There were lives lost too, and it is important not to lose sight of the human cost, even in the context of our present story. But monuments are meant to stand forever, and so when one is battered in this way it serves as an acute reminder of the lasting havoc wreaked by military conflict. In destroying this testament to the past, the attackers ruptured a very tangible link between past and later generations. Despite changes amongst empires, regimes and religions, this monument had remained standing, structurally intact, providing the people of the city with a symbol that could ennoble their survival, while inspiring them to rebuild the fractured pieces of their identity after each succeeding misfortune.[50]

And for what grand purpose was the building half obliterated? Was this attack somehow necessary in the context of the war between the Holy Alliance and the Ottomans? The Venetian forces did evict the Turks from Athens in the autumn of 1687, but in the following winter, the city became unmanageable. Athens was exposed, clearly indefensible against reprisals from the much larger Ottoman army. A plague had also broken out amongst the local population which had affected some of the soldiers. Count Morosini and the Venetians abandoned the city six months after their arrival, and the replenished Turkish forces soon slouched back in.[51] Because of the irreparable damage done to the Parthenon, the attack on Athens had proved, in the words of one nineteenth-century historian, a 'calamity rather than a stroke of fortune'.[52]

When we read about the Parthenon, Lord Elgin and the famous Marbles, 1687 is often relegated to a brief preamble or a footnote. But should we really be so forgiving? Why place the entirety of the blame on Elgin for the violation of the Parthenon, while the two seventeenth-century aristocrats, Morosini and Koenigsmark, escape with relative impunity? Were it not for this bombardment, Elgin's men, when they arrived on the scene over a century later, would have been unable to remove fallen pieces from the vicinity of the monument. The building would have remained (almost certainly) a mosque and access to its upper reaches would have been strictly forbidden. But with the Parthenon now a ruin, the opportunity presented itself.

Some pilfering on the site would begin in the years that followed. The great building now lay open and half-demolished, many of its sculptures scattered on the ground or buried beneath the rubble. It would only be a matter of time before well-to-do opportunists moved in. The first of the looters was General Morosini himself. Just after defeating the Turks, the commander of the Venetian forces ordered his men to remove the central figures from the west pediment. But the attempts were slipshod and, on their way down, three of the figures (Poseidon and his two full-sized horses) fell to the ground and broke into pieces. Some of Morosini's officers nevertheless took away fragments – and the undeterred general brought an ancient marble lion from the port of Piraeus back to Venice. A Danish soldier took away two fallen metope heads, which soon became the first items from the Parthenon to be publicly displayed in Europe, as star artefacts of the Royal Danish *kunstkammer* (they remain to this day at the National Museum of Denmark).[53] Although these early takings were hardly unbridled, the examples set a dangerous precedent. Once the Europeans were given broader access to ancient sites, there would be little in the way of morality or self-restraint that would stop them from acquiring as much loot as possible.

Following the re-occupation of Athens by the Turks in 1688, such acquisitions would not necessarily be easy. The Ottomans still ran the most feared empire of the day and were no immediate friend to European travellers. There had been only a handful of visitors in the seventeenth century. A French ambassador, the Marquis de Nointel, for instance, made a visit to the Acropolis in 1674, some

13 years before the Venetians went to war with the Turks. He happened to bring along a talented artist who made an exceptional series of drawings of the 'mosque' on the Acropolis with much of its ancient sculpture still in place. But no one would have been allowed to scale the façade, nor take pieces away. Most attempts at drawing the buildings were curtailed and any images were confiscated by the authorities. In one case, a man was nearly shot for taking measurements of the Parthenon.[54]

This protectionism cannot be mistaken for an Ottoman love of ancient monuments. The animus had more to do with a dislike of Europeans and a desire to keep the buildings, which included military stations, a holy mosque and a harem, away from the prying eyes of foreigners. The occupants of the garrison also used many of the fallen pieces of marble for their own purposes, including incorporating large blocks into fortifications or makeshift buildings on the site. There were even stories of Turks grinding down marble to make mortar needed for construction.[55] Needless to say, the minor officials and soldiers of this far-flung part of the empire were hardly paragons of custodianship.

Nevertheless, with the eighteenth century came an increasing level of foreign access to the Acropolis. Because of the sheer availability of pieces, many of which were still lying near the ancient monument, it was inevitable that they would begin to be coveted, representing as they did potential souvenirs of a nobleman's visit to Athens. The rummaging for pieces on the ground had begun; what Mary Beard has called 'open season' on the site.[56] But still, even though small items were spirited away, nothing significant could be removed, such as the large pieces of frieze, many of which were scattered across the site, the major pediment sculptures or the metopes. The takings had been for the most part opportunistic in nature, casually executed and somewhat discrete. No major archaeological project could be undertaken. Not, that is, until the Embassy of Thomas Bruce, the seventh Earl of Elgin, Ambassador Extraordinary and Plenipotentiary of His Britannic Majesty to the Sublime Porte of the Ottoman Sultan.

2

A Story with Neither Hero Nor Villain

When we tell stories, we often like to focus our attention on the individuals involved. Perhaps it says something about human nature that we almost invariably try to find someone who can play the hero or the villain in any given story. This person then becomes the cause of all major developments in the narrative; and upon them we heap praise, or we place blame. And this is exactly what has happened to Lord Elgin. He has been made to stand tall at the centre of the story and, depending on one's viewpoint, is portrayed either as a saviour or as a scoundrel. To many of his contemporaries he was the 'noble Earl' who adeptly salvaged invaluable pieces of antiquity from looming barbarism, while for others he was the 'dull spoiler', the 'paltry antiquarian', the 'marble stealer'.[1]

The problem with recounting the story of the Parthenon Marbles in the usual way is that far too much emphasis is placed on one individual. What kind of a man was Lord Elgin? Was he an honourable diplomat, a rescuer of antiquities, a selfless proponent of the progression of fine arts in Britain? Or was he an acquisitive rake, looking only to profit his own private collection, without the slightest qualm for the interests of the local population at Athens? In truth, the answer lies somewhere in the middle: he was all of these things, but none of them entirely. He represented a mixture of motives, abilities and middling desires. Whatever it may have amounted to, he is hardly worthy of playing the hero – or the villain – in the story. The focus should instead shift to what happened on the ground in Athens during that crucial period, and the wider context that made it all possible.

In fact, the seventh Earl of Elgin cut a somewhat pitiable figure, a case of thwarted ambition and unfulfilled potential more than the decisiveness of a man of action. Lord Elgin's Embassy at the 'Sublime Porte' of the Ottoman Sultan began in 1799 and ended less than four years later.[2] Before he had arrived at the Ottoman capital of Constantinople, the main purposes for which he had been sent – to sign a peace treaty with Ottoman Turkey and to open up the Black Sea for British traders – had already been achieved by others.[3] And the greatest diplomatic success of his time in the East had little to do with him, but was a direct result of the triumphs of the British Navy under Admiral Nelson in chasing Napoleon out of Egypt. The Ottomans were relieved that their empire was no longer under threat from Revolutionary France and so plied Great Britain's chief representative with whatever favours they could, including acquiescing to a very ambitious project in Athens.

Beyond his time at Constantinople, his career as a whole was unremarkable. While that particular Embassy may have been expected to serve as a stepping-stone to a distinguished career in His Majesty's foreign service, it ended up instead as its peak. After Turkey, he would spend three years under house arrest in France as prisoner of war (1803–1806), he would lose his wife to the seductive charms of a neighbour (the divorce proceedings playing out through scandalous trials in 1808–1809), he would contract a disease that disfigured part of his face, he would hover on the brink of insolvency and, after his death in 1841, he would leave his family with debts that took a further generation to repay.[4] He would also attempt – and fail – many times over to seek a lifetime peerage from the British Government, the requests for which are still recorded in a series of excruciating letters to the Prime Minister and members of Cabinet.[5]

When it comes to the operation in Athens, it is likewise difficult to give Elgin much credit: he was not present in the city as the work of removing the famed sculptures began in the summer of 1801, remaining instead at his post in the imperial capital. He had also been absent from Constantinople at the time the infamous permission had been secured from the Sultan's court.[6] He would send a series of dispatches to his agents on the ground, with some of these revealing the extent of his acquisitive aspirations: 'I should wish to have, of the Acropolis, examples in the actual object', he would write to his head contractor in December 1801, 'of each thing, and architectural ornament – of each cornice, each frieze, each capital – of the decorated ceilings, of the fluted columns … of metopes and the like, as much as possible'.[7] He would be paying for the enterprise as well, though payment would at times be far from prompt (and, towards the end, practically non-existent).[8] But the day-to-day manoeuvring in Athens had little to do with him. When he at last arrived on the scene in the spring of 1802, almost a year into the project, for a relatively short review of the work before commencing a tour of the Greek Islands with his wife, there was little he did to affect the machinery which was already in place and churning along relentlessly.

To do justice to the story, rather than Elgin, a separate list of colourful actors should instead be presented. The men working in Athens when the sculptures were removed between 1801 and 1804 were for the most part *artistes* who had been recruited in southern Italy by Elgin's secretary on the ambassadorial team's stop in Sicily during the sea journey from England. Were it not for them, for their work ethic and their devious creativity, for the types of people they were, the enterprise would almost surely have failed.

How unlikely it would have seemed at the outset that they would amount to much. The chief artist was Giovanni Battista Lusieri, a talented painter of enormous Italian panoramas whose one shortcoming was that he had trouble finishing his artistic projects. Lusieri would oversee a team that included a painter, Feodor Ivanovitch, referred to as 'the Calmuck', a former slave from the court of St Petersburg in Russia and a monumental drinker; an architectural draughtsman, Vincenzo Balestra, who was a hunchback (though this deformity would allegedly not affect the work of his hands), along with his young apprentice;[9] and two men spirited out of French-occupied Rome who would make plaster moulds of the sculptures. Add to this Elgin's chaplain, Philip Hunt, an energetic agent without doubt, but a shrewd and opportunistic man above all else. It would be the chaplain Hunt who would play a major role in securing permission for Elgin, and it was the artist Lusieri who would succeed at the long game, overseeing the daily work, and orchestrating various plots along the way, in order to ensure that the sculptures were taken away and removed to England once and for all.

But the result of the enterprise had little to do with the actions of any single individual, and much more to do with the larger context. As we shall see, the historical backdrop played a major role, as indeed did the coincidences and vicissitudes that often accompany large undertakings such as this. And there was a part too for the equipment on the scene: the tools without which no excavation, no removal of large pieces of sculpture and no evacuation would have ever been possible. It is this larger network – of characters, situations, historical circumstance, tools and so on – that can help to explain what transpired during those eventful years in the first decade of the nineteenth century.

The Turning Tide of Ottoman Support

When the artists first arrived in Athens in August 1800[10] they had been sent by Elgin with the task of making drawings, paintings, architectural measurements and plaster moulds of the classical sites of Athens. The kernel of the idea came not from Elgin himself, but from Elgin's private architect in Scotland, the man who had earlier been renovating the Elgin family estate at Broomhall.[11] The architect, Thomas Harrison, was typical of the new generation of aesthetes in that he saw true beauty not in the Roman and Palladian forms that had been in vogue throughout the eighteenth century, but in the original Greek models, the ones that until recently very few western Europeans had been fortunate enough to see with their own eyes. The suggestion from Harrison, and it was an effective one, was for Elgin to utilise his Embassy to obtain accurate renderings of the remnants of classical genius scattered about Athens, and to do this to inform tastes back home in Britain. Making models of the sculptures and architectural features by way of casts was the main goal; this way young artists and architects would be able to see the work of the masters, even if only in facsimile form. Elgin admired the idea and, though he failed to obtain financial support from the Government of the day, went ahead with the enterprise, promising to underwrite it all himself.[12]

What was noteworthy about the plan was that it did not include any intention to take away the artefacts themselves. This was not wished for – or even conceivable – at the time. The group sent to Athens did not include an archaeologist in their number (nor, what might have been more common at the time, an antiquarian); they were skilled in the arts of reproduction, not scientific extraction. Their actions would eventually demonstrate this dilettantism when it came to dismantling the sculptures, which included sawing and chiselling pieces from their backings, with devastating effects on the material itself. No detailed record was kept of the finds around the site, meaning that little is known about precise find spots of most of the pieces excavated from the ground or extracted from the walls of the other houses on the Acropolis.[13]

Setting out on their mission, the men began with some of the more accessible sites around Athens, sketching ancient buildings such as the Temple of Hephaestus in the Agora and the Monument of Lysicrates, which had been incorporated into the walls of the local Capuchin Monastery where most of the westerners stayed during their visits. It took six months to obtain access to the Acropolis itself because, as in 1687, the hill was still being used as a garrison. Even upon obtaining permission to enter, they were faced with the inconvenience of having to pay the local military commander, the Turkish Disdar, the enormous sum of five guineas a day.[14] This was typical baksheesh at the time, but it was a lot of money for Athens: it was said to be the daily equivalent of hiring over 60 local labourers.[15] Not a situation that could persist for very long.

It appears likely that the artists would have sought some sort of formal permission to enter the Acropolis as early as May 1801, though the details of this attempt have not been preserved.[16] Whatever form it took, this would have allowed the artists the ability to shift their subject matter from the remains of the lower town to the more formidable monuments of the citadel. But even this was not to last. The wider geo-political context would have an impact when news reached the Ottomans that the French were amassing a fleet in Toulon to send across the Mediterranean, with the supposed intention of launching an attack on the Greek mainland.

Frictions between France and the Ottoman Empire had reached a high point. The two powers had been historic allies since the sixteenth century. France had never joined the Pope's famous Holy Alliance that had caused so much destruction in 1687, and it was Louis XIV's Ambassador, the Marquis de Nointel, who had been the only westerner afforded unfettered access to the Acropolis some 13 years prior, which included the ability to make drawings. But all this had changed following the French Revolution. The Directory in charge of France had sent a young general, Napoleon Bonaparte, fresh from his military successes in Italy, to conquer Egypt in 1798. Egypt was then controlled by the Mamluks, vassals of the Ottoman Sultans, allowed by the latter to govern the region. An attempted regime change in Egypt was like a dagger to the flank of empire. Napoleon's initial success caused great distress at Constantinople and the gathering ships at Toulon sparked fears of a reinforcement of the French position. Instructions were immediately sent from the capital to Athens that the military garrison be closed to all foreigners, regardless of nationality; and this would inevitably include Elgin's artists.

The men were thus shut out of the Acropolis and had to again make do with the less-desired monuments of the lower town. It was at this very moment – by sheer coincidence – that Elgin's chaplain made a trip to Athens from Constantinople, effectively as a chaperone to Elgin's wife and visiting in-laws who wanted to tour Greece. Though a man of the church, Philip Hunt was, it should be repeated, a very ambitious, even unscrupulous, figure who saw the position of chaplain to a well-known diplomat as one that would inevitably lead to fame and fortune. He was one of these characters so acutely aware of the power structures of the time, and so willing to reaffirm them in his actions, that he was as servile to his superiors as he was callous to his underlings.[17] As such, Hunt was more than willing to do whatever it took to please his employer back in the capital and had very little regard for the honour or esteem of the locals. His time in Athens coincided with the ban imposed on foreigners and so he saw first-hand its impact on the attempted work of the artists, who were by this point at loose ends. Hunt came to the realisation that another permission was needed, this one coming directly from Constantinople and setting out in clear terms what was needed for the artists to complete their tasks.[18]

And so he returned to the capital and set about drafting a memorandum that would be shown to the Ottoman authorities as a basis for negotiating what he hoped would be a more robust clearance note for the artists.[19] Not only did it seek permission for the men to have unobstructed access to the Acropolis for the purposes of drawing, painting, erecting scaffolding and making moulds, it added two new heads of claim: digging to 'discover the ancient foundations' and the liberty to 'take away any sculptures or inscriptions which do not interfere with the works or walls of the Citadel'.[20]

In the normal course, the demands of Hunt's memorandum would have been cast aside by the Ottoman officials who had more pressing matters to contend with. And, in fact, since Lord Elgin had first triggered negotiations with the relevant Turkish representative several weeks earlier, he had been met with little in the way of enthusiasm. But something was happening, well beyond either Elgin or Hunt's control, that would rescue the memorandum and turn it into one of the most auspicious and controversial documents of the entire period of Ottoman control over Greece. It would form a turning point in the possibilities afforded for the Parthenon, as Elgin himself would later admit when questioned on the topic by a Parliamentary Select Committee: 'the whole system of Turkish feeling', he said, 'met with a revolution'.[21] Had it not occurred, there would have been little chance for the men at Athens to obtain the kind of latitude, at least on paper, that they would need to begin the infamous enterprise of removing the sculptures and carting them away.

The change was brought about by news relating to the situation in Egypt. Napoleon's foray into Egypt had been interpreted by the British as an attempt to block access to India via the Red Sea and thus served as an affront to their own imperial designs. And so the Royal Navy was sent after Napoleon. Following success at the Battle of the Nile in 1798, the British were able to isolate Napoleon and 40,000 French troops from aid or reinforcement from France. Thus, by the happenstance of history, the Ottoman Empire found itself militarily aligned with Great Britain for the first time in centuries, even if only by the adage that the enemy of its enemy was now its friend. But victory at the Nile was not enough. The French were still active in Egypt, which included lending support to the *égyptologistes* who would help introduce the study of Ancient Egypt back in France, and indeed across Europe. Napoleon himself had escaped to France in the middle of 1799 and the French were now pushing into Syria and the Holy Land. A decisive victory by the British was needed.

And that is exactly what happened. Following British success at the Battle of Alexandria in March 1801, the French besieged at Cairo finally surrendered in June, which signalled the end of French ambitions in Egypt and the surrounding areas. While the removal of the final vestiges of the French army would not be complete until September of that year, the shifting tides would have felt like nothing short of a miracle to the Ottomans in Constantinople. They at last felt the threat of French Republicanism (with all its talk of nationalism, liberty, and 'rights of man') removed from their midst and they were highly appreciative. The British – especially the British Ambassador – became heroes of the town. The Embassy was offered gifts: aigrettes, pelisses, horses, snuff boxes, medals ... and essentially anything that had been requested for Athens.[22]

Permission Granted

A permission was thus secured on 6 July 1801 and came as a token of Ottoman appreciation for the military shift that had taken place: a revolution in feeling indeed. This permission came in the form of a letter from Constantinople signed by the Ottoman Kaimacam, Seged (Seyyid) Abdullah, who was acting head of the Ottoman Porte while the Grand Vizier was away with the army in Egypt. It was addressed to two Ottoman officials in Athens, the governor (Voivode) and the chief justice (Cadi). The Kaimacam's letter was referred to by Hunt and the foreigners as a '*firman*', that is an edict issued by the Sultan – though as we shall see in chapter three, it almost certainly was something less than this. It nevertheless was a letter with the authority to command, and it acceded almost exactly to Hunt's requests: it offered free access to the Acropolis, the ability to put up scaffolding, to draw, to make moulds, to remove obstructions, to make excavations, and – most exceptionally – the freedom to remove pieces of stone from the site. The wording of this last grant was that no opposition be made to the 'taking away of some pieces of stone with inscriptions, and figures', language that comes not from the Ottoman original, which no longer exists, but from a contemporaneous Italian copy. The letter, and its legal implications, will be assessed further in the next chapter.

It was clear that Hunt's memorandum formed the basis for the text of the permission, which, in all likelihood, comprised a translation into Turkish of much of his English draft. The actual negotiation was undertaken by an Italian working for the Embassy named Bartolomeo Pisani. Pisani was placed as middle-man in dealings between the Embassy and the Ottoman Government. He was the Embassy's 'dragoman', a role roughly equivalent to that of an interpreter, though one who wielded enormous power over both sides of the negotiation, neither of which was able to know for sure whether his translation reflected the other's true intention. 'God save me from the dragomans', went a well-known saying of the period, 'and I will save myself from the dogs'.[23] The Italian copy, issued at Hunt's request so that he could better understand the content of the original, had been drafted by another Italian working at the court, Antonio Dané.[24]

Hunt happened to be in Constantinople when the document was issued, preparing to set out for Athens once more. Because the English were held in such high regard in the capital, he was appointed an official Ottoman escort, Mubashir Raschid Aga, a name which translates as 'bringer of good news'. The two would travel together to Athens, and later to the Peloponnese, and the Mubashir would be entrusted with this essential piece of paperwork.[25]

Upon arriving in Athens on 22 July, Hunt went straight to the Voivode, the governor of the city, to present the Kaimacam's letter and secure for the men the liberties granted therein. He was successful, although the question of the 'taking away' power seems not to have been broached. It would only be a few days later, once Hunt had visited and inspected the Parthenon, that the idea would come to him. In such auspicious times, he must have reckoned, why stop at copies of the magnificent pieces? Looking up at the southeast corner, considering the five columns and, above them, the metope figures (seven remained in relatively good condition on this part of the building), his cupidity, his vanity and his misplaced sense of duty must have gotten the best of him. He went back to the Voivode to seek approval for removing the second metope of the series.[26]

The Voivode was no dullard. He would have known there was no express language in the instructions from Constantinople that allowed the removal of integral elements from the building. One passage in the text presupposed that 'no harm' would be caused by the buildings being 'viewed, contemplated and designed'. But there was some dispute between Hunt and the Voivode over how far the 'taking away' provision could extend. It was, after all, the final concession at the end of a long document, seemingly included as an afterthought. The passage required that no opposition be made to the removal of 'pieces of stone'. Did this mean loose pieces lying around the site? Or could it possibly refer to more?

The letter at this point became the basis for additional negotiations, ones in which Hunt did his best to convince the Voivode to allow for a more expansive reading of the text. There were others present at the session. The Mubashir, who had accompanied Hunt to Athens, was there and acted completely on the side of the foreigners. As Hunt would later report to his Ambassador, the man 'behaved on this occasion with uncommon energy and propriety; he entered completely into your Lordship's views'.[27] The British Consul was also there, a native-born Greek named Logotheti. Logotheti was at first uneasy with the new demand from

Hunt and suggested that the Voivode not extend the interpretation quite so far. But he eventually gave in.

The final decision and its implications were again products of chance, brought about by the wider historical context surrounding the characters. The Voivode would have been well aware of the good stead in which the British were held by the Porte and that refusing the agent of an ambassador would have had repercussions on the Voivode's own station and career. Again, much relied upon the success at Cairo, news of which had reached Athens around this time.[28] This would also have an impact on the other major figure in town: the Disdar, or military commander, who was quartered in the garrison and who would be tasked with the day-to-day application of the concession. Coincidentally the previous Disdar had died several days before the meeting. The man's son (who had already caused the artists much distress during their earlier attempts at gaining access to the Acropolis) was now in a position to inherit the title, or so he would have hoped. His accession would depend upon favourable words making their way back to Constantinople. Suddenly, and ashamed of his earlier actions, the young man obliged Hunt in whatever way he could. He knew his fate would lie in Hunt's hands – because the chaplain had the ear of the Ambassador and the Ambassador the ear of the Grand Vizier.[29] The official who would play the crucial role of overseeing the Acropolis in the years to come was now strategically aligned in the foreigners' favour.

But Hunt's good fortune also came from his ability to pay. He had arrived in Athens with gifts in tow for the local officials, including chandeliers, firearms, telescopes, jewellery, pieces of cloth and more.[30] As for the specifics of what exactly had changed hands during and after Hunt's discussions with the Voivode, Hunt was conveniently vague when asked about it later by the Parliamentary Select Committee in London, though he did admit to having made presents of 'lustres, fire arms, and other articles of English manufacture'.[31] A later visitor would estimate the value at between £45 and £65 per piece of sculpture removed from the site.[32]

When later asked by the Select Committee whether Hunt thought the '*firman*' expressly permitted the removal of sculptures from the buildings themselves, he responded cannily that this was the interpretation which the Voivode had been 'induced to allow it to bear'. Pressed further, he admitted that this inducement was the result of the good stead in which Elgin was held amongst the Turks. As for bribes, Hunt would continue to claim that there was nothing 'sufficiently precise' to allow him to 'conjecture the amount'.[33] In exchange, it appears, he did not leave empty-handed. Hunt was given three sheep a day and a quantity of fruit from the Voivode, which, according to one author, was part of a 'normal two-way gift-exchange process' in the region.[34]

We will consider the Kaimacam's letter in further detail in the next chapter, but for now, whatever the reasons may have been, the Voivode agreed to allow the removal of that important first metope, and the Disdar-in-waiting could do nothing but comply. The change for the artists themselves was remarkable. No longer would they be stopped, diverted or harassed when trying to access the site each morning. For the time being at least, the local authorities would do nothing to interfere with their work.

The Removals Begin

The first metope was removed on 31 July 1801, a little over a week after Hunt's return to Athens. Windlasses from a ship at port were erected over the south-east corner, while rope and tackle were put to use. The ship's carpenter and 20 local labourers climbed up on the scaffolding and went to work removing the piece of marble from its backing, dislodging it from between two neighbouring triglyphs and lowering it to the ground.[35] A second metope (eastern-most in the sequence) was brought down the following day.[36] This time the operation did not run smoothly. As we know from chapter one, the metopes, like the frieze and other sculptures on the Parthenon, were not simply decorative elements tacked onto an existing building; they had been integrated into the architecture itself. A piece of cornice remained above the second metope, somewhat like a protective awning, which had first to be removed. As none of the men were trained for this sort of operation, the procedure was far from clinical – and the cornice crashed to the ground. An English traveller present at the removal wrote about the episode: 'down came the fine masses of Pentelican marble, scattering their white fragments with thundering noise among the ruins.'[37] It was clear that none of this would be easy.

Despite the destructive commencement, we must remember that many of the Parthenon Marbles – most, in fact – would not be taken directly from the building itself, but would instead be pulled off the ground, excavated from beneath the rubble or cut or removed from fortifications and makeshift structures over the following two-and-a-half years.[38] This is because much of the building's remaining sculptural elements had been so violently dispersed due to the disastrous bombardment of 1687. A review of the drawings and watercolours of the monument from the period reveals that what remained of the structure at the time were the extreme east and west ends of the colonnade (totalling 30 of the original 58 columns), the pediments on each side (with remnants of only 10 of the original two dozen figures) and a narrow part of the cella wall from the west with its corresponding frieze. The more significant stretches of frieze lay buried, scattered about or built into Ottoman constructions. The crucial central sequence of the east frieze, for example, a scene that featured the principal gods seated around the enigmatic presentation of the peplos robe – probably the single most important block of the entire Parthenon – was being used as a nearby retaining wall by the janissaries.[39]

Much of the work that followed therefore involved more primitive forms of excavation. Many pieces of the south frieze, depicting men on horseback in a long procession, were uncovered where they had lain for over a century. The remnants of the large sculptures from the west pediment were found during digs near that part of the building.[40] In total, about one third of what was taken was removed directly from the building itself; the rest was found below or nearby. The relative ease with which the men could excavate and remove the majority of items was therefore due in no small part to the earlier bombardment. The damage caused by war was therefore at least partly to blame for the situation that presented itself in 1801, arguably even more so than the audacity of the Voivode or the rapacity of Elgin's men.

The methods used, however, were nonetheless damaging. In most instances, when loose frieze blocks were found, the men resorted to saws and chisels to remove the sculpted part from the weightier backside. Recent research has revealed that this occurred with 32 of the pieces, while a total of 56 had been chiselled down in one form or another.[41] The capital from one of the columns was considered too large to carry and so was cut down the middle. After being dislodged, the long central block of the east frieze was dropped by the workmen and broke in two. The resulting rift through the centre of the peplos scene remains visible today at the British Museum, cutting through the arm of a priestess and forever marking the piece with a reminder of the injurious labour needed to recuperate it (see Figure 2).

Figure 2 The central figures of the Parthenon frieze, Block V of the east frieze, form the 'peplos' scene, with a rift at the centre caused by workmen during the block's removal from the Acropolis
Source: PRISMA ARCHIVO / Alamy Stock Photo.

The work on the Acropolis was overseen by the chief artist Lusieri. He would have seemed benign and almost comical were the results of his efforts not so controversial today. He appears in drawings of the Acropolis from the period, shading himself from the Greek sun with an effeminate parasol in his hands and then between two Doric columns, his arms folded as the Disdar wags a disapproving finger in his direction.[42] Lusieri, it should be recalled, was not an archaeologist but an artist, known for his enormous Italian landscapes. Though a skilled painter, he seemed to lack the energy or attention span to complete many of his artistic works. But the removal of Marbles in Athens would be an undertaking to which he could commit himself entirely; and it would prove to be his one monumental completion, condemned though it is by many today. Reverend Hunt left later that summer, but Lusieri continued to work away. Within a year, seven metopes, roughly 20 blocks of frieze and most of the pediment sculpture had been taken from the Parthenon and the surrounding area.[43] They were carried down to the British Consul's house in the town, before being carted off 8 km to the port at Piraeus.[44]

The practicalities of managing such an enormous enterprise are worth noting. Certain pieces of equipment would prove vital. These included the windlass taken from the ship in the harbour, the rope and the tackle, all of which allowed for the removal of the metopes (and later the pediment sculptures) from high atop the Parthenon; also included was a cart large and sturdy enough to transport the pieces out of the town. Lusieri had use of such material because it had earlier been brought to Athens from France for the purpose of assisting another actor engaged in a similar enterprise: the French antiquarian Louis-François-Sébastien Fauvel, the former agent of the aristocratic Ambassador of France, the Comte de Choiseul-Gouffier.[45] However, unlike Lusieri, Fauvel would never be blessed by circumstance. The French, longtime allies of the Ottomans, were never able to secure the delicate combination of military dependence and good fortune that had benefited the Elgin project. Fauvel, who would have liked nothing more than to take away as many pieces from the Acropolis as possible, was consistently rebuffed by both Voivode and Disdar. In all his time operating in Athens to that point, nearly 20 years from 1780 to 1798, he had managed to secure only one block of frieze and two fallen metopes for the Comte, which were discovered by chance on the ground near the Parthenon.[46]

When the tide turned following Napoleon's conquest of Egypt in 1798, all French citizens in Ottoman territory were placed under arrest, including Fauvel. Thus, at the critical moment when Hunt and Lusieri were beginning to orchestrate the removal of the sculptures from the Parthenon, no imperial nemesis was in place to press the Voivode against them. Perhaps more importantly, an imprisoned Fauvel meant his equipment was free for the taking. Thus, Lusieri obtained the necessary tools for the project with little effort and at no expense. Without them, neither the removal nor the transport would have been conceivable, let alone possible.

When Lord Elgin first arrived in Athens in April 1802, 10 months after the Acropolis removals had begun, his men had already taken away more than half the sculptures that would one day bear his name. His appearance amounted to little more than a largely superfluous encouragement to the men and the apparent offer of a blank cheque to cover the expenditures. As William St Clair writes, 'He urged his agents on, telling them to dig and buy and take away. No effort or money was to be spared to get what was wanted from the Acropolis, and that work was to have priority over everything else.'[47]

Elgin's Embassy would draw to a close within a year of that time, in January 1803, at which point he would begin the long journey back to Britain – but en route he would be placed under house arrest in France, following a renewed declaration of war between France and Great Britain.[48] From that point onwards, Lusieri would be operating almost entirely independently.[49] By 1804, Fauvel had been released from prison and was back in Athens, successfully applying pressure on the Voivode to put a stop to Lusieri's free reign; further work on the Acropolis was promptly banned. But there was still much to be done elsewhere, including the packing of antiquities into crates, and arranging the necessary shipments from Piraeus, something that would be completed only by 1811. Lusieri became increasingly frustrated with the lack of correspondence from Elgin, even after the latter's release from France and his return to England in 1806.[50] The oft-promised money dried up. Lusieri nevertheless persevered, perhaps seeking to redeem himself for the unfinished projects of his artistic past, and was still nominally acting as Elgin's agent when he died in Athens in 1821, dejected, at the age of 67.[51]

Events, Context and Tools

And so we can try to better understand the story of the Parthenon Marbles and their removal by highlighting the role played by Lusieri throughout the period, but also by Hunt at the critical juncture of 1801, and by the workmen who did the lifting and the prising, the sawing and chiselling, the packing and carting, that resulted in over 90 large pieces of sculpted marble leaving the Acropolis between 1801 and 1804. In consequence, we can also appreciate the relatively minimal role played by Elgin himself. He was not central to the narrative and as such the sobriquets clinging to him over the years – saviour, plunderer, thief – are best left out of the final equation, as a way of offering a more honest assessment of what actually happened in Athens at the relevant time.

Historical accounts often focus on select individuals – kings, queens, generals, earls – and while this makes for good armchair reading, it in no way allows us to uncover the whole picture regarding a particular situation. There is a school of thought that instead sees history as the product of larger mechanisms. Rather than focus on the statesman or the politician, this approach analyses the socioeconomic forces that prompted change at different moments in human history. The approach owes much to the philosophies of Hegel and Marx. This branch of history, that of the 'structuralist' historian, prefers to recount the events of the past not as the consequence of decisions and actions of leading figures, but as the product of changes in technology, population, the economy, geo-politics and general human understanding.[52] Names such as Napoleon and Churchill are minimised in this structuralist account: had it not been these particular individuals who acted, others might have done so in their place. Could we say the same in relation to Elgin?

More recently, one branch of sociology has also begun to describe the context of all activity as an 'actor-network', that is an all-encompassing, interconnected network of humans and non-humans – a category that can include technological instruments, commodities and even changes in the environment.[53] As a result, it is no longer safe to see history (or any area of study) as the result of free choices made by powerful individuals. Instead we must try to understand the overall context of these choices: the complete network of all relevant 'actors' involved.

This actor-network approach offers a more constructive avenue for understanding the situation that prevailed in Athens at the time: as a vast field of interconnected actors endowed with agency and unfolding in relation to changing events, none fully under the control of any one individual. The historical context set the scene with three crucial events which in no way predetermined the result, but were critical in shaping the proceedings of the project. The first of these, which we saw in chapter one, was the explosion of 1687. The Venetian blast half-obliterated the Parthenon, destroying some of the sculptural features and placing a good number of pieces within the reach of Elgin's men. Without 1687, the Parthenon would probably have remained a relatively complete structural entity, no doubt still functioning as a mosque, and would have remained off-limits to foreign visitors. Put simply: without 1687 there can be no 1801.

The second contextual event was the steady decline of the Ottoman Empire. Beginning with its surprise conquest of Constantinople in 1453 (and Athens five years later), the Empire had for generations struck fear into the heart of Christendom. But by the late eighteenth century the situation had changed dramatically. Slowly European coalitions and local insurgents began defeating the Ottomans, one battle at a time, until it appeared to most that this was an empire in retreat. Soon the Ottoman Empire would become the veritable 'sick man of Europe', but the game was already being played at this point by western powers keen to accelerate the decline and trying in whatever way they could to secure advantages from it.[54]

While this geo-political shift played out on the larger world stage, it had an effect on the domestic scene in Athens as well. It meant European travellers could at last find their way deep into the Empire without having to fear janissaries brandishing scimitars; money could now solve most problems. And this was nothing new. When a country is weakened, when its revenues and influence are minimal, petty corruption tends to prevail, especially amongst provincial officials. Alternative sources of income become essential, and a greater openness to foreigners willing to pay for the privilege of measuring old ruins or scraping away at half-buried stones then seemed inevitable.[55]

The third event was the threat and eventual failure of Napoleon's foray into Egypt. As mentioned, this had the effect of pivoting the Ottomans away from the French towards an alliance with Britain and then – following the surrender at Cairo – inspiring unrestrained amity between Turks and British. This was a proximate cause, and led directly to Hunt's ability to secure, deliver and ultimately act on the permission of July 1801, but it too was assisted by the general Ottoman decline over the preceding century. Had the Empire remained a force to be reckoned with in the East, it would have had little to fear from the threat of French incursion, and may have been able to fight off Napoleon on its own. With the decline came the need to rely on others, placing the British Embassy in a particularly powerful position.

In addition to this, there was a vast interconnected network of people and things that can help explain the occurrence of certain historical events. Here we can distribute 'agency' more widely, in a way that covers the tools and equipment on the scene, without which nothing would have been possible. These included the roads, communication lines, livestock used for travel, legal documents and the paper upon which they were written, the capital released for the project, and of course Fauvel's ropes, tackle and cart that Lusieri had opportunistically secured. As the initial intention was merely to paint, measure and make moulds, Elgin's men had not come to Athens prepared to excavate, let alone to remove, large pieces of stone, and so, without these it would have been impossible for the operation to succeed. Taken together, the physical actors provided for the removal, perhaps as much as any living being involved in the story.

With all of this taken into account, the decisions of one man, as well as his character, seem rather trivial by comparison. To argue over whether Lord Elgin was a hero or a villain is to miss the point. The result in the past of placing him at the centre of the action has been to mislead the narrative, focusing instead on the feelings associated with liking or disliking a particular person. Thus, by downplaying the figure we can offer something of a counterbalance to this approach, removing at least some of the emotion and misplaced attention, and allowing us to view the history with a fresh outlook. Rather than hauling Elgin before the court of public opinion, as has so often been done in the past, why not try and start again?

Perhaps coming at it in this way can have an impact on the larger dispute around the Parthenon Marbles. Both sides may be able to find more areas of consensus than they otherwise thought possible. As such, a method for achieving a workable solution on the Parthenon Marbles may be closer to hand. But we will have to return to that.

3

A *Firman* by Any Other Name

Let us now turn to the question of permission. This inevitably involves a full consideration of the documents secured by those operating under Lord Elgin from the Ottoman Court in Constantinople. Amongst these are of course the letter of permission that Philip Hunt obtained from the Kaimacam in July 1801, which was said to have allowed the removals of the Parthenon Marbles from the Acropolis in the first instance. Also to be considered are documents obtained in the years that followed: a letter of approval from the Grand Vizier of October 1802, a copy of which was recently uncovered amongst the Elgin papers at Broomhall, and a permit allowing the export of the final 40 crates from the port of Piraeus in 1811 obtained by Elgin's successor as Ambassador, Lord Adair. We will consider each of these in turn to see what insights they can provide on the question of legality.

Following this, we will turn our attention to some of the external factors that facilitated the procurement of such documents at the time, to see what light they may shed on the overall legality. Such factors include the payments and gifts made by Elgin's men to officials in Athens and the overall context of Ottoman rule at the time, which was both repressive and brutal. What impact might these have on the validity of the authorisation? Do they serve to undermine it? Or is their impact largely negligible? Once the legal question has been posed – and answered, insofar as possible – we will turn to the ethical question. Even if they had been legally authorised, were the actions nevertheless morally questionable? And what implications might the ethical position have on our understanding of the status of the Marbles today?

We begin with the Kaimacam's letter of July 1801. As mentioned in chapter two, the text of this letter was largely based on the points set out in Hunt's memorandum of the same month, which had requested a *firman* for the men in Athens to access the Acropolis, to draw and make models of the buildings on the site, to erect scaffolding around said buildings, to dig for the foundations and – finally, and most crucially – to take away 'any sculptures or inscriptions which did not interfere with the works or walls of the Citadel'.

A *firman* was an imperial order emanating from the Sultan and written in Ottoman Turkish. To this day, no such document has ever been found. Researchers have searched in vain through the Ottoman Archives in Istanbul, which hold copies of *firmans* from the Ottoman era, but have found no record of any such document from 1801 issued to Hunt.[1] Even at the time, the true nature of the document would have remained a mystery to the foreigners. Only two individuals working for Elgin's Embassy would have understood the original text: Pisani, the dragoman (or interpreter), and Antonio Dané, the Venetian who would have translated the original into Italian for the benefit of Hunt.[2] The reason for the translation was that Hunt, who had found himself in the dark when earlier trying to enforce a *firman* with an Ottoman official, wanted the comfort of knowing the exact content of the document in a language he understood. He was therefore well equipped when he arrived in Athens on 22 July 1801 and subsequently met with the Voivode. Hunt kept the Italian translation in his possession and later brought it back with him to England. He furnished a copy of it to the Select Committee of the House of Commons in 1816 and kept the original in his possession: this then passed privately to his descendants before resurfacing in the 1960s thanks to Elgin's biographer William St Clair; it was acquired in 2006 by the British Museum, where it remains today.[3]

The word '*firman*' appears to have tripped rather lightly from the lips of foreigners in Turkey at the time. They used the term to refer to a great number of Ottoman texts, such as travel permits, employment appointments and imperial instructions.[4] Lady Elgin, for instance, wrote in a letter about the present document that 'Hunt is in raptures, for the Firman is perfection'.[5] A true *firman* derived its authority from the Sultan, and would have included the Sultan's emblem and a number of other formalities, such as an invocation to Allah and the full date of the order in Arabic.[6] What is clear from the Italian translation is that the original document was signed by neither the Sultan nor his Grand Vizier, but by the Kaimacam, Seged (Seyyid) Abdullah, who had been acting for the Grand Vizier while the latter was away with the army in Egypt. The original also lacked the Sultan's emblem and any reference thereto as attestation of the authority of its content, which were necessary for a *firman*.[7]

These lacunae, along with the absence of any copy left in the Ottoman Archive, have led scholars to conclude that the original was something less than a *firman*.[8] But even if it were a mere letter from the Kaimacam, what sort of authority did it have within the Ottoman legal system? Was it a command to its recipient or a simple request, capable of being ignored? While we do not have the original, we must nevertheless try to draw conclusions from the context in which the document was used, as well as from the words of the Italian translation itself. While we might never know with absolute certainty, we can still offer a plausible account of the document's legal status at the time.

So how might the Kaimacam's letter have been understood within the Ottoman legal system? First of all, with the Grand Vizier away, the Kaimacam was the most senior official at the Ottoman Porte during the period. Secondly, it was addressed to two Ottoman officials in Athens, the local Judge ('Giudice' in Italian, usually interpreted as Cadi or Qadi, the religious judge for the area) and the Voivode (the local governor), the latter of which, as we have seen, complied with its requests over a period of time stretching well beyond a year. The inclusion of the Judge as recipient was also telling: as the chief judicial figure in Athens, he would have been the one charged with resolving any dispute that arose in the interpretation of the letter and, if necessary, with its ultimate enforcement. This is an indication that the letter expressed far more than a wish on the part of the Kaimacam, as it was part of the role of the Cadi to enforce legal obligations.[9] Taken together, these indicate that the document had been a command from the acting head of the Porte to two inferior officials, a letter with the name *buyuruldu* (derived from the term 'to order') within the legal system of the time.[10]

Those involved in negotiating, securing, transmitting and applying the document seemed to understand it to be an order from the capital, and would have acted very differently had they been dealing with anything less. Hunt, a shrewd operator familiar from his time in Turkey with the functioning of *firmans*,[11] was very emphatic when he met with the Voivode. And his official escort from the Court, the Mubashir, whose presence underscored the document's importance, had been assertive with the Voivode, behaving 'with uncommon energy and propriety', as Hunt later put it in a report to Elgin.[12] The Voivode, who would have clearly been aware of the difference between a command from his superiors and a letter of request, would have otherwise given the chaplain short shrift. As soon as he read the document and 'perceived the determined tone with which we spoke', again according to Hunt, 'he became submissive in the extremist degree'.[13] It therefore appears likely that the letter comprised an order – a *buyuruldu* – from the Ottoman Court that needed to be obeyed. Otherwise, the response in Athens would have been very different. None of what followed would have been remotely possible.[14]

The Text of the Kaimacam Letter

If we turn now to the text of the Italian translation, we can try to determine the sort of liberties the original might have granted Lord Elgin's men in Athens. The translation was written on a sheet of laid paper with a contemporaneous watermark from a paper manufacturer near Venice known to have exported to the East, all consistent with the materials used by Italians such as Pisani or Dané.[15] Despite what one scholar has suggested, this document was certainly not a later forgery composed by Hunt prior to his appearance before the Select Committee in 1816.[16]

The translation was set out in two parts and was without paragraph numbers or clauses; it reads very much like two long run-on sentences, a typical style called by Professor Edhem Eldem 'the nightmare of students of Ottoman history'.[17] It began by stating that it was – as we know – a translation of a letter written by the Kaimacam and addressed to the 'Giudice' and the Voivode of Athens. The first part of the body outlined the request made by Lord Elgin, Ambassador 'della corte d'Inghilterra' (from the court of England) to 'la porta della felicità' (the 'Porte of happiness'). The Ambassador, having explained the importance of the writings, artworks and scientific theories of the Ancient Greeks, and that he had himself commissioned five 'Pittori Inglesi' (*English* painters, sic) in Athens to examine, study and draw the artefacts of the town, expressly asked that a written order be made ('scritto ed ordinato'). What was asked for was that the men not be interrupted or obstructed by the local authorities when going to and from the 'Castello' (the castle, ie the Acropolis), placing scaffolding around the temples, copying or making mouldings, measuring the remains or excavating the foundations of the buildings in order to find 'mattoni inscritti' (inscribed bricks) and that no opposition be made if they wish to take away 'qualche pezzi di pietra' (some pieces of stone) with old inscriptions and figures. It is clear that the request half of the document was made to echo Hunt's original memorandum.

The text then introduced the individual carrying the letter. The Italian version had left the generic initials 'NN', which probably stood for *nescio nomen* ('I do not know the name'), meant as a placeholder for the name of the eventual courier.[18] While the later translation into English provided by Hunt to the Select Committee in 1816 had rather presumptuously included Hunt's own name here (described as 'an English gentleman'), this is almost certainly incorrect since the official holder of the letter would have been the Ottoman Mubashir.[19]

Then came the second, more important part of the letter whereby the Kaimacam commanded the Cadi/judge and Voivode/governor on behalf of the 'Excelso Impero' (Excellent Empire) to act in conformity with the request of Lord Elgin as set out above. This in large part mirrored what had already been asked for, wording it as a direct order to the two officials. It was the 'chiaro l'impegna' (clear commitment) of the Empire to favour the Ambassador's request; being 'incombente' (incumbent) upon the officials not to oppose it, they were to use their utmost 'attenzione' (attention) to act in conformity with that request. One expert in Ottoman law has said that this part of the document showed only a wish and not an order or enforcement of a law or of the Sultan's command.[20] With respect, though, it is difficult to square the words ('clear commitment', 'incumbent upon', 'attention to act in conformity with') with a mere wish on the part of the sender. And then there were the letter's concluding words: 'e nella su rifferita maniera operiate, e vi comportiate' (in the aforesaid manner you must operate and comport yourselves). It therefore appears like the command of a superior, one which afforded relatively little discretion in complying with its terms.

What then did that order require? First was to comply with the request as set out in the first part of the text. This meant the artists were free to enter and leave the 'castle' as and when they wished, to set up scaffolding around the monuments, to make mouldings of the features of the buildings and to take measurements of the remains. Next was the ability to excavate, which was itself significant since no foreign visitor had previously been granted such a privilege.[21] Lord Elgin wrote to Lusieri at once, proclaiming that with this new power 'a great field is opened for medals, and for the remains both of sculpture and architecture'.[22]

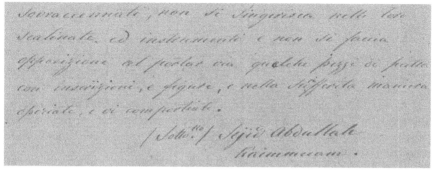

Figure 3 The concluding lines of the Italian translation of the Kaimacam letter of July 1801 comprise the infamous permission to remove from the site some pieces of stone ('qualche pezzi di pietra') with inscriptions and figures
Source: © Trustees of the British Museum.

The final order was that no opposition be made to the taking away of pieces of stone with inscriptions and figures ('e non si faccia opposizione al portar via qualche pezzi di pietra con inscrizione, e figure') (see Figure 3). This has become the most controversial line of the entire document, one that is still debated today. What did the words, coming as they did at the end of a 700-word letter, really permit? In the logic of the preceding text, it would seem to have related to the excavations ('scavare') that the men would undertake in the hopes of uncovering the ancient foundations of the buildings and any remaining 'inscribed bricks' amongst the rubble; if pieces of stone were unearthed in the process, they could then be taken away.[23] But what exactly was the meaning of 'al portar via' (taking away)? Did it mean that the men could pull buried artefacts from the soil and rearrange them on the ground? Or did it actually extend further, to permit them to take pieces off the Acropolis and into the lower town? The language is somewhat open-ended. In Italian, 'al portar via' can mean either of these things, or both, and without the original Turkish document, we can only assume that the order gave a certain amount of discretion on this point to the local officials implementing it.

And did the permission extend beyond excavation to the prising of architectural sculptures from the edifices themselves? Lord Elgin, when asked about it before the Select Committee in 1816, seemed to think so.[24] But nowhere in the document is such an authorisation expressly granted. Some commentators have deemed this sufficient to conclude that the letter explicitly forbade such dismemberment.[25] A certain logic runs through the argument. If, as a premise, we accept that all property on a military site such as this was property of the Sultan, then presumably only permission from the Sultan could validly transfer ownership.[26] Putting aside the fact that the permission came not from the Sultan, but from the Kaimacam, can we nevertheless say that the permission authorised the removal of sculptures from the buildings, like the metopes taken down under Hunt's watchful eye at the end of July 1801?

Nowhere in the text of the letter are there words to that effect. This led the eminent legal scholar John Henry Merryman to write in 1985 that, 'While it is possible to read the firman as a flowery concession of everything for which Elgin asked, it is more reasonable to conclude that the Ottomans had a narrower intention, and that the firman provides slender authority for the massive removals from the Parthenon.' Merryman concluded that the reference to taking away pieces of stone 'seems incidental, intended to apply to objects found while excavating.'[27]

Could the permission extend to *any* artefact found on the site? The phrase used in the translation is 'qualche pezzi di pietra', with 'qualche' generally understood to mean 'some'. Philip Hunt, in providing a translation for the Select Committee in 1816, had rendered the word into 'any', giving the critical phrase a much wider interpretation: 'when they wish to take away *any* pieces of stone'. This is no doubt a serious variance, with consequences as to how far the legal interpretation might extend. The British politician and diplomat Harold Nicolson, writing about the matter after the Second World War, drew attention to this discrepancy, concluding that the correct translation was most likely 'some' and not 'any'.[28] More recently, the leading scholar of the Ottoman period, Edhem Eldem, has found that the liberal use of a term such as 'any' in a document of this nature would have been highly unlikely for the Ottomans. Eldem surmises instead that they would have used a less expansive, though purposefully vague term (like 'some') in order to allow officials to interpret it as best suited the circumstances on the ground at the time.[29]

The drafting of Ottoman documents did leave open possible alternative interpretations. Lord Elgin said before the Select Committee in 1816 that 'permission issuing from the Porte for any of the distant provinces, is little better than an authority to make the best bargain you can with the local authorities'.[30] And he was not entirely wrong. In one example recounted in the 1840s, English travellers to Bodrum were given a *firman* from Constantinople that allowed them to 'go round the fortifications' of the town's castle. But the local Voivode, adhering to the strict language in the text, refused to allow them entry *within* the castle. In another, written permission given to French travellers to 'go within and examine' the same castle was interpreted by the Voivode so as not to permit them to leave! And in yet another, the liberty given by a *firman* to an English collector to 'take down' sculptures from the ruins at Ephesus was not in itself enough for the local official to allow the sculptures to then be 'taken away'.[31] Much seemed to rely on the interpretation made by officials on the ground, who could prove to be as cruel or as fastidious as they desired at any given time.

Assembling these interpretations and anecdotes is a little like counting angels on a pinhead. Whatever our conclusions, we are left largely with conjecture. We will never know for certain what form the original document took, nor indeed the precise extent of its contents. As such, we cannot answer with certainty that the removals were permitted under the concession, nor that they were not. The only standard that might allow us to move beyond the irksome question is that of evidentiary interpretation used by courts of law in interpreting documents such as this one. Courts employ a balance of probabilities, not seeking certainty, but instead asking which of the many conflicting interpretations is more probable than any of the others. This is how legal determinations are ultimately made, appropriate within the environment in which they operate.[32] Because we are considering the legal effect of the Kaimacam letter, we should take the approach we would assume a court of law would take. We must therefore ask whether it appears, on a balance of probabilities, that authorisation to remove the Marbles had indeed been given. Judging by the above – the text used, the context in which the letter was obtained and interpreted at the time, comparisons with other official documents – it appears more likely than not that the letter *did* in fact provide authorisation for Elgin's men to remove the Marbles, at least according to the Ottoman legal system. But, as we shall see, that is by no means the only consideration.

Later Ottoman Documents

The Kaimacam letter of July 1801 is not the only hinge by which the enterprise hangs. There were subsequent documents which may be interpreted as providing further evidence of authorisation by the Ottomans of the activities that took place on the Acropolis. As appears from the letters of Lusieri to Elgin from 1802, a year into the removals the Voivode (governor) and the Disdar (commander of the garrison) started to cool on the project. Lusieri asked Elgin to obtain further authorisation from Constantinople, as a way of clarifying the Porte's initial intentions, while providing a necessary stamp of approval. In a letter dated 28 October 1802, Lusieri reported that this had arrived from Constantinople and, when presented to the officials, was immediately effective: 'I calmed the Disdar with our action so that he could live in peace', a relieved Lusieri wrote.[33]

The content of such additional authorising documents had for many years remained a mystery. Reliance was placed by some on Lusieri's 28 October letter to demonstrate a form of official acquiescence, as indirect proof that the actions of the men had indeed been sanctioned after the fact. John Henry Merryman, quoted above for his circumspection about the Kaimacam letter, adduced the later documents as evidence of retroactive 'ratification' by the authorities that effectively rendered the removals lawful after the fact. Even if the earlier letter had been imperfect, the subsequent letters demonstrated a form of official approval. 'It is the law everywhere', he wrote, 'that an act in excess of the authority originally granted can be ratified, expressly or by implication, from conduct indicating acquiescence'; the later events therefore 'make a strong case for ratification of the removal, even if it exceeded the authority given' in the original document.[34]

Now, thanks to the work of Elena Korka of the Hellenic Ministry of Culture and Sport, after many hours in the Elgin archive at Broomhall, an Italian translation has been found that reveals the content of one of the Ottoman orders from October 1802.[35] This is quite a remarkable find and has been said by Korka to illustrate the 'magic' that occasionally comes from the tedious research process.[36] The contents of the find, however, do not necessarily help those looking to undermine the legality of the initial removal. On the contrary, the uncovered document appears to show official approval of what had taken place – with the explicit encouragement that it continue.

Like the Kaimacam letter, this letter appears to be a *buyuruldu*, an order from the Ottoman Court. Due to its form and the lack of any mention of the Sultan it is not a *firman*. Yet unlike the earlier letter, this one is signed by the Grand Vizier, who had by this point returned to Constantinople following the retreat of the French. The letter is addressed to the Voivode of Athens, thanking him for the hospitality he had shown Elgin on the latter's visit to the city earlier that year. The letter also recognised the reception given to Lusieri, who had remained at Athens to 'prepare some drawings'. The final part of the letter – the order to the subordinate – requires the Voivode to continue to act with goodwill towards Elgin's men and to cooperate and support the 'work' entrusted to them in the best way possible. It is assumed by Korka (quite wisely) that another version of this letter, practically identical to the first, was addressed to the Disdar.[37]

This recently discovered translation does appear to demonstrate official approval for what had occurred in Athens. Korka has said that the terms are vague and, notably, that the Vizier might have been given some misinformation about the extent of the work undertaken by Lusieri and the men: we know, for instance, that they were doing more than simply 'preparing drawings'.[38] Yet the Vizier's letter, taken together with the earlier Kaimacam letter, does indicate a form of approval by the Porte. The translation demonstrates approval for the 'work' entrusted to the men by Elgin, which is to be supported going forward by the Voivode (and presumably the Disdar in the accompanying letter).

Certain subsequent actions may, however, give reason to doubt that removal remained perpetually permissible. The first was the apparent revocation of earlier excavation permissions in 1804 and the second was a ban in 1805 imposed on the removal of sculptures from the Acropolis.[39] Both were the result of the changing tide in Athens at the time, with the French now in favour and Fauvel back on the scene to press the Voivode against Lusieri and the Elgin project. In fact, the 1805 ban appears to have been issued at the behest of the French Ambassador in Constantinople to the delight of Fauvel, who claimed that it alone was what saved the Parthenon's west frieze *in situ*.[40]

While the revocation of 1804 and the ban of 1805 may have had an impact on excavations going forward, there is no evidence to show that they could, or indeed did, operate retroactively. In fact, the bulk of Lusieri's work on the Acropolis had finished by the end of 1804 and this mostly affected the excavations he had undertaken elsewhere in Athens, though even these seem to have continued (illegally) for at least six months.[41] More importantly, a revocation and ban, though certainly having a practical impact on the day-to-day operations, do not seem to have been capable of affecting the legality of the earlier orders from Constantinople. So these changes of 1804 and 1805 did not appear to affect the pieces that had already been removed from the Acropolis, nor indeed those already shipped from the Port of Piraeus and on their way to England.[42]

A second remarkable find was made recently in the Ottoman Archives in Istanbul. This relates to the final export permission obtained from the Ottoman Court to allow the departure of the remaining Marbles from Piraeus. There was much hypothesising over the years in the absence of such a document, including as part of the ratification theory espoused by Merryman to show official acquiescence in the taking of the Marbles.[43] No fewer than 40 crates of antiquities were still awaiting shipment at Piraeus in 1806 when war was declared between Britain and the Ottoman Empire. Remarkably, the cases remained at the port throughout the war and, at the cessation of hostilities in 1809, Lusieri asked the new British Ambassador in Constantinople to obtain an export permission to allow the crates to leave.

The Ambassador, Lord Adair, began negotiations with the Porte, but it soon came to light that the Turks were refusing to recognise the permission to remove the objects in the first place.[44] Only after six months of bargaining was Adair able to obtain authorisation, which he reported in a dispatch to the British Foreign Secretary. The permission eventually reached Lusieri in Athens and he set about securing the final shipments to Malta. One major load departed on a chartered ship in March (with military escort), while the remaining five cases would leave the following April on the HMS *Hydra*.[45]

Three documents from the period have now been located in the Ottoman Archive and go to prove this state of affairs – and more. The first, dating from 1810, is an internal message from the Grand Vizier to the Sultan, Mahmud II. It explains that the Ambassador 'of England' had sought permission to transport 'image-bearing stones' that his predecessor Lord Elgin had 'purchased' in Athens, and that it had been 'verified' that such stones had indeed 'previously been given to the English'. In a rather revealing passage, it explains that the delay caused in providing this permission was not due to any inconvenience in granting it, but rather because the Court was using delay tactics as a diplomatic manoeuvre. The idea being that the longer the Ambassador had to wait, the more appreciative he would be to receive the eventual permission. A draft letter is provided for the Voivode in Athens, to which the Sultan has stamped his approval with a few words in imperial Turkish.[46]

The second document dates from the following year, 1811, and demonstrates that the matter still had not been resolved – or rather that the Ottoman stalling tactics had indeed been working. In this missive, the Grand Vizier again writes to the Sultan seeking approval of an order to be sent to the Voivode in Athens, again upon the Ambassador's request. The third document is that final order, a copy of which was forwarded to Athens: 'Concerning the matter of the transport of some broken marble pieces and earthen pots decorated with figures …. There is no harm in granting permission for the transport and passage of the said stones, and this letter [is written so that] no impediment be offered to the transport and passage of the said stones that have been placed in crates located there.'[47]

Now few doubts should remain as to the permission which allowed the final shipment of sculptures to depart. Taken together with the letters of 1801 and 1802, this is surely sufficient proof that the Elgin party had secured authorisation, once again assessed on a balance of probabilities, and considering the entirety of evidence available. The purpose of this conclusion should not of course serve to deflate the legitimacy of the argument for the restitution of the Parthenon Marbles. Its ambition is far narrower: to serve as a dispassionate attempt to lay out the most logical interpretation of the documents and the context in which they were first issued and later enforced. If anything, such conclusions could perhaps allow for a fresh approach to the matter. Rather than rehearsing the arguments over 'theft' or 'unlawful removal' of the Marbles, discussions could instead move beyond this. It may even offer a more fruitful territory for compromise.

Bribery in the Ottoman Empire

There remain two lingering questions that relate to the legitimacy of Ottoman authorisation. The first of these is the question of payments and gifts made by Elgin and his men to obtain the necessary favours from the Ottomans. Did these constitute bribes? And, if so, might they serve to undermine the legitimacy of the ultimate permission given? The second question relates to the historical context, viz. Ottoman rule over the territory that would soon become the Kingdom of Greece. As some have argued, is the fact that authorisation came from a hostile and oppressive power enough to undermine the legitimacy of that authorisation? On both counts, we must consider the question of legal legitimacy, but this may not be enough. Clearly there are moral implications to these acts as well, ones which are still being felt today. What impact might these have on the assessment?

Let us begin with the question of bribery. Gifts, in the form of western goods, were handed over to Ottoman officials in both Constantinople and Athens throughout the period. From the beginning, Elgin's artists had to pay the five guineas for access to the Acropolis. Recall too that when Hunt returned to Athens in July 1801, accompanying the Mubashir and the order from the Kaimacam, he came bearing gifts.[48] Lusieri reported that he had given the Voivode and Disdar money, telescopes, horses, shawls and a green cape.[49] Based on later estimations provided by Lord Elgin in England, it would appear that at least £5,000 was spent on 'presents' to Ottoman officials over the 12-year period beginning in 1799 (equivalent to approximately £150,000 today).[50] Add to this Ambassador Adair's request to export the remaining Marbles from Piraeus in 1810, which was accompanied by a payment of some £100 to officials and a further 'gift' of 1480 piastres to the Kaimacam.[51] As Elgin would later admit to the Select Committee, in their negotiations with Europeans, the Ottomans were unaffected by anything but 'weight of gold'.[52]

Do such disbursements constitute bribes? As elsewhere, there is much debate on the point. Merryman concluded in 1985 that bribery was 'hardly a significant legal consideration' in the East at the time, and would not have vitiated the decisions of the officials involved.[53] One British Museum curator has gone further, characterising these as part of a 'two-way gift exchange process', using as evidence the presentation of sheep and fruit to Hunt while he was in Athens.[54] Others, such as David Rudenstine, have argued that the gifts clearly did constitute bribes, with Rudenstine disputing Merryman's conclusions by drawing attention to the fact that, at least under English law, paying off officials had been forbidden since at least the time of Magna Carta (by which King John promised to 'sell to no man … either Justice or Right').[55]

Elgin's biographer, William St Clair, who initially agreed with Merryman that bribes were 'technically lawful' under the circumstances,[56] later discovered that the Disdar would have received in this manner an amount 35 times his annual salary, the Voivode even more.[57] St Clair thus changed his view: 'No administrative or judicial system', he wrote in 2006, 'can be expected to withstand such a weight of political influence and money. This is imperialism in action, destroying not only monuments but the local administrative and legal infrastructure.' Decisions made at Constantinople and Athens were, in his view, contaminated by the corruption, and rendered legally questionable: 'Decisions by public officials to exceed their authority that are obtained by inducements are questionable under most systems of law, and I know no lawyer who says Ottoman law was exceptional.'[58]

Let us try to understand then the legal effect that bribery might have had at the time. A bribe can be described as an undue reward offered to, or received by, a public official in order to influence their behaviour in acting out their duties.[59] Though this particular definition may be rooted in a western legal tradition, the principle is accepted throughout the world today and similar language can be found in international conventions.[60] The taking of money and gifts by Ottoman officials would certainly fit within our definition of bribery, but how exactly was bribery treated within the Ottoman Empire? According to the *Encyclopaedia of Islam*, the word for bribe (*rashwa* in Arabic and *rüsvet* in Turkish) had the same negative connotation in the Islamic world as it did in the west and had long been forbidden by law.[61] According to Sharia, bribery is considered a major sin for both the one making the bribe and the official receiving it. This has its roots in the Koran,[62] but even more so in the words of the Prophet Mohammad who invoked a divine curse upon those who offered or took bribes.[63] While bribing an official so that a deserved right is enforced may not be sinful for the one making the bribe, it remains so for the official receiving the payment.

When Elgin's Embassy began, the ships carried from England chandeliers, clocks, watches, jewelled boxes, ermine, pistols, and yards of satin, brocade, velvet and damask. Of course, many of these would not be used as bribes, but would serve as ceremonial gifts to the Sultan, Grand Vizier, Kaimacam and others in the Ottoman administration at Constantinople.[64] Interestingly, when the Kaimacam letter was being negotiated in July 1801, there does not appear to be evidence of gifts or money being offered in exchange. As we know, the permission was given largely due to Ottoman appreciation for the defeat of the French in Egypt. Lord Elgin spoke later only of his 'trouble and patient solicitation' in obtaining the permission.[65]

The situation in Athens was different. In a remote outpost it was a matter of course to offer emoluments to officials, a practice that was established long before Elgin's time.[66] Elgin would even admit to the British Government that permission from the Porte was 'nothing more [than] an introduction, by means of which secret negotiations may be carried on with such persons in office or in power, as have some superintendence, or immediate concern with the objects in question'.[67] But the explanation does not excuse the crime. As the *Encyclopaedia of Islam* puts it, European visitors often assumed bribery was 'a way of life' in the East, but it remained anathema there as anywhere else.[68] Even if the Kaimacam's letter had been clear, the acceptance of bribes by the officials required to enforce it would have been contrary even to the precepts of Sharia; if it was unclear, then the foreigners too would be inculpated in the wrong.

But if the acts involved were wrongful at the time, punishment would be subject only to Ottoman law. This could have meant the prompt dismissal of the guilty officials or, worse, a summons to Constantinople for the necessary punishment dispensed by the Porte.[69] Punishment from his superiors was precisely what the Voivode had dreaded in September 1802, prompting Lusieri to ask Elgin for additional letters from the Porte, the ones he happily received the following month. The feared reprimand from Constantinople, while entirely conceivable, never in fact materialised. The activities of the officials in Athens went unrepudiated; the officials unpunished. The Porte could have sought to correct the situation, but it never did. As such, the activities were tacitly tolerated by the authorities at the time. While the acts could have conceivably been seen as wrongful, no legal pronouncement was made upon them, meaning that they were ultimately never declared 'unlawful' within the Ottoman legal system.

Ottoman Rule as 'Occupation'?

A second question that continues to linger relates to the context of Ottoman rule over Athens at the time. It has been suggested by some that authority derived from Ottoman documents should be considered null and void, as the instruments of a foreign power imposed upon a conquered people.[70] 'Foreign occupation' was referred to in the first Greek claim for the Marbles in 1983.[71] In 1986, Melina Mercouri famously asked the members of the Oxford Union, 'is it proper to transact with the Turks for the most treasured of Greek possessions when Greece is under Turkish invasion and subjugation?'[72] Even today, the position of the Greek Government continues to refer to Athens at the time as being 'under Ottoman occupation.'[73]

Military occupation occurs when the army of one country controls some or all of the territory of another. For the purposes of international law an 'occupied territory' was formally defined only in 1899, within regulations to the first Hague Convention, as territory 'actually placed under the authority of the hostile army' and only extending where that authority 'is established, and in a position to assert itself'.[74] Occupations arise during or after armed conflicts and are usually short-lived affairs. After one army defeats the other, it is usually only a matter of time before a peace treaty establishes a new territorial delineation: the occupier then returns the conquered region, the territory is annexed to the victorious power or the territory becomes an independent entity.[75] For example, the Allies occupied Germany in 1945, dividing it into the four zones of occupation; by the early 1950s the armies had retreated, leaving in place civilian governments in both West and East Germany. In other situations, occupation can lead to annexation such as what followed North Vietnam's conquest of South Vietnam in 1975, after which the countries were united.

But was Greece occupied in this way at the time of the Marbles' removal? By 1801, it may have been difficult to conceive of Ottoman rule as an 'occupation', even by the terms of the modern definition stemming from the Hague Convention. The Ottomans had conquered Athens from the Florentines by 1458, nearly three and a half centuries earlier. In fact, Athens had been under foreign control more or less continually since the fourth century BCE when the city was conquered by Philip II of Macedon (a mere century after the Parthenon's construction). After the Macedonians came the Romans, the Goths, the Byzantines, the Burgundians, the Catalans and the Florentines, before the Ottomans finally took over. Athens had been only sporadically independent over the previous 2,000 years. In addition, Greeks had become involved, to a certain extent, within parts of the civil administration of the Ottoman Empire, though this tended to be in Constantinople, the Aegean islands, Wallachia and Moldavia, not in Athens itself.[76]

The Turkish presence in Athens did, however, possess the trappings of military rule. Control of the local population was enforced by janissaries who worshipped a different god and took their orders from across the Aegean. Soldiers were stationed on the Acropolis, which served as a garrison, with its cannons aimed down at the city, though these had apparently been dismantled by 1800 and were only for show.[77] Over the centuries, there had been attempts from the outside to cast off the Ottoman yoke: in 1687, two deputations of Greeks had gone out to welcome Morosini and the Venetians as liberators; later, an ill-fated rebellion 'under the Muscovite flag' took place in Salamis; and in 1770, Catherine the Great of Russia tried to foment a Greek rebellion during the Orlov Revolt, though ultimately without success.[78] All this might lead some to conclude, along with the historian Molly Mackenzie, that 'it was as conquerors that [the Turks] had come to Athens and it was by right of conquest that they remained there'.[79]

Evidence exists of a recalcitrant, even rebellious, sentiment amongst the local population which helped lay the groundwork for Greek independence a generation later. Liberal Greeks had, by the late eighteenth century, begun to dream of an emancipated homeland, following the model of the French Revolution. As early as 1797, the revolutionary writer Rigas Feraios composed his patriotic *Thourios* hymn ('Better an hour of freedom than forty years a slave') and published his political map of Greece, known today as the 'Greek Magna Carta', a year before his execution at the hands of the Ottomans.[80] And despite an apparent docility, the Athenians evinced a clear dislike for their overlords. Englishman John Galt, in Athens from 1809 to 1811, wrote that the Greeks 'consider their oppressors as having only a temporary possession and, to the most careless observer, it must be evident that the opportunity only is wanting to combine them as one man against the Turks'.[81] Lord Byron saw them in *Childe Harold's Pilgrimage* 'trembling beneath the scourge of Turkish hand, from birth to death enslaved, in word and deed unmanned',[82] and in his notes to the poem held that the Greeks had 'never lost hope' in being delivered by a sympathetic foreign power.[83] Byron's friend John Cam Hobhouse commented in 1809 that the Greeks were 'devotedly attached to their country and nation and, even to a degree which may appear foolish and incautious, continually express their hatred of their masters and their confidence in themselves'.[84]

If we tilt the historical telescope only slightly towards the period following the removal of the Marbles, the status of Ottoman authority can more easily be called into question. Within a decade of the final shipment leaving Piraeus (April 1811), the first call was made for the Greeks to rise in revolt against the Ottomans. Athens itself was liberated as early as 1822, the same year as the first National Assembly sat in Epidaurus, a Provisional Administration was established for Greece and a new Constitution was adopted.[85] In 1823, Great Britain would recognise 'belligerent rights' for Greece, hence downgrading the sovereign claim of Ottoman Turkey over the territory.[86] And it was the solidarity of the many philhellenes returning to Europe after visits to Athens that would help maintain support for the Greek cause throughout the War of Independence. Be that as it may, the idea of Greek statehood would have appeared fanciful – at best poetic – back in 1801.

That said, the modern term 'occupation' is not necessarily circumscribed by the passage of time.[87] Under the Hague definition, an occupation can persist provided the territory remains 'placed under the authority of the hostile army', without any explicit expiration period. Examples of long occupations do exist, though the longer they continue the less certain their status.[88] Israel's control of the West Bank for example, begun in 1967, is still considered an occupation by the United Nations General Assembly, the International Court of Justice and Israel's own High Court,[89] although the Israeli Government continues to dispute this categorisation; Indigenous groups in Canada, Australia and the United States occasionally refer to the conquest of their lands by European settlers as a continuing occupation. And some in Ireland, describing English rule over that island, still talk of '800 years of occupation'.[90] Such examples, however, do seem somewhat tenuous. And the notion of a 350-year *occupation*, especially by the terms of the early nineteenth century, would have seemed an anomaly, if not a complete absurdity.

Even if this had been an occupation, what effect might that characterisation have on the acquisition of the Marbles? While an occupation today might denote a series of onerous obligations on the occupying power (respecting legal rights of civilians and private property, refraining from destroying or damaging cultural monuments, etc), few, if any, of these existed prior to the twentieth century.[91] Occupations used to exist almost entirely to the advantage of the occupier, with express benefits such as a guarantee of obedience from the local population, the ability to requisition public property and impose taxes and, perhaps most importantly, the ability to force a favourable peace settlement.[92] Occupation at the time did not impose limits upon the occupier, a situation very different from today. As such, the particular actions of occupiers would not have been overridden by the European powers acting in concert. There was simply no basis under the law of nations to do so.

The only method of unwinding the decrees of an occupier would have been through the eventual passage of some negatory Act by the newly independent successor state. After 1832, the Kingdom of Greece could have disavowed enactments made by the Ottomans. However, nothing was done regarding the permissions relating to the Acropolis. Short of this, the rules governing private affairs from the Ottoman period would have continued much as they had previously, as they did, for example, with the ownership of land.[93] Without an existing international principle to wield, and with no targeted action by the fledgling Greek state, there would have been no way of nullifying the loathsome acts of the Ottomans, regardless of whether or not they were considered veritable occupiers of Athens at the time.

Law and Morality

Whether we like it or not, there is little way of impugning the legality of the permission given for the removal of the Marbles. We have seen this already in the balance of probabilities approach, an approach used widely as the common civil standard for assessing the legality of any action or situation. On balance, then, the Kaimacam's letter of July 1801 does appear to provide authorisation, while additional evidence can be adduced from the Grand Vizier's letter of September 1802 and the final export permission of 1811. Any acts of bribery paid to obtain permission were never punished. And the legal consequence of the permission was not formally retracted once Greece was freed of Ottoman rule. Taken together, the enterprise appears to have been legal at the time (again, on balance) and the activities were not overridden by later acts by those in authority.

But surely that is not enough … surely more than the strict legality of the operation must be considered. What of its morality? Law and morality are of course very different. The source of law is a precise set of rules. Those rules are objective in nature and imposed by the relevant legal authority. If those rules are followed, an action is considered lawful; if not, it is unlawful. Morality, on the other hand, is less precise, but can develop steadily as the mores of society change: such decisions relate not to a clear set of mandatory rules, but to a constellation of ethical factors, each one complex, nuanced, affecting the overall matter in subtle but significant ways.

Morality is at its core a personal matter. It stems from the individual conscience. Through it we feel that certain actions are right or wrong, regardless of what the law might tell us to do (or not to do). Ethics can then develop out of a shared morality, largely accepted across a community but not imposed by a superior force like the courts, police or military powers.[94] In a sense, it arises from the ground up based on a moral consensus. Sometimes ethics can be reflected in particular instruments: the best examples of these are ethical codes that apply within specific professions, as well as to particular industries or fields.[95] In particular, the antiq uities trade and the museum sector each operate according to specific codes of ethics, and the best known of these (for museums) is the Code of Ethics of the International Council of Museums (ICOM).[96] Such codes are meant to reflect principles that are generally accepted within the community.[97]

In the case of the Marbles' removal, the morality of the taking looks far less certain than its legality. The morality of the act was questioned even at the time, especially by English visitors to Athens, including most famously Lord Byron. It was also questioned in strident terms by Members of Parliament during a House of Commons debate in June 1816, who referred to the removal as 'unjustified' and as an act of 'spoliation' (as we will see in the next chapter). Furthermore, would the actions of Elgin's men be considered morally appropriate had they occurred today? What would we think, for instance, of excavations with little consideration for the principles of archaeology, the prising of architectural sculpture from edifices, the sawing and chiselling of sculpted marble in order to facilitate transport and the paying of local warlords to ease the overall process? Would it matter that the project had been lawfully sanctioned by the powers that be? The point is not whether the specific acts violate a subsequent ethical position, but whether the retention in the present of material obtained in such a way can be deemed ethically problematic.

Let us briefly consider the actions against the ICOM Code of Ethics, as a guide to how they might be seen within the current landscape.[98] To begin, the ICOM Code requires that museums acquire objects only where they are satisfied that valid title is held and that the objects were not illegally obtained or illegally exported.[99] Based on the above analysis, the removal of the Marbles would appear to comply with these requirements. However, the Code goes on to proscribe the acquisition of objects where there is 'reasonable cause' to believe their recovery had involved the 'intentional destruction or damage of monuments [or] archaeological sites', or where there was a 'failure to disclose the finds to the owner or occupier of the land, or to the proper legal or governmental authorities'.[100] It would appear that the removal of the Marbles would violate such a proscription: for instance, the sawing or chiseling of entire blocks of marble and the lack of a detailed account of any of the findspots. Lastly, there is a requirement in the Code for acquisitions that involve a 'contemporary community' to be made based on the 'informed and mutual consent' of the community involved, and that the respect for the wishes of the community should be paramount.[101] While the Code is by no means retroactive, it helps to indicate how the removals from Athens might be considered today from an ethical perspective.[102]

This is not to say that these ethical principles can allow us to undo the actions of the past. While the law provides us with the ability to force a particular outcome, the law can also impose certain barriers to prevent legal action in relation to isolated events of the distant past (most notably limitations of action in civil cases, to be discussed in chapter six).[103] Ethics is different. While ethics cannot allow us to force a particular outcome on the relevant parties, ethics is also free of some of the barriers imposed by law.[104] This is what permits us to assess actions that occurred long ago through our own particular ethical lens. It remains our prerogative to judge the morality of those actions, especially when they have direct consequences today.[105] An example of such a situation might occur when the tangible outcome of an act we consider immoral continues to manifest itself in the present: for instance when important property remains in one particular location as the result of that act; or when the consequences of that act continue to resound within certain communities.

While these ethical positions cannot allow us to force a particular outcome – no ethical code would presume to do as much – they do serve two purposes. First, they problematise the present situation. The retention of property that was removed in ways now considered morally troubling must be assessed on such a basis. The status quo remains volatile, which can serve as a prompt for further action, such as an attempt to seek a meaningful resolution. The second purpose served by the ethical analysis is to set out a broad range of possible solutions, each of which may be considered ethically defensible. Taking action by employing one of these solutions in an attempt to break the deadlock is therefore wholly justified, even if the action itself does not take a prescribed form.

Different approaches to the ethical problem will be considered later in the book. For now, let us pause the discussion on ethics and return to it in chapter six. We will then be able to contrast more concretely the ethics of today with the structures imposed by law upon the British Museum. But first let us turn back to the Marbles and consider their treatment following their arrival and assembly in Britain during the early nineteenth century.

4

Albion's Verdict

Once the Marbles had made the voyage overseas and were assembled in London, it remained to be seen what was to be done with them. Lord Elgin had hoped at the outset to keep the finds in his private collection. With Broomhall in Scotland completed in 1799, the year he left for Constantinople, the initial plan had been to decorate it with the antiquities and reproductions taken from Athens.[1] But upon his release from France in 1806, his priorities began to shift, and he envisaged setting them up for public display in London. Time had taken its toll on Elgin: the imprisonment in France, a costly divorce, his physical ailments – and, most importantly, his debts. He had spent a significant amount on the acquisition and transport of the Marbles. According to his accounts, by 1811 expenses for the project had exceeded £60,000 (nearly £2 million in today's money) and, as the sculptures were being expensively stored in London, the outlay was growing by the day.[2]

The solution was not immediately clear. Elgin had published a short reader on the topic of the Marbles in 1810, as a way of promoting his newly acquired collection amongst the British public. Before long, many of the artistic luminaries of the time had given their views on the quality of the pieces, and the response was overwhelmingly positive. The president of the Royal Academy, Benjamin West, had told Elgin that they were 'unrivalled works of genius' in a letter that was quickly appended to the publication.[3] The great Italian sculptor Antonio Canova, when propositioned by Elgin to restore the semi-ruined pieces, refused, saying it would be a sacrilege to 'presume to touch them with a chisel'.[4] The artist JMW Turner was impressed; as was the poet John Keats, who would go on to compose a sonnet entitled 'On Seeing the Elgin Marbles'. This all looked promising for enhancing the value of the collection. However, Elgin's proposal to the Paymaster General in 1811 to sell the collection to the nation for £70,000 was promptly declined.

It was only in 1815, after further refusals from the Government and the Trustees of the British Museum, that Elgin took the initiative of petitioning Parliament directly.[5] A petition was prepared and presented to the House of Commons on 15 June. By this point Elgin was in need of the money. But going through Parliament would be slow, then as now. Added to this were the distracting influences of world events: led by the British, the Seventh Coalition had defeated Napoleon at Waterloo, and the matter of purchasing a collection of antique marble for the nation would have to wait.

Fortunately for Elgin, the postponement was short-lived. In February 1816, he was able to reintroduce his petition and the House of Commons debated it, before deciding to establish a Select Committee to further examine the matter.[6] The Committee, consisting of 18 MPs of varying political stripes, was tasked with answering certain questions about Elgin's collection. First and foremost, was whether the collection was of sufficiently high quality. There were rumours that Elgin's finds were unimpressive. Many pieces were in a state of sad disrepair. Lord Byron had called them 'Phidian freaks', 'misshapen monuments and maim'd antiques'.[7] Others, including the well-known classicist Richard Payne Knight, thought the works were not Greek at all, but Roman. The objective of this Committee would be to establish, once and for all, their authenticity and consequently their financial value.

Another matter it had to investigate was whether Lord Elgin had indeed obtained authority from the Ottomans to remove the Marbles in the first place. This is perhaps a surprising part of the brief, demonstrating the extent to which British institutions of the early nineteenth century were concerned with matters of propriety. Although the events had occurred many years earlier – and in a foreign country – it was still incumbent upon the Committee to assess the situation as best it could. The Report and transcript of its hearings are, if nothing else, a stellar example of British bureaucracy at work.

But the goal was not entirely altruistic. The reason the Committee needed to investigate the circumstances of the original acquisition was not because of some public disgust at the looting of ancient temples, but rather to ensure that Elgin had not used his role as Ambassador for private gain. Although the Government had earlier refused to fund the project in Athens, it was felt that, had Elgin obtained privileges by virtue of his position, and had he materially benefited from these, it would be inappropriate for Parliament to reward his unscrupulous actions by paying for the goods obtained as a result. Concern was also expressed at whether public money should be spent on property that might, if acquired by an ambassador in the course of his functions, belong by right to the State.

The Select Committee Gets to Work

In its considerations, the Committee left no stone unturned. Elgin was interviewed, followed by his erstwhile secretary, William Richard Hamilton, and a number of eminent artists. The question for the artists was how they rated the collection and to what aesthetic level, using Roman models as comparatives. The answer on this point was nearly unanimous. The Marbles were great works of art, the artists said ('the finest things that ever came to this country', beamed one),[8] and it would be a privilege for the nation to acquire them. After the artists came the scholars, including Payne Knight, who persisted in his views, though now admitting that *some* of the sculptures may have been Greek originals. Finally came Elgin's former chaplain, the upwardly mobile Philip Hunt, who had long since left the employ of Elgin and was now working for the rather more impressive Duke of Bedford.

The Committee's Report was an enterprise in staggering meticulousness. Long before the Greeks lodged their claim for the Marbles, long before the impassioned pleas of Melina Mercouri, this humble Westminster body, operating like dozens of others at the time, plodded through the testimonies and gathered the facts as best it could under the circumstances. Some commentators have been critical of the approach. The American law professor David Rudenstine, for example, has suggested that the parliamentarians should have sought statements from Turkish officials and others on the ground in Athens.[9] But of course this would have been impossible at the time: while committees today are able to resort to video calls, emails and extensive powers of compulsion, it remains commendable that this one, within two short weeks, was able to hear from all the major figures from the Elgin side (apart from Lusieri, who was still in Athens), as well as countless artists and other experts. The members remained persistent and tenacious throughout. None of the witnesses, Elgin included, escaped the Committee's inquisitive eye.

Of the four specific questions the Committee eventually reported on, two are of primary interest here. These relate, first, to the authority by which Elgin had acquired the collection and, second, to the circumstances in which that authority had been obtained. On the first of these, the Committee considered the 'fermaun' [sic] acquired for the artists in Athens, basing itself on a surprisingly, and perhaps suspiciously, detailed recollection of the document by the witness Hunt. While the Committee did not provide a firm conclusion on whether the text did or did not provide the necessary authorisation, it weighed the evidence surrounding its execution and came down on the side of Elgin and Hunt, but only just. There was an implication, drawn from Hunt, that the text itself may have been deficient (requiring a generosity of interpretation by the Voivode), as discussed in the previous chapter, but the Committee accepted evidence from Hunt (corroborated by Elgin's secretary, Hamilton) that the excavations and removals had continued for months, even years, without remonstration from the Turks at Athens or Constantinople, nor indeed from the local population.[10] This last point was the furthest the Select Committee would go towards querying the impact of the removal on the Greeks. Nowhere did the Committee slip into Byronic mode and bemoan the deleterious effects on a once proud land, nor the damage done to the structural integrity of Minerva's great temple.

The response to the second question still proves to this day a thing of judicious beauty. The scrutiny here was on whether Elgin had used his position as Ambassador to gain favour, and ultimately permission, from the Ottoman authorities. Firstly, it was asked whether Elgin undertook this mission on his own behalf. We already know this to have been the case, since the earlier proposal to invest in a speculative foreign venture had proven too much for the Government. But this point was quickly brushed aside by the Committee. The importance was not Elgin's own impression, but how the Ottomans with whom he was dealing understood matters. Did they afford him permission as a private citizen? Or did it flow from his position as chief representative of a distinguished ally? Tantalising questions, no doubt, the answers to which might have been impossible to ascertain. The Committee, in its wisdom, did not attempt to divine Ottoman intentions. Whether the officials had considered Elgin to be acting entirely in his personal capacity, the Committee held to be:

> a question which can be solved only by conjecture and reasoning, in the absence and deficiency of all positive testimony. The Turkish Ministers of that day are, in fact, the only persons in the world capable (if they are still alive) of deciding the doubt; and it is probable that even they, if it were possible to consult them, might be unable to form any very distinct discrimination as to the character in consideration of which they acceded to Lord Elgin's request.[11]

A clearer recognition by a public body of the ill-suited nature of parliaments and courts for processing the complexities of the world at large has seldom been made. The analysis would instead rely on 'conjecture and reasoning'. And the best evidence in this regard came from another traveller, the Earl of Aberdeen – future Prime Minister as well (1852–1855) – who had been in Athens at the time, informing the Committee that he did not deem it possible for a private individual to have succeeded as Elgin had. Even Philip Hunt supported the premise that 'a British subject not in the situation of Ambassador, could not have been able to obtain from the Turkish Government a fermaun of such extensive powers.'[12] And so the Committee left it. There was no way of knowing for sure, within the limits of time and space, the exact basis on which the permission had been obtained, but it appeared doubtful that anyone but an Ambassador could have obtained it.

The other two questions related respectively to the merit of the Marbles as works of sculpture and the value of the Marbles 'as objects of sale'. Were they peerless examples of Greek antiquity, useful for promoting the study of fine art in Britain? And, if so, how much should be offered for their acquisition? Thanks to the supporting testimony of the artists, the merit was considered of the first rank. As for the purchase price, this was placed at £35,000, a sizeable amount for the time (equivalent to just over £1 million today), but only half the amount Elgin had itemised in his earlier expenditures.

The last point – the matter of price – irritated Elgin. He wrote to Hamilton and complained of the 'manifest coldness and ill-will' of the Report,[13] though there was little else he could do at this late stage. In Elgin's view, the Report displayed an unnerving inconsistency. If the Committee had decided with the artists, and against the view advanced by Payne Knight, that the sculptures were marvellous and genuine, why such a low price? The answer seems to lie not in the logic of aesthetic valuation, but in the Committee's attempt, subtle though it may have been, to suggest a price low enough to discourage future British ambassadors from emulating Elgin: using their position, even indirectly, for personal advantage and then selling the fruits of the endeavour to the nation. This reading squares neatly with the answer to the second question above. Perhaps Elgin did benefit from his ambassadorship to obtain the authorisation, but if the reimbursement were limited to half his expenditure, the acquisition of the collection would hardly encourage similar behaviour by others.

The Report was signed on 25 March 1816 and made public over the course of the following month.[14] It was now left to the House of Commons to consider the matter. This time the MPs had the Report as ammunition when they began their debate on 7 June 1816. And the battle lines were clearly drawn. On one side were those who felt Elgin had emerged from the Committee hearings rather well and that his actions had succeeded in saving a mistreated monument at risk of further ruin by the Turks and the acquisitiveness of European visitors.[15] On the other side were myriad reasons to reject the Committee's recommendation. Firstly, it would be a drain on the public purse. Britain had only just come out of the Napoleonic conflicts that had engulfed Europe for 15 years and, though victorious, had the wellbeing of thousands of demobilised soldiers to consider. The country's deficit was reported by one MP at almost £17 million (equivalent to £500 million today). Another warned that the 'want of subsistence was the cause of riot and disturbances in many parts of the country', an ominous note that seemed to presage the Peterloo Massacre three years later.[16]

There were still some who did not think Parliament should reward Elgin for abusing his ambassadorial post. The Committee's Report, having been somewhat equivocal on the point, was used to show that no private citizen could have achieved what Elgin had done. Added to this were the accusations of bribery, supported by Hunt's admissions before the Committee that he had offered many presents, as discussed in chapter three. Then came the cries of 'spoliation', of the 'unjustified nature of the transaction', of the dishonour caused by Elgin to the people of Athens and to his own nation. Members were exhorted by one amongst their number to 'wipe off the stain, and not place in our museum a monument of our disgrace'.[17]

This last imperative came from MP Hugh Hammersley, and it was Hammersley who seemed to dominate the floor during the debate, at least in terms of the tone of his harangue. He was 'not so enamoured of those headless ladies', he began sententiously, 'as to forget another lady, which is justice.' He was also rather forward thinking. For it was Hammersley who proposed an amendment to the Bill with the following effect:

> that Great Britain holds these marbles only in trust till they are demanded by the present, or any future, possessors of the city of Athens, and upon such demand, engages, without question or negociation, to restore them …

It is no wonder the echoes of Hammersley have come down through the ages, reverberating through the legislative chambers of the Hellenic Republic and the hallowed halls of the Oxford Union. At a time when few could imagine Athens relieved of Turkish rule, Hammersley's pleas that the Marbles be held 'in trust' were remarkably prescient.

But poor Hammersley, whose career in Parliament would otherwise prove unremarkable,[18] undermined his own argument. He recommended that an amount of £25,000 be nevertheless offered Elgin, despite proposing the return of the Marbles to their homeland. Why, came the response, in these trying times, should Britain spend money on something only to forgo the ultimate benefit? Were there a time for benevolence, it certainly was not on the back of a post-war economy. In addition, Hammersley's suggestion came with the prediction that it would be Tsarist Russia that would soon liberate Greece. The notion that Britain would have to then send the Marbles to Russian conquerors was too much for the other side to bear: the proposition was, according to one MP, 'one of the most absurd ever heard in that House'.[19] Hammersley's amendment was promptly voted down.

The House of Commons then divided for the final vote. The tally was 82 in favour of purchasing the Marbles, with 30 against. And so it was concluded: a bill providing further detail was passed and soon had force of law as *An Act to vest the Elgin Collection of ancient Marbles and Sculptures in the Trustees of the British Museum for the Use of the Public*.[20] The recommended amount of £35,000 was transferred from the Treasury to the Trustees of the British Museum who then purchased the collection from Elgin. Thereafter it would be kept whole and inviolate in the Museum, distinguished by the name 'The Elgin Collection', with ownership vested in the Trustees. One final point was added: Elgin would become a Trustee himself, and this privilege would then pass to his heirs (a practice that continued until 1963).[21] A form of recognition, no doubt, but not quite the British peerage he had so ardently hoped for.

The overall process deserves comment from our own perspective. Not only was the taking of the Marbles scrutinised by a Parliamentary committee, but so too was it debated in the House of Commons, with the acquisition and vesting of the Marbles ultimately confirmed by Act of Parliament. As AH Smith would write 100 years later, in 1916, the 'great Elgin controversy' had effectively been 'settled by two of the most authoritative tribunals known to the constitution of this country'. Despite opposition raised, both at the time and since, 'the great body of responsible and informed opinion has endorsed the verdict of the Committee and of Parliament'.[22] Regardless of whether we agree with that verdict, or indeed with Smith's conclusions, the point here is that a thorough process was indeed followed, one that involved two of modern Britain's foundational institutions. This was not some slipshod acquisition, but rather the parliamentary process playing out in all its glorious efficiency. To simply dismiss it as a sort of laundering operation is to miss the point: denying the method of acquisition (as some have done)[23] is, in a way, denying the legitimacy of those institutions that assessed and ultimately approved of it.

Recognising this connection does not mean that the acquisition of 1816 settled the matter once and for all, nor that further debate should thereafter cease. In fact, as we have seen, the Select Committee remained circumspect with regard to

Elgin's approach to the removal, and the House of Commons was far from unanimous. This gives the familiar line repeated by the British Museum and its Trustees a rather disingenuous ring: according to past statements, and the current website, Elgin's activities were investigated by the Committee and 'found to be entirely legal'.[24] The use of the word 'entirely' raises concern, as it seems to brush over the Committee's notable ambivalence and the admonition of Elgin's use of his role as Ambassador. What we know, rather, is that the Committee did its best with the evidence at its disposal, refraining from dressing its conclusions in the language of certainty. This nuance needs better appreciation in future, not least in public statements issued by the British Museum, in order to offer a more accurate account of the full history of acquisition.

Regardless of the ultimate conclusions reached by the Committee, though, and by the House of Commons as a whole, the point here is not that the institutions were necessarily correct, although their work was certainly admirable, but about how they performed the roles expected of them, as similar Committees and Parliaments have done across time, and as they continue to do today. That process goes to the very core of British democracy – then as now – and forsaking one particular outcome would seem to cast aspersions on the institutions themselves, accusations that should never be made lightly.

The Continuing Debate

Despite AH Smith's view in 1916 that 'the great body of responsible and informed opinion' had accepted the conclusions of a century earlier, there remained in his time, and indeed to this day, a vehement debate over the acquisition of the Marbles. Interestingly, two vital points of disagreement were already present in the considerations of the Select Committee and the House of Commons that are still argued over now. The first relates to the response by Greeks at the time of the removal, while the second deals with the categorisation of the removal as a putative 'rescue operation'.

On the first point, there appeared from the evidence considered by the Committee to have been little discomfort, let alone protest, amongst those living in Athens during the time of the removal. In fact, a labour force of some several hundred locals had been employed for this very purpose from July 1801 until the final batch of Marbles was taken away.[25] This point was of course noted by the Committee, which saw it as confirmation that the removals must have been permitted de facto since there appeared to be an absence of any remonstration. Were the Greeks not bothered by the removal of the very things that would one day be called the 'essence of Greekness'?[26]

The lack of protest has been adduced by some to show that the Marbles did not mean as much to the Greek people as politicians such as Melina Mercouri would later claim.[27] Back in 1816, Hunt and Hamilton stated before the Select

Committee that the locals must have wanted the sculptures removed because it offered employment and brought in money, a rather cynical view largely supported in the Report.[28] But this was by no means the unanimous position. One witness before the Committee, John Morritt, an MP himself, said that the Greeks in Athens, which he had visited in 1795, 'were decidedly and strongly desirous that [the sculptures] should not be removed'.[29] One Greek scholar from Athens, Ioannes Benizelos, had written to Hunt in January 1803, referring to the 'last deplorable stripping of the Temple of Athena on the Acropolis ... like a noble and wealthy lady who has lost all her diamonds and jewellery',[30] though Hunt never mentioned this to the Committee. And John Cam Hobhouse, Byron's travelling companion, reported a discussion he had had with an educated man from Ioannina at the time who told him: 'You English are carrying off the works of the Greeks, our forefathers – preserve them well – we Greeks will come and redemand them.'[31]

So there exists some contemporaneous evidence of Greek discontent, though it did not appear to be widespread. Let us recall, though, that Athens was at the time only a very small town within the Ottoman Empire, and could not be considered a centre of Greek learning: it might seem unfair to assume, as the Committee had done and as others have done since, that a failure to protest by the simple labourers of Athens was tantamount to popular approval for the project as a whole.

In the end, we might conclude that whichever way we consider it, the matter is of little import to the status of the Marbles today. The heritage of a people, like that of the Greek nation, is by no means static. Regardless of what an antiquity might have meant in the past, the question should more appropriately be focused on what it means to a people *today* – and, in any case, what it has come to mean for them. That is the crux of the matter, and part of the reason why the dispute over the Marbles has continued for so many years.

The second point of division inherited from 1816 relates to the hypothetical question of whether the removal of the sculptures from the Acropolis could be termed a rescue operation – or whether it was instead an act of wanton destruction? Many of the facts upon which conclusions have been drawn, then as now, have already been discussed. We know that the Parthenon itself had been a ruin since 1687 and, while some of the sculptures remained on the edifice, many had been knocked to the ground or destroyed. We know that the local Turks were more or less indifferent to ancient sculpture and, on a number of occasions, used the pieces as building material for their homes and for the fortifications of the citadel. We know too that western travellers were keen to take away small pieces on their visits. But we also know that these removals involved little more than fragments. Even Fauvel, during his long tenure at Athens, with the twin blessings of money and the support of his own Ambassador, was able to take only two metopes and one piece of frieze: nothing on the scale of what Lusieri would later achieve.

Those arguing against restitution often take it as given that the condition of the Marbles in Athens would have deteriorated over time. This argument is set forth rather cogently in a 2002 article by Ellis Tinios with the telling title 'A Short History of the Parthenon Marbles: Why Restitution is Not Always the Answer.'[32] In it, Tinios surveys the significant damage suffered by the Parthenon and its remaining pieces since Lord Elgin's time. He explains how moulds taken in the late eighteenth century indicate the extent of destruction and effacement undergone by the Marbles in the intervening period. He concludes that 'destruction on this scale would have continued unabated for several more decades and far less sculpture would survive in readable form today if Elgin had not acted.'[33] One visible example is the cast made by Elgin's men of west frieze block VIII, which features a bearded horseman reining in his horse. It is in a better state of preservation today than the original which remained on the building (the rider having lost his head sometime in the nineteenth century).[34] And the sculptures that did remain *in situ* would be subjected to the smog and acid rain that would overtake Athens by the late twentieth century, which had a deleterious effect on the substance of the marble until they were finally removed and placed indoors for safekeeping, and eventually cleaned.[35]

Meanwhile, those advocating return prefer to emphasise the mistreatment of the Marbles, first by Elgin's men and then at the hands of the British Museum itself. We have already seen how Lusieri instructed the labourers to use chisels and saws to remove pieces from the building and to make others more easily transportable.[36] In Britain, when casts were made of the sculptures, lye and acids were used to remove the plaster at each round, to the chagrin of certain contemporaries.[37] Then came the scrubbing scandal of the 1930s, when copper tools and coarse carborundum were used by staff under orders from a major British Museum benefactor, Lord Joseph Duveen, to strip away the outer surface of the Marbles in order for them to appear more appropriately 'white'.[38] On the basis of this evidence, certain commentators have concluded that the British Museum has forfeited whatever moral claim it had over the Marbles.[39]

The problem with this particular debate is that the views expressed, whether for or against restitution, tend to colour the interpretation of the facts themselves. Thus Tinios, who supports the British Museum's position, inevitably overlooks the obvious damage done by Lusieri and minimises the effects of the 1930s episode; while those on the other side often underplay the actual damage done to the pieces that remained behind.[40] The truth is that both arguments hover in the realm of the hypothetical. They each try to imagine what might have happened had Elgin's men not succeeded in their endeavours.

But, frankly, what difference does it make today? Does a nineteenth century 'rescue' operation somehow secure a continuing right of possession for the British Museum on moral grounds? Or if the sculptures would have remained untouched in Athens, would this truly favour the argument for return? Each side may attempt to gain the moral high ground here, but in doing so, tends to rely on its own version of an alternative history. This results in a battle of the counterfactuals, which is never a particularly satisfying engagement. Perhaps, instead, the value in all this should not be in understanding what might have been. Rather, the question should be what can be done with the Marbles today – to seek a better understanding of the pieces that remain and to use them as the basis for a reconciliation between the parties themselves.

A Museum Gets its Star Attraction

In the year following Parliament's passage of the Act, the collection went on display at Montagu House in Bloomsbury. And the British Museum, which had first opened its doors in 1759 to all 'studious and curious Persons',[41] took on its star attraction.[42] Visitors poured in, no doubt inspired by the coverage in the papers and the debate in Parliament. More people came to see the new acquisitions than had ever before visited the Museum: soon there were more than 1,000 visitors a day,[43] a far cry from the five-at-a-time guided tours offered by the Under-Librarian when the Museum first opened.[44] And the visitors were not grandees whiling away their afternoons: all social classes were duly represented. One Trustee meeting reported that, at a certain point, the audience 'consisted chiefly of Mechanics and persons of the lower Classes'.[45]

The British Museum was now a truly popular institution, open to visitors from across the spectrum, and appreciated by them all in turn. A newspaper reporter at the time overheard one saying to another about the Marbles, 'How broken they are! a'ant they?' And the other responding, 'Yes, but how *like life*?' The reporter then added: 'The profoundest artist, after years of thinking, could not have uttered a truer conclusion.'[46] The impact of the Marbles in Britain cannot be overstated. Until then, the classical museum piece had been quintessentially Roman, judged predominantly on aesthetic grounds, like the Apollo Belvedere, with its patrician arms and dignified head neatly in place. Figures, vases and sarcophagi from Italy had constituted the only conceivable harvest of noblemen on their Grand Tours, while Greece under the Ottomans had been largely off limits; its great works could thus only be gleaned from books.[47] Now, genuine Greek sculpture was on display in London, and there was an entire collection of it to be admired. As Mary Beard has written, the Marbles were 'the first examples of sculpture from what was believed to be the Golden Age of Art that most people in Britain had ever clapped eyes on'.[48]

And so the early museum would see the nature of its collections change. No longer was its purpose to edify the public with faithful copies of ancient forms; now it was to display, insofar as possible, genuine originals. So much the better if an original was missing a head or an arm (or both arms, like the Venus de Milo which would come to the Louvre in the 1820s). In fact, the incompleteness of a work tended to emphasise its age and pedigree, a way of placing the ravages of time on display. As Keats wrote in his sonnet on the Marbles, they revealed the agonis-ing mingling of 'Grecian grandeur with the rude / Wasting of old time'.[49] Praise of beauty soon became praise of authenticity; pursuit of the ideal became the pursuit of the real.[50]

The success of the Marbles also allowed the pieces to transcend the Museum itself. They would soon travel beyond the institutional walls, even if only in repro-duced form. The metopes and frieze were moulded and made into casts, many times over. Cast-making like this was not necessarily without its side effects: as mentioned, the process required lye and acid to remove the moulding from the sculptures, and so had a caustic, if visually imperceptible, effect on the patina of the marble. The process nonetheless allowed the 'Elgin Marbles' to multiply, with offspring sent to museums at Liverpool and Plymouth in England, and to Tuscany, Rome, Naples, Venice, Prussia, St Petersburg and beyond. Each major institution seemed to want a complete set.[51] Miniature versions were made for members of the public. The Marbles helped bring the trade of cast-making into the industrial era. The scale was enormous, the possibilities of machine-like replication endless; and the works themselves, advertised around the world, became the celebrities of their age.

And what of Lord Elgin's original goal of encouraging 'the progress of the fine arts' in Britain? Reproduction of the originals was one thing, but did mass expo-sure lead to a groundswell amongst artists, designers and architects? One need not travel far beyond the British Museum to appreciate the effects. On Pall Mall one spots the Athenaeum, a gentleman's club completed in 1830, topped by a version of the Parthenon frieze in cream and Wedgwood blue, above a golden statue of Pallas Athena. Along Piccadilly, next to the Duke of Wellington's former residence, is the Hyde Park Screen of the same period, which again displays an adaptation of the famous frieze, here above a colonnade, as part of a grand entrance to one of London's great parks. And the inspired idea of incorporating figures into the pedi-ment of a classical structure seems to have re-entered the architectural lexicon at about this time. Façades could now be used to recount narratives in stone about the buildings they adorned.

The structure of the British Museum might be the clearest example of this. The new building would be complete by the late 1840s and would come to house the Marbles. This is the one familiar to visitors today on Great Russell Street. It was designed by philhellene Robert Smirke, who as a young man had visited Athens in 1803 and written in his journal upon seeing Elgin's labourers pulling parts of the frieze from the Parthenon cella: 'Each stone as it fell shook the ground with its ponderous weight with a deep hollow noise; it seemed like a convulsive groan of the injured spirit of the Temple'.[52] Despite his denunciation, Smirke's conception of the British Museum many years later would owe much to what he saw of the Parthenon, with its massive columns, its colonnaded entranceway, its symmetry and its overarching pediment.

Figure 4 The pediment sculptures by Richard Westmacott above the entrance to the British Museum were sculpted in 1852, offering a creation myth for all humanity
Source: © Alexander Herman, 2018.

Most interesting perhaps would be the addition in 1852 of a composition for the pediment by Richard Westmacott high above the Museum's entrance, the spirit of Ancient Greece clearly in mind (see Figure 4). Westmacott was well aware of the Elgin Collection, as he had been one of the witnesses called before the Select Committee in 1816 and examined on the artistic value of the pieces. Just as the Parthenon had displayed the creation myths of the city of Athens, the British Museum (thanks to Westmacott) would offer a creation myth for all humanity, as displayed in the pediment: the progress of Man from primitive life and agriculture towards science and understanding, eventually arriving at a worldly satisfaction. As with Smirke's architecture, the plan here was to take the Parthenon as inspiration, but to outdo it in terms of reach. The Enlightenment ideal was blossoming in Britain at the time, stretching well beyond a single temple, religion or people. The story of this museum would be one for all of humanity. This was how Victorian London, with its educational, cultural and financial institutions, perceived itself: as the true centre of the world. And this perception owed much, for better or for worse, to the collection of sculptures taken from Athens by artists working for Lord Elgin half a century earlier.

5

The History of a Claim

In Athens, from 1821 to 1832, the focus was on matters of significantly greater urgency. The War of Independence was being fought against the Ottomans, during which the buildings on the Acropolis would be seriously damaged. Yet even at the most trying of times, the preservation of the Parthenon seemed a priority. One story tells of Greek forces willingly offering bullets to Turkish soldiers barricaded in the Acropolis to persuade them to stop dismantling the blocks and columns in search of the lead fittings inside.[1] The tale was repeated long after the war, as a sort of foundation myth for Greek reverence of ancient monuments. Whether or not this was true, we cannot know, but concrete (and verifiable) measures were indeed taken, such as decrees issued by the revolutionary government and the early National Assembly during the 1820s to preserve antiquities and ancient monuments and to prohibit their sale and export from the territory.[2] In the midst of a bitter war, such consideration for ancient heritage was quite remarkable.

Also surprising at the time was the solicitude shown by the English. Much is known of Lord Byron's commitment to the cause, making the long journey to help the Greek side in 1824, before ultimately succumbing to malaria during the long siege of Missolonghi. Two years later, the British Ambassador, Sir Stratford Canning, wrote a diplomatic letter to the Turkish commander-in-chief, urging restraint during the siege of the Greeks on the Acropolis so that the ancient buildings could be spared (they were 'objects of extraordinary beauty … examples to the entire world'). Canning pleaded that destruction of these 'contributes no glory to the nation and will never be a concern or a worry to you', while their preservation would 'greatly increase Your Excellency's glory and fame.' A similar plea came from the French, but to no avail. The Turkish bombardment of the site proceeded in the year that followed, with the use of artillery and mines, leading to significant damage to the Parthenon and the near destruction of many of the other remains on the Acropolis.[3]

After the War of Independence and the establishment of the Kingdom of Greece in 1832, perhaps understandably, the new nation began to look to the Acropolis as a symbol of identity and unity. This was encouraged by the newly crowned King Othon, a teenaged Bavarian prince ('Otto') placed on the throne by the European powers, along with his enlightened German entourage. The

Acropolis became hallowed ground and would soon be dubbed the 'Sacred' Rock (Ιερός Βραχος, as it is still known today).[4] The Turkish buildings, including the little mosque, would eventually be cleared from the hill, along with a number of the earlier medieval and renaissance structures, in order to let the classical monuments stand tall: the Parthenon, the Propylaia, the Erechtheion and the now-rebuilt Temple of Athena Nike.[5] The Acropolis became a listed national monument in 1835, to be cared for by the newly-established Greek Archaeological Service, and from that date forward the removal of artefacts from the site would be prohibited, while the export of antiquities from the country, first barred during the War of Independence, would be heavily regulated by new legislation.[6]

The *Act on the Discovery of Antiquities and the Use Thereof* was passed as one of the first laws of the new state in 1834.[7] The breadth of its scope and the restrictions it imposed on the collecting and removal of antiquities surprised many European visitors, some of whom had volunteered (like Byron) as pro-Greek fighters during the War, and who might have expected that the 'open season' on pilfered antiquities would continue much as it had under the Ottomans.[8] But a rechristening of Greek identity seemed to have taken hold. A shift of consciousness too, one which would draw significantly on the ancient past. To be Greek now meant to be a descendant of the people of Hellas – a Hellene. The ancient sculptures and fragments collected into the first National Museum, established on the island of Aegina in 1829, were said to 'stir the spirit of the modern Hellenes to imitate and call to mind the brilliance and glory of their ancestors' and ultimately to 'bring honour to the nation.'[9] The 1834 law explicitly provided that 'works of the ancestors of the Hellenic people shall be regarded as national property of all Hellenes', a major step towards codifying state ownership of classical artefacts.[10] In fact, this was the first national legislation in the world to provide comprehensive protection for antiquities, as well as to embed ancient history so firmly within the modern notion of statehood.[11] By contrast, the British Parliament only passed its first statute preserving ancient monuments some 50 years later, the Ancient Monuments Protection Act 1882.

The plea, in one form or another, for the reconstitution of ancient monuments such as those on the Acropolis would become a distinctive feature of the national narrative. During this period, the Archaeological Society was founded in Athens, a nominally independent group that worked in conjunction with the government, and whose mandate was to research and excavate the city's classical sites. A leading member of that society would declare in 1838, pointing to the remains on the Acropolis, that 'it is to these stones that we owe our political renaissance'.[12] Four years later the Society's general secretary publicly urged England to return, 'as a token of reverence to the cradle of civilization, the temple's jewels which were snatched from it and lie now, far away and of little value, while the temple itself remains truncated and formless.'[13] A comparison was made with a drawing by

Raphael tragically torn in two for the purposes of transportation. The recovery of removed antiquities, it seems, was a top priority from the dawn of the new nation state.

During this period, an official request was made by King Othon for the return of four pieces of frieze taken by Elgin's men from the Temple of Athena Nike. The Greeks had finished reconstructing this small structure at the entrance to the Acropolis and the frieze was all that remained outstanding. The Greek Minister for Ecclesiastical Affairs and Public Education referred to the 'abundantly doubtful' legality of the removal by Elgin's men and stressed that the taking of works of art 'that are so closely associated with the ancient glory of Greece could have been disputed in the name of the rights of man.'[14] The request was transmitted through diplomatic channels and presented to the British Foreign Secretary, Lord Palmerston, in 1836, but was rejected without explanation.[15]

Several years later, the Archaeological Society made a request to the British Museum for copies of several pieces – the caryatid and column from the Erechtheion and the still-unreturned frieze slabs from the Nike Temple – as well as funds to help clear the remaining debris from the Acropolis.[16] The letter was recorded in the Trustees' minutes of 22 June 1844 and seems to have been passed on to the British Government. The response came two years later from the British Ambassador at Athens, who expressed that it was the 'pleasure' of Queen Victoria to present a complete set of casts of the Parthenon frieze, the fulfilment of a plan that had apparently been forming for a decade or more. Given that several such casts were already in circulation, it probably seemed appropriate that the Greeks, like the Prussians and others, should have their own set. The Ambassador noted that the casts were already on their way and were being sent 'free of all expense'.[17]

Much later, in 1890, following the publication of an article favourable to the return of the Marbles in a popular British journal,[18] an appeal was made by the City of Athens to the British Ambassador, inviting the Government of Queen Victoria and the British Parliament to return the Parthenon frieze.[19] In 1927 another attempt was made when the Greek Ambassador to London asked the Director of the British Museum for two pieces of the collection (a capital and column-drum) which were considered essential to the ongoing restoration of the Parthenon.[20] The response was that the Trustees were precluded by statute from returning anything beyond duplicates and useless items.[21] And so it went.

From the British side, the possibility of returning the Marbles only began to receive serious consideration by the mid-twentieth century. Remarkably, it was in the midst of the Second World War that the matter came as close as ever to being resolved. In January 1941, Britain and Greece were the only two countries in Europe fighting the Fascists. A question was raised in Parliament by Tory MP Thelma Cazalet-Keir asking the Prime Minister to introduce legislation providing for the Marbles' return after the War 'as some recognition of the Greeks' magnificent stand for civilisation'. The matter went for internal consideration at the Foreign Office, which came 'as close as makes no difference' (the indicative phrase used by Christopher Hitchens) to agreeing to return in principle. Informed opinion was sought from Professors at the Courtauld Institute, who supported the principle, and from the British Museum itself, which was only slightly more equivocal (admitting, for the first time, that the Greeks considered the removals 'spoliation of their national heritage under Turkish tyranny'), while public opinion, in the form of letters to *The Times*, also seemed to favour return. A Foreign Office recommendation was made for a return after hostilities, on the basis of a 'gesture of friendship' (as a way to avoid setting precedent for other antiquities), provided the pieces were properly housed and cared for by the Greeks, and that the UK Government was given a share of control over arrangements for the pieces' future preservation.[22] It was the existence of these final conditions that would eventually stall the project. The internal correspondence was kept sealed, Cazalet-Keir's question was answered in the negative and, when the War concluded, priorities had moved on. The great symbol of Anglo-Hellenic friendship was never to be.

The matter raised its head periodically in the decades that followed. In 1961 a parliamentary question regarding return was put to Prime Minister Harold Macmillan, who responded with characteristic evasion.[23] This prompted a plea from the City of Athens, some 70 years after its previous request, along with appeals from the city's Academy and its School of Fine Arts. The precise response can only be imagined. It would take only a *deus ex machina* to bring the matter to the forefront of the British cultural agenda. And that is exactly what arrived in the remarkable figure of Melina Mercouri.

Enter Melina

Melina Mercouri became Minister of Culture of the Hellenic Republic in 1981. She was unquestionably the most glamorous person to fill such a role. She had been an actress, having starred in classics of 1960s Greek cinema such as *Never on a Sunday* and *Phaedra*, but she had always been political. She had been forced into exile by the Colonels in 1967 for her liberal and pro-democratic views. After the Junta's defeat in 1974, she was elected to the Hellenic Parliament in 1978 and her credentials within the Pan-Hellenic Socialist (PASOK) party made her the obvious choice to represent the cultural resurgence of late-twentieth-century Greece (see Figure 5).

Figure 5 The great campaigner for the return of the Parthenon Marbles, Greek Minister of Culture Melina Mercouri attends the opening of an exhibition on the Acropolis in Amsterdam, 1985

Source: Bart Molendijk / Anefo, CC0, via Wikimedia Commons (with thanks to the Melina Mercouri Foundation, Athens).

With Mercouri at the helm of the Ministry, the timing was right to make the first official request for the return of the Marbles. The chance came in the summer of 1982 at the World Conference on Cultural Policies organised by UNESCO in Mexico City. During this distinguished gathering of Culture Ministers from around the world, Mercouri announced that Greece would soon be lodging a claim for the Marbles. 'I am glad that relations between Greece and England are so friendly that I can speak simply and directly, from the heart', she began, and quickly pointed out that her intention was not to empty the great museums of their collections: 'we are not asking for the return of a painting or a statue. We are asking for the return of a portion of a unique monument, the privileged symbol of a whole culture.'[24]

The Conference's ensuing recommendation was supported by 55 countries, with only 12 voting against it (including, with no great surprise, the United Kingdom). The recommendation included statements that the removal had disfigured the Parthenon, that it was 'right and just' for the Marbles to return to Greece and that UNESCO's Director-General should give full support to the demand. It was also affirmed that the return should be considered as 'an instance of the application of the principle that elements abstracted from national monuments should be returned to those monuments'.[25]

The response from the UK Arts Minister, articulated to Parliament in March 1983, was that the Government's position was that the Marbles should remain at the British Museum and, in any event, this was a matter for the Trustees to decide, not elected officials.[26] Mercouri visited the UK in May and caused a sensation, giving televised interviews and going so far as to hold an impromptu press conference in the Duveen Gallery itself. She did not hold back, approaching the Marbles and at one point even caressing them, seemingly on the verge of tears, before entering into a vociferous exchange with the Museum's director David Wilson in front of the cameras. 'I don't want to ruin the British Museum', she can be heard saying in the footage, 'I want my Marbles back. These are part of a unique monument. *They* have torn down and destroyed this monument.'[27]

When the claim arrived from Greece on 12 October 1983 it set out the case in slightly more prosaic terms. Greece sought 'the return of all the sculptures which were removed from the Acropolis of Athens and are at present in the British Museum' on several enumerated grounds: the Marbles were an integral part of a unique building that was symbolic of Greek culture; works of art belonged to the cultural context in which and for which they were created; and the removal had occurred during 'a period of foreign occupation' which had left Greeks with no say in the matter.[28] After some delay, the UK response came in April the following year: an outright rejection.

Not to be defeated, Greece turned more formally to UNESCO and lodged another claim on 20 September 1984, this one through the procedures established by the Intergovernmental Committee for Promoting the Return of Cultural Property to its Countries of Origin or its Restitution in Case of Illicit Appropriation (Intergovernmental Committee). The claim relied on several international instruments: the 1954 Hague Convention for the Protection of Cultural Property in the Event of Armed Conflict, the 1969 Council of Europe Convention on the Protection of Archaeological Heritage and the 1972 UNESCO Convention Concerning the Protection of the World Cultural and Natural Heritage. The central argument was that the items removed from the Parthenon formed part of a Greek cultural treasure. The response from the UK came the following year, again stating that the matter was best dealt with by the Museum's Trustees who were, in any event, prevented by their governing statute from returning collection items.[29] And that was the end of it: the UK formally withdrew from UNESCO in 1985; Mercouri finished her tenure in 1989 and with her went much of the enthusiasm for the crusade. She returned to the post of Minister in October 1993, but in the brief period that followed her focus was on saving the environment around the Aegean. She died of cancer in March 1994.

The early part of Mercouri's ministry may prompt us to ask whether her approach ultimately proved beneficial to the cause of seeing the Marbles reunited in Greece. Of course she brought the issue into the spotlight, perhaps like no public figure since Byron, and galvanised support for the issue in Britain, Greece, and indeed around the world. According to David Wilson (a source to be considered with considerable caution), prior to Mercouri only a handful of philhellenes had any interest in the matter.[30] After her, it became the quintessential case of disputed heritage and of restitution. 'The Parthenon Marbles are our pride', she had said in one of her English interviews. 'They are our identity. They are today's link with Greek excellence. They are creations synonymous with our concepts of democracy and freedom. They are to us the sublime testimony offered to us by Greek artists that man can be noble.'[31] She was often emotional – a feature perhaps overemphasised by her critics – but had she not been, would she have had the same impact? Watching the old footage, one recognises that, while she was clearly a superlative performer, the return of the Marbles was a cause to which she had committed herself wholly, and she did so with every ounce of her conviction.

But such an approach can be dangerous. In this case, it raised the stakes to dizzying heights and painted the British Museum into a corner. In seeking nothing less than the complete return of the Marbles, it may have pre-empted less grandiose resolutions. Early in this period, in April 1982, before the claim and before the fanfare of Mexico City, the Museum's Keeper of Greek and Roman Antiquities, BF Cook, had stated at a conference that it was 'perfectly possible in principle for the British Museum to lend fragments of the Parthenon sculptures to the Acropolis Museum for an agreed period.' Apparently he had discussed the matter with the Greek Inspector General of Antiquities and both men had agreed that 'it is in principle desirable that small fragments should be re-united with the sculptures to which they belong.'[32] It was hardly a radical proposal. But coming after decades of inaction and obfuscation, it could have perhaps kick-started a more productive discussion around the Marbles, a sign of willingness on both sides to collaborate, offering a first step towards fulfilling the promise of that tantalising symbol of friendship between nations. But with the claim and Mercouri's visit to London, the matter would no longer be susceptible to such tidy manoeuvres. It was now an all-or-nothing tug-of-war being fought on political, diplomatic and communications fronts.

In 1994, not long after Mercouri's death, an informal proposal from the new Greek Minister of Culture was quietly put to the Trustees. Perhaps it was done in the hope that, with her passing, the matter could return to some level of normality. The proposal suggested a 'low profile' return of the pediment pieces, in exchange for Greece agreeing to put aside its claim to the frieze. But the Trustees rejected it outright: according to the minutes, they decided that 'there was nothing in the offer to cause them to change their existing position'.[33]

It seems the battle lines had been drawn and the positions were now firmly entrenched. More than discreet machinations would be needed to shake the Trustees into action.

Another Select Committee Takes a Look

The persisting disagreements, as well as the wider and more contemporary problem of trafficking in looted antiquities, finally made their mark on the UK Parliament in 2000.[34] A Select Committee on Culture, Media and Sport had been tasked by the House of Commons to look into the return and the illicit trade of cultural property. The goal of this Committee went well beyond the Marbles, although this was at times hard to discern from some of the testimony presented, or indeed from a great number of memoranda submitted thereafter. Amongst the many witnesses were three representatives from the British Museum and three from Greece.[35] The Greek team was composed of the country's Foreign Minister George Papandreou, a representative of the Culture Ministry (Lina Mendoni) and Mercouri's ageing widower, the filmmaker Jules Dassin. The spokesman for the group, Papandreou (who would go on to serve as Prime Minister from 2009 to 2011) spoke of the need to put aside legal questions around ownership and focus instead on returning the Marbles to their original context, something the Greeks hoped could be done in time for the 2004 Olympic Games in Athens.

Those who spoke on behalf of the British Museum, including the Chair of Trustees and Director, proclaimed that the Museum held clear and unequivocal title to the Marbles, that the risks to the sculptures if returned to Greece were too great and that accepting the Greek claim would open the floodgates to many other demands from source countries, which would ultimately lead to the emptying out of the world's great museums. About 100 memoranda were submitted in total, including briefs from the Museums Association, the major auction houses, trade representatives and international advocacy groups.

The Select Committee Report, published in July 2000, contained surprisingly little on the Parthenon Marbles, though it was again emphasised that the Trustees were unable, without another Act of Parliament, to offer, or even negotiate, the return of objects from the collection.[36] The UK Government was said to be 'happy to discuss the issue of the marbles' and the Under-Secretary of State for the Arts, Alan Howarth, even said that progress would depend upon 'a closer meeting of minds, a closer mutual understanding of each other's point of view'. But no procedures were recommended by the Committee to facilitate the return of cultural material, from the British Museum or any other institution, except for cases involving human remains or Nazi-looted art.[37] The Committee did make a recommendation that the UK accede to the UNIDROIT Convention on Stolen or Illegally Exported Cultural Objects from 1995, though this was never followed.[38]

Two years after the Select Committee sessions, the British Museum Trustees appointed a new Director, Neil MacGregor, who had recently completed a successful tenure as Director of the National Gallery. The appointment came after a period of some difficulty and in-fighting between the Museum and the Government over financial matters and questions of management.[39] Hopes were high in some quarters that, under MacGregor's new brand of leadership, the British Museum might abandon its curmudgeonly stance in relation to restitution. But he delivered something else entirely. One of MacGregor's first major moves was to meet, in November 2002, with the then Greek Minister for Culture Evangelos Venizelos and discuss a way forward on the Parthenon Marbles. This was after a 'new' proposal had been unfurled from Greece over the previous year on the basis of reciprocal loans.[40] By all accounts, the meeting did not go well.[41] A few days later, a letter came from the Chairman of Trustees, couching in genteel terms a formal rejection of any possible agreement on the return of the Marbles, even on the basis of a temporary loan.[42] It did not seem as though direct negotiations would get Greece very far.

As the Athens Olympic Games approached, and the desperation to achieve a resolution increased, the Greeks attempted other approaches. Prime Minister Kostas Simitis tried to move things along in October 2003, resorting at one point to a rather pathetic measure when he asked Tony Blair at a summit in Brussels, during an exchange picked up by television cameras, 'I have an election to fight next year – could you do something about the Marbles?'[43] When nothing came of this, Culture Minister Venizelos returned to London at the end of 2003 and used the incongruous but generally sympathetic forum of the Trade Union Council to set out in broad terms his public request to the British Museum. In this new position the old claim from the days of Melina Mercouri was put aside. Greece would not demand the outright restitution of the Marbles. Instead, the proposal focused on a potential 'cooperation' between the British Museum and the Acropolis Museum in Athens that could facilitate the return of the Marbles to Greece as a long-term loan in exchange for a selection of high-quality sculptures and other artefacts from museums in Greece.[44] The proposal had the merit of offering something to the British Museum in exchange for the long-term loan of the sculptures and may well have succeeded had it not been for a change of regime following the 2004 election. Greece's ruling PASOK party – the party of Mercouri, Venizelos and the hapless Simitis – suffered a heavy defeat after 10 years in power and its ambitious proposals regarding the Parthenon Marbles fell with the Government. It was not that the leadership of the new centre-right Government wanted to return to a more entrenched position; in truth, there were other more pressing matters to attend to. This party, New Democracy, had just inherited the Olympics and the Acropolis Museum – and the exorbitant costs associated with both projects. The proposals for cultural cooperation and reciprocal loans naturally fell by the wayside.[45]

A New Museum for Athens

The construction of a new state-of-the-art museum to replace the small and rather dilapidated one near the Parthenon had been discussed as far back as the 1970s. There had been a total of four international competitions and a number of false starts, but by 2001 architectural plans by celebrated Swiss-American architect Bernard Tschumi (partnering with a Greek colleague, Michael Photiadis) had been accepted and work started on the project. The museum was to be located not on the Acropolis itself, but some 200 metres to the south of the ancient site. The opening, which had been promised in time for the 2004 Olympics, had been held back on multiple occasions, first to care for the ancient structural remains discovered under the building site and then due to lawsuits and protests in relation to the proposed demolition of two Art Deco apartment blocks to make way for the museum.[46] It was not until June 2009 that the Acropolis Museum finally opened its doors.

Even without the return of the Marbles from the UK, there remained in Athens a significant collection of sculptures from the Parthenon, as well as from other parts of the Acropolis. These had been kept since the nineteenth century in the small museum on the hill. The collection included 51 metopes, 37 blocks of frieze and eight partial figures from the pediments along with fragments from others (the chest of Poseidon, the hand of Zeus, part of Athena's head and so on): in total just under half of the extant sculptures were in Athens, but it remains difficult to compare these to what had been taken by Elgin's men.[47] Many of the best-preserved metopes were in London, as well as the more prominent pieces from the pediments. With the frieze, the distinction was perhaps less stark, since certain slabs left on the west cella by Elgin's men were in a fair condition, especially after cleaning, as were others excavated after Greek independence. This included half of Block VI of the east frieze featuring Poseidon, Apollo and Artemis, the best-preserved passage of the entire east frieze.[48] But in that little museum it was difficult to do justice even to these remaining pieces; some had to be kept in storage.

The building of a suitable museum in Athens would certainly provide added momentum to the Parthenon Marbles debate – and this fact was not lost on the politicians who helped secure the project. As the Greek Prime Minister said in 2007, 'the reunification of the Parthenon Sculptures remains the great goal. I am confident that the new Acropolis Museum, work for whose completion is now going on with a speedy pace, will add new and very strong arguments to this effort.'[49] One of the arguments that had earlier been used by some opposed to restitution was that there was no adequate place to house and display the Marbles if they were sent back to Athens.[50] At least as far back as the 1980s, it was under-stood by both sides that the sculptures could not be replaced on the monument, since the caustic conditions of the Athenian atmosphere would cause significant damage to the surface of the pieces. And the existing museum did not have the space. With such limited alternatives, the British Museum may have seemed at the time the more suitable home.

The new museum would provide an obvious solution to this shortcoming. And, in the manner in which it chose to display the pieces, the Acropolis Museum would in many ways surpass the British Museum. In London the frieze pieces and metopes were placed against the walls of the Duveen Gallery, facing inwards rather than out, demanding of the visitor a considerable mental endeavour to understand their original placement on the building. And while the Marbles were once shown at the British Museum in conjunction with plaster casts representing those pieces still in Athens and elsewhere, after the opening of the Duveen Gallery in 1962 the casts were gone. This effectively hid from the viewer the fact that parts of the sculptural scheme were in existence elsewhere but nevertheless absent. As Mary Beard has put it, 'the overall effect (and the intention) of the gallery design is to efface what remains in Athens.'[51]

At the new Acropolis Museum, the sculptures would instead be set out exactly as they would have been on the building, in their respective places and according to the appropriate dimensions of the overall architectural scheme. Empty spaces representing the missing Marbles, used for largely political reasons in the initial period, were soon filled by plaster casts, giving the visitor a proper sense of how each sculptural element of the Parthenon would have related to the others (the casts are eye-catchingly white, just so no one gets the impression that they are authentic). The geographical positioning in Athens was also apt: the east pediment faced east and the west faced west; meaning that the birth of Athena could reflect the rising sun and Poseidon could contemplate the sea.[52] Moreover, the glass walls of the Museum provided sightlines over to the Acropolis, allowing visitors to look across and see the original structure.

As lauded as the new Museum may have been, its opening did not resolve the debate. Following the completion of a suitable home in Athens, the ammunition in the British Museum's arsenal had to adapt. The arguments developed and became somewhat more tendentious. No longer could it be said that the Greeks were without a facility to care for the pieces to the same standard as the British Museum. Now it was said that returning the Marbles would not be returning them to the monument for which they were built, but simply moving them from one museum to another.[53] If neither institution was intrinsically better placed than the other to do this then why bother returning them at all?

But the line of defence under MacGregor soon became a line of attack. He subtly sought to diminish the role of the Acropolis Museum, painting it as an institution set up to portray only the very narrow Athenian view. It was at the British Museum that the Marbles could be seen as great works of art for a global community, only properly understood within the larger context of comparable civilisations. This angle had always been espoused by the Museum, but now it was brought to the logical extreme. Display panels in the Duveen Gallery began inviting visitors to compare the Parthenon frieze to the work of the Persians at Persepolis. A book on the Marbles published by the Museum counterpoised images of the gathering horsemen with photographs of the English fox hunt and Maasai hunters in Africa.[54] The two-fold purpose here was to paint the Greek claim as a cry of primitive nationalism and to reduce it to something very parochial. Only the 'universal museum', a cosmopolitan centre for competing narratives that espoused tolerance through the equal treatment of all cultures, could possibly live up to the task at hand. The institution was fully invested in its self-appointed duty to tell the story of all humanity, from the Stone Age to the modern era, passing through Sumer, Ur, Ancient Egypt, Persia and, of course, Classical Greece.

Much had changed since the days of Mercouri; a simple reactive position, such as that of David Wilson, had proven to be ineffective. And so it would be up to the great universal museum, with MacGregor at its helm, to tell the global story, which of course included the Marbles at its heart. It was an ingenious move, turning what had once been viewed as the quaint old vessel of a reactionary establishment into the sleek ship of progress. In many ways, he sought to outflank the restitutionists from the left, taking a stand that unashamedly supported globalism, diversity and inclusion.

Added to this was the persistence of the more technical points of argument. The official museum position remained that Elgin's actions had been deemed 'entirely legal' by the 1816 Select Committee (a conclusion not without its problems, as discussed in chapter four) and that the Trustees had acquired lawful title to the sculptures that year following the passage of the Act of Parliament. The current British Museum Act 1963 forbids disposals from the collection, with exceptions only for duplicates, objects deemed 'unfit' for the collection and those considered 'useless' (as to which, see chapter six).

As for the point about putting title aside and seeking out a collaboration based on a long-term loan, like the one proposed by Venizelos some years earlier, it was made manifestly clear that this was a non-starter. The refusal was predicated on what could be termed a technicality, but it was something the Museum now deemed essential. If the Greek Government refused to accept the lawful title of the Trustees, how could the Trustees undertake to lend the Marbles to Greece? This would appear to mean there was no guarantee for their ultimate return, with the added risk that some legal mechanism might be used to retain the pieces in Greece indefinitely. In the absence of any acknowledgement of Trustee title, sending them to Greece (it was argued) would be tantamount to bidding adieu to a fundamental part of the Museum's collection.[55] This stance will be more fully assessed in the following chapter.

The Legal Case is Presented

By the time the socialist PASOK party returned to power in Greece in 2009, the Olympics were a distant memory and the Acropolis Museum had already opened, but Greece had far bigger problems on the horizon. The debt crisis, spurred on by the global recession of the previous year, was beginning and it would consume political capital in Greece over the following years. It would also consume governments. PASOK would lose to New Democracy in 2012, and New Democracy would in turn lose to the more radical Syriza in 2015, elections decided on fundamentally economic terms: austerity, debt and bail-outs from international sources. The Marbles understandably fell down the list of priorities.

It was during this period of uncertainty, however, that a proposal was put together by one of the foreign associations lobbying for the Marbles' return. These bodies are made up of supporters of the Greek cause, campaigners who in times past might have self-described as 'philhellene', and who take their cue in many ways from Lord Byron. There are a confusing number of such groups, compounded by periodic name changes. The oldest, and most established, is the British Committee for the Reunification of the Parthenon Marbles, established in the midst of the Mercouri extravaganza of 1983 as the British Committee for the Restitution of the Parthenon Marbles (the change from 'restitution' to 'reunification' in its title suggesting a more recent shift in the campaign's approach). This body has counted among its members university professors, actors and Members of Parliament. It has found support among the likes of Tom Hanks, Judi Dench, Vanessa Redgrave, Ian McKellen, Joanna Lumley, Stephen Fry and Liam Neeson. The British body spawned national committees in other countries too, numbering nearly 20 today, each with its own leadership and identity. Another such group was called 'Parthenon 2004', a UK entity set up as a grassroots counterpart to the more establishment British Committee, employing what have been called 'guerrilla' tactics with the media in order to secure the return in time for the Athens Olympics.[56] When its initial purpose went unfulfilled, the name changed to 'Marbles Reunited'. A further group was the loosely-formed international body that sought to unite them all, the International Association for the Reunification of the Parthenon Marbles.

The chairman of the last of these groups, an Australian named David Hill who had long been anxious to explore a more assertive approach, was behind the new proposal. A secret meeting was convened in London in early 2011 with 'unofficial' representation from the Greek Government (a Deputy Minister arrived covertly without his entourage) to consider the possibility of bringing a restitution claim through the courts.[57] It was felt that, after 30 years of diplomatic requests, nothing had been achieved: the British Museum had not relented in the least. The only remaining option, according to those assembled, was to seek an order from a court, but there was disagreement as to which court would be appropriate to hear such a claim. Two legal options were presented at the occasion: one from a team of American attorneys and another from a team of English barristers.[58]

The American approach was to bring a claim through the courts of Washington DC as a way of putting pressure on the UK Government. Whilst this argument might have appeared on its face implausible, it took inspiration from a lawsuit brought several years earlier by an elderly Austrian émigrée living in Los Angeles before the California courts against her native Austria for the return of five Gustav Klimt paintings, including the famous *Portrait of Adele Bloch-Bauer I* (the 'Woman in Gold' from the 2015 film of the same name), which had been taken from her family by the Nazis in 1938. By succeeding at the US Supreme Court, Altmann was able to force the arbitration that eventually allowed the paintings to be returned, an outcome which at the outset had appeared impossible.[59] The Klimt paintings had become national treasures in Austria and the Austrian authorities had initially been unprepared to alter their position. It was the legal victory in America that paved the way for restitution.[60] The thinking was that the same approach could be followed with the Parthenon Marbles. In a similar way, the US courts may accept jurisdiction for the Greek claim even though it related to property situated well beyond US territory and involved actions that had occurred long ago.

The English team proposed an action before one of two international courts: the International Court of Justice in The Hague and the European Court of Human Rights in Strasbourg. The human rights claim, it was thought, could succeed on the basis that the continued retention of the sculptures constituted a breach of the right to property and a 'right to culture'.[61] It was generally accepted by the team that a civil claim brought by Greece before the domestic courts of the UK would be doomed to fail and that alternative avenues should be explored.

The proposal from the English barristers was ultimately chosen due in part to concerns that, while the US approach may have brought success in Washington, any judgment in favour of Greece would have been difficult (if not impossible) to enforce on UK territory.[62] The international courts, on the other hand, seemed to offer a more substantial prospect of success for the Greek cause. The jurisdiction of both courts was recognised by the UK and they were venerable institutions whose judges (many of whom had been British over the years) were highly esteemed.

The English team was led by Geoffrey Robertson QC of Doughty Street Chambers. Robertson was a renowned human rights lawyer, who, in addition to taking on high-profile defamation and international criminal trials, had successfully assisted a group of Aboriginals from Tasmania in reclaiming the bones of their ancestors held at the Natural History Museum in London where they had been undergoing invasive scientific testing.[63] The location of the bones was a sad testimonial to the nineteenth-century zeal for collecting what was deemed exotic and depositing the finds in European museums. The team that Robertson put together for the Parthenon Marbles would be very similar to the one he had assembled in 2010 to defend WikiLeaks founder Julian Assange from extradition – with one notable exception.

The exception was Norman Palmer QC. Palmer was the country's leading expert on cultural property matters, as both a barrister and a professor, having taught the subject for many years at University College London. He had also chaired parliamentary bodies dealing with a range of cultural heritage issues, including the black-market trade in looted antiquities (as chair of the Advisory Panel on Illicit Trade), human remains in museum collections (as chair of the Working Group on Human Remains) and the classification and valuation of treasure discoveries (as a member of the Treasure Valuation Committee). He had worked with Robertson in assisting the Tasmanians and had more recently represented the Government of Iran in an action to recover a number of priceless Bronze Age artefacts that had been illegally excavated and brought to London for sale at a prestigious gallery.[64] He had also inspired, through his work at the Institute of Art and Law, an entire generation of art lawyers. He seemed the logical choice.

The English team produced a short legal opinion which provided a brief overview of the argument, eschewing significant detail. This was soon presented to the Greek Ministry for Culture in early 2011. However, nothing further happened. The PASOK party, which had tacitly sanctioned the instructions, lost power following the Greek election the following year. Once again, a political shift would delay any progress in the matter.

Nevertheless, two years later, the new Greek Minister for Culture and Sports, Konstantinos Tasoulas, agreed to fully investigate the English team's suggestion of bringing a claim before an international court. With this in mind, an invitation was extended to the barristers to visit Athens and meet face-to-face with the Minister and Prime Minister, both of whom were members of New Democracy. The meeting was scheduled for October 2014.

The timing was in many ways fortuitous: it followed the wedding of a junior member of the team, Amal Alamuddin, to Hollywood movie star George Clooney on 27 September of that year. This would result in a wholly unexpected level of media attention throughout the visit. Whilst the focus was largely on Amal (now) Clooney, it had the effect of bringing attention to an issue that had been dormant for the past decade, especially in Greece. In the course of one of the many press conferences during the team's stay in Athens, Palmer was asked by a journalist whether he thought that Greece could regain the Marbles. He replied: 'I am extremely optimistic that a conciliatory and amicable solution can be reached. And if it can't, then other considerations will have to be examined.'[65] This unexpected attention compelled the Greek Government to pursue the matter in the hope that the three legal minds might find an international legal solution to the intractable problem.

However, just as momentum was gaining on the Greek side, the situation changed once more. This was the result of the last major move by MacGregor before the end of his 13-year tenure at the British Museum. On Friday 5 December

2014, less than two months after the visit to Athens, he announced the loan of one of the major pieces from the Parthenon collection, the River God from the west pediment. This was the first time any of the Marbles had left the country since their arrival 200 years earlier. And the recipient institution was the Hermitage in St Petersburg. Russia was, at that time, the target of major international sanctions (and public censure) for its invasion and occupation of Crimea earlier that year, as well as its ongoing involvement in the bloody Syrian civil war. However, nothing could be done to stop the loan: when MacGregor made the announcement, the sculpture was already in place at the Hermitage.

The Director expressed his view that even Pericles himself would 'applaud' such a journey. There were remonstrations from the Greek Government,[66] criticism from some quarters, but – surprisingly – a number of positive responses. 'Sending Putin the Elgin Marbles is barmy', wrote London's then-mayor Boris Johnson in an exercise of convoluted logic, 'but it's what makes Britain great.' The idea was that arm's-length institutions were unfettered in their decision-making, even if this clashed with government policy, and such was the sign of a healthy democracy. The move also marked a new era in the British Museum's treatment of the Marbles. No longer would they be excluded from the Museum's extensive loan programme, through which some 4,000 works were sent out each year.[67] MacGregor's plan was to 'normalise' the Marbles, to ensure that they were treated no differently from the other eight million items in the collection.[68] This meant showing the pieces in a new light and not isolating them in the Duveen Gallery. It also meant acquiescing to international loan requests such as the one from St Petersburg.

As though to follow through on the promise, upon the sculpture's return from Russia in early 2015, it was placed in an exhibition at the British Museum called *Defining Beauty: the Human Body in Ancient Greek Art*. The curatorial intention was to attract comparisons between the muscular body of the River God and other works of classical art, such as the Belvedere Torso (loaned from the Vatican) and the British Museum's own Discobolus (a Roman copy of a lost Greek original). This was the first time key pieces from the Elgin Collection had been placed comparatively – and indeed purposefully – amongst other works of classical art. To the *Guardian* art critic, the exhibition was enough to make a retentionist out of a former restitutionist: 'By its sheer passion, this exhibition makes … a case for spreading the beauty of Greek art and thought worldwide, for showing it in a global centre like the British Museum. In short, it is an argument for keeping the sculptures where they are.'[69] The sculptures from the Parthenon were back on the agenda in Britain. And not, as before, framed solely by Greece's claim for return.

By the time the barristers presented their longer legal opinion to the Greek Government in the summer of 2015, the excitement over their previous visit had worn off significantly. The Hermitage loan had elicited circumspection and criticism from some, but had been successfully brought to its conclusion by the Museum. Meanwhile Greece was undergoing the worst throes of the financial crisis, with another election, bank closures, a third proposed bailout and a public referendum on austerity. The country was on its way to becoming the first in the developed world to default on a loan from the International Monetary Fund. It is not surprising that there was little consideration being given at that time to the plight of the Marbles.

A Realignment?

Despite the long history of rejection, each newly elected Greek Government seems to hold out hope that it can find a solution to the impasse. Under Syriza, elected in 2015, Culture Minister Lydia Koniordou (who, like Mercouri, had previously been an actress) put forward an impassioned plea: 'This is a request – a claim – that no government and no minister of culture will part from. From Melina on, we continue serving this claim. We will never give up.'[70] Then, with New Democracy back in power in 2019, Prime Minister Kyriakos Mitsotakis tried to seize the issue and resolve it once and for all. Leading up to his first official visit to the UK in November 2021, Mitsotakis made it clear that the Marbles were a top priority – and that he would offer a 'new way forward' on the matter.[71]

There were perhaps reasons to be optimistic. Mitsotakis was meeting with his UK counterpart, Prime Minister Boris Johnson, an avowed lover of Classics who was no stranger to the Marbles issue. As a student, Johnson had been president of the Oxford Union when the Marbles were debated in June 1986 and it was he who had invited Melina Mercouri to speak. A famous photograph of the two of them together was taken at the time. He had also penned a heartfelt appeal in the pages of *Debate*, the Union's newsletter, calling for the Marbles' return, an article more recently unearthed by a Greek journalist.[72] In it, Johnson recognised the 'passionate feeling of the Greek people' and criticised the 'sophistry and intransigence of the British Government', concluding that the Marbles 'should leave this northern whisky-drinking guilt-culture, and be displayed where they belong: in a country of bright sunlight and the landscape of Achilles'.[73]

Much had changed too in the preceding years. Restitution had gone from a relatively arcane issue affecting only museums to the mainstream of political debate. President Emmanuel Macron of France had moved his country towards engagement with former French colonies in Africa by announcing his intention to return 'African heritage' to Africa.[74] Germany was making restitution a public matter, announcing the coordinated return of hundreds of Benin Bronzes from its collections.[75] The Dutch and the Belgian Governments were also moving in this direction. And of course, much had happened since the turn of the millennium in relation to restituting Nazi-looted art to the heirs of victims of the Holocaust.[76]

Added to this was a strongly-worded recommendation aimed at the UK in late September 2021 from UNESCO's Intergovernmental Committee, the same body first seized of Greece's claim back in 1984, a matter that had remained before the Committee for some 40 years. In it, the body expressed 'deep concern' that the issue remained pending and 'disappointment' that its past recommendations had not been observed by the UK, calling on the UK to 'reconsider its stand and proceed to a bona fide dialogue with Greece on the matter.'[77]

Other Parthenon fragments had begun to move as well, each forming a precedent of sorts and adding incremental pressure on the British Museum. Along with his promise to Africa, France's Macron also suggested in 2019 sending to Greece part of the Parthenon frieze from the Louvre.[78] In January 2022, the Salinas Museum in Palermo, Sicily returned a small fragment of a foot from the east frieze to the Acropolis Museum. This was done on the basis of an eight-year loan (a similar loan of the piece had taken place from 2002 to 2008), but was soon turned from a 'deposit' – the word used in the press release – into a permanent transfer.[79] Then in December of that year, the Pope announced a similar arrangement to send three Parthenon fragments from the Vatican Collections as a 'donation' to the Archbishop of Athens, who then proceeded to place them in the Acropolis Museum.[80] These pieces had left the Acropolis well over 200 years earlier and had been bequeathed a long time ago to their respective holding institutions. If those institutions could return, the logic might run, why not the British Museum? However, the objects being returned were fragments, small if important parts of larger figures (the foot of Artemis, the heads of a bearded man and a tray-bearer, and part of a horse), on a very different scale from the hall-sized collection in the Duveen Gallery.

When Mitsotakis did meet with Boris Johnson in November 2021, he argued for the full restitution of the Marbles. As he explained on British television at the time: 'I will be making my case to the British Prime Minister ... Where there's a will, I'm sure we can find a solution.'[81] He made clear that he would not accept a loan, only the permanent return of the sculptures. In exchange he promised a rotating collection of 'artefacts and treasures that have never left the country' as an enticement to the British Museum.[82] It sounded a little like the offer put forward by Evangelos Venizelos some 20 years earlier, but few seemed to pick up on the similarity. In fact, by ruling out the loan possibility, it was even less conciliatory than that earlier proposal.

But it was not to be. Despite his undergraduate sympathies, Johnson seemed to have wholeheartedly adopted the stance of the UK Government. At the meeting on 16 November, Johnson told Mitsotakis that, while he understood the 'strength of feeling' in Greece on the issue, he would not involve the Government or Parliament in seeking a resolution. He reiterated the UK's longstanding position that 'this matter is one for the trustees of the British Museum'.[83] Once again, any glimmer of hope was quickly extinguished.

Still the Greek side did not appear to have relinquished either interest or hope in the crusade. In the memorandum submitted to the 2000 Select Committee, the Government had said the time was then 'ripe' for bringing the Marbles home to 'redress the cultural and moral injustice' of their original removal and that it was confident the UK would 'demonstrate its willingness to address this important issue.' Seven years later, the Greek Prime Minister stated that the Greeks were 'dedicated' to the goal of the Marbles' return 'and we shall remain so', feeling optimistic that 'in the end, even the most doubtful will be convinced and will change their attitude toward the matter.'[84] And then Mitsotakis incorporated much of that same language into his own admirable attempts.

Not one of these sallies has had success. The doubtful remain so. The British Museum remained firm in its position, even if, under MacGregor, it was required to update its arguments for the twenty-first century. The UK Government has also remained unconvinced and largely unwilling to steer the issue towards resolution, offering at best no more than a few sympathetic words. But whether it was Howarth's 'closer meeting of the minds' or Johnson understanding 'the strength of feeling' – whether it was a Labour or Tory Government – little seemed to change. Johnson himself was a case in point, revealing how the idealism of youth could so easily dissipate after time spent within the country's political establishment. The position he ended up taking was entirely institutional, far beyond the powers of any one individual to alter or overturn.

Charity to the Rescue

And yet, even after this, many are saying that change is in the air. Is the current restitution paradigm bringing with it a mighty wind that will prove unavoidable even to the most conservative of institutions? The unlikely instigator has been the Chair of Trustees of the British Museum, George Osborne. Former Chancellor of the Exchequer under David Cameron, Osborne's Tory credentials are beyond dispute. But, after becoming Chair in the summer of 2021, he must have sensed that, when it came to the Marbles, the status quo was not wholly satisfactory. When asked about the issue during a televised interview in June 2022, he surprised many by saying that he thought there was 'a deal to be done'. This was prefaced by the familiar statement that the Marbles played a central role in the British Museum's civilisation-spanning collection, but he did add that 'sensible people' working from both sides might be able to reach an arrangement if they approached the matter 'without a load of preconditions' and 'without a load of red lines'.[85]

Following Osborne's pronouncements, the Museum began to soften its tone very slightly, with its representatives beginning to speak of a potential 'Parthenon Partnership' with Greece.[86] It was also reported that secret talks had been taking place between the British Museum and the Greek side since late 2021, coinciding with the time of Mitsotakis's state visit.[87] The details – and potential outcome – of some of these negotiations will be dealt with in the next chapter. Meanwhile, a former Conservative Arts Minister, Lord Ed Vaizey, publicly declared his support for the Marbles' return and joined the advisory board of an organisation called

'The Parthenon Project', the goal of which was to seek out 'win-win' solutions to the longstanding dispute. While this might appear to be yet another of the many non-governmental bodies with an interest in the matter, the organisation does seem to have attracted impressive recruits from the corridors of power, with a number of former politicians, journalists, authors and Members of the House of Lords, such as Vaizey, joining its advisory board.[88]

While these appear to be promising signs, will they alone shake the status quo? Osborne's words do show an openness to compromise, but they are not miles apart from past statements by MacGregor and others over the years. 'Yes, we hear the voices calling for restitution', Osborne said in his speech at the annual Trustees dinner in November 2022. 'But creating this global British Museum was the dedicated work of many generations. Dismantling it must not become the careless act of a single generation.' This hardly sounded like a man about to hand over the family silver. It was clear that, whatever long-term partnership may be struck with Greece, the Museum would not soon become an active enabler of restitution.

The Government also reaffirmed its position against returning the Marbles, with the Secretary of State, Michelle Donelan, explaining how doing so would 'open a can of worms' and be a 'dangerous road to go down' and Prime Minister Rishi Sunak stating that 'the UK has cared for the Elgin Marbles for generations' and that the 'collection of the British Museum is protected by law, and we have no plans to change it'.[89] It remains unclear what impact the governmental view could have on the supposedly ongoing negotiations.

A further development from 2022 may also have an impact going forward. This was the passage on 24 February of the Charities Act 2022, a law intended to address some of the technical inconsistencies in the rules governing charities in England and Wales. As will be explained more fully in the next chapter, a provision of this law, when it comes into force, would allow trustees like those of the British Museum to return property if there is a 'moral obligation' to do so, upon receiving approval from the Charity Commission, Attorney General or the Courts, regardless of the restrictions found in statute.[90] This offers a new angle for discussions around restitution – and not one that was expected by many. While decisions on moral grounds would always be up to the Trustees, and would require approval from one of the requisite bodies, the change would nevertheless signal the demise of the frequently employed defence: that the Trustees are 'prevented by law' from returning items from their collection. In theory, they could agree to return the Marbles to Greece upon a moral obligation. But how such morality would be defined is a matter of some discussion.[91]

So where does this leave us? Are the times truly changing? While coverage and commentary of the latest developments in the matter have been fulsome and (largely) positive, when placed against the backdrop of the long-running dispute, signs of hope may quickly fade. Is there enough in these glimmering possibilities to shift the burden set by two centuries of debate, discussion, dashed hopes and recriminations? Are the forces gathering now weighty and numerous enough to affect real change? If precedent has taught us anything, it is that the parties are so set in their ways, the entrenchment so deep, that the situation may be in need of more than a simple quick-fix, whether couched as a 'partnership' or as a 'win-win'. Undoing the swollen knot of disagreement will require many hands working together over a long period of time, not one solitary figure cutting through it all with one grand gesture.

6

The (un)titled Masterpiece

To most people, title to property would appear clear-cut and, in most cases, permanent. When we own goods, we have the strong sense that they belong to us: that we can sell them if we like, or lend them, exchange them, pledge them or simply give them away. We assume they are *ours*. But very rarely do we investigate this assumption. Very rarely do we question whether we have title at all.

In truth, questions of title have never been easy. As one London solicitor once said to me, if you try to pin title down with any kind of precise definition, it simply slithers away.[1] It is no surprise that one of the leading experts in the area, Sir Roy Goode, has called ownership 'one of the most elusive concepts of English law'.[2] In relation to real property (such as land and buildings), it will involve complexities of tenures and estates. If it relates to movable property – known as 'chattels' at common law – there can be legal and equitable rights, the property can be exposed to trusts and successive interests, and it can be subject to 'two concurrent legal interests and to an indefinite number of concurrent equitable interests'.[3] And this is only under English law! Because chattels, unlike real property, have the feature of being transportable, they can travel easily from one jurisdiction to the next, with each jurisdiction capable of imposing upon them its own distinct rules around title.

It is precisely this transportability, along with the potential frequency of transaction, that underpins the law's acceptance of the informality of title when it comes to chattels. Transactions involving real property are formalised, normally requiring deeds of title and registration in a land registry. Not so for chattels. Under English law, for example, there is no general requirement for a deed to be drawn up when transferring chattels, nor is there a requirement to register one's title (with the exception of automobiles).[4] Were it otherwise, the sale of even a modest object would be overburdened with paperwork, something that would unnecessarily raise the transaction costs for even the simplest of transactions and undermine the fluidity of our advanced commercial system.

In the case of chattels, the law offers a presumption. This presumption forms the basis of our entitlement to own, and thus to sell, pledge and lease, or to give away our property entirely. If we possess a chattel (if we exercise custody over it, with intent) we are presumed in law to be the owner. Possession is therefore an essential ingredient of title, serving to explain the common saying that 'possession is nine-tenths of the law'. Such a phrase of course offers no statistical exactitude as to ownership, but it does serve as an indication that with possession comes an often overwhelming claim to full ownership. This was expressed with much clarity by the great nineteenth-century jurist Sir Fredrick Pollock:

> Possession is *prima facie* evidence of ownership … for the very reason that possession is the visible exercise of ownership, the fact of possession, so long as it is not otherwise explained, tends to show that the possessor is the owner: though it may appear by further enquiry that he is exercising either a limited right derived from the owner and consistent with his title, or a wrongful power assumed adversely to the true owner.[5]

Possession is not the absolute entitlement to ownership. Thus the phrase sets it at nine-tenths, rather than the full whole. If we possess a chattel, we are presumed to be its owner. But it is a presumption that can be rebutted by anyone with a superior claim to title. There are therefore two forms of title: possessory title (title that relies entirely on possession) and proprietary title (title that can be proven by some other evidentiary means). We might enjoy possessory title in a chattel which we have in our custody, but a third party may demonstrate that they have proprietary title, which would allow them to reclaim that chattel in law.[6] If a painting is in our possession, for instance, we are presumed to be its owner by dint of possession, but the true owner may be able to prove that it is in fact on loan to us, and that they would like to recall such a loan. In this way they can rebut the possessory presumption.

But how does one acquire title in the first place? This can be *ab initio*: as a finder or potentially as a landowner on whose property a chattel is discovered.[7] Title may also vest by statute in the way that 'treasure' discovered in England vests in the Crown.[8] Other examples of vesting statutes, of special importance in our matter, are statutes that vest title to collection objects in the trustees of national institutions, such as the National Gallery, the Victoria and Albert Museum and, of course, the British Museum.

It is also possible to acquire title in property belonging to another. The most obvious form of such acquisition would be a voluntary transfer by way of sale, gift or bequest. The transfer of property by sale is usually set out in the relevant contract between the parties, though occasionally default rules will apply, such as those found within the Sale of Goods Act 1979 in England. Transfer by way of gift can be completed by delivery at common law (requiring delivery, acceptance and a donative intent on the part of the donor) or else by an executed deed (the deed must be signed, witnessed and delivered in order to be valid).[9] And transfer by way of bequest will occur according to the terms of a will or, failing such, according to the rules of intestacy. In these examples, the title holder transfers title directly, though the transfer can occur via an agent acting on their behalf as well.[10]

Title can also be acquired in situations lacking voluntariness. This might appear at first to contradict one of the fundamental principles of the common law, which is the rule of *nemo dat quod non habet*. By the operation of this old principle, 'no one gives what they do not have', meaning, in the context of title to chattels, that one cannot bestow title on another if one does not have title in the first place. If one maintains only possessory title, then one passes on no better title to the other party. Such a rule applies generally in relation to sales, gifts and bequests.[11] The rule makes it easier, in principle, for original owners to claim back lost or stolen property, even from those who might have found or acquired such property innocently, because the latter will not have acquired more than mere possessory title in the property. The proprietary title remains with the original owner.

There are exceptions to the *nemo dat quod non habet* principle. The most prominent operates by way of the expiry of the limitation period, the period of time in which a claim must be brought to court. In England, this is governed by the Limitation Act 1980. In many cases, the limitation period is six years, beginning 'when the cause of action accrued'.[12] If the cause of action is the tort of conversion (the mistreatment of another's chattel that prevents the other's use and possession thereof),[13] the owner's original title will extinguish at the moment the limitation period expires.[14] Should the owner's title be extinguished, the party in possession of the chattel would then have an impregnable title: their possessory title would effectively be upgraded to a proprietary title, at the expense of the proprietary title of the original owner.

In cases of successive conversions, under the Limitation Act 1980 the six-year period does not begin anew with each fresh conversion: it is calculated from the original conversion.[15] But, pursuant to section 4 of the Act, if that first conversion is a theft, the limitation period does not begin until there has been a conversion not 'related to the theft': for instance, a good faith purchase (to be proven by whosoever relies upon it).[16] A good faith purchase is understood to be a purchase by a party that is acting honestly and has no notice of any defect in title.[17] Thus the Act will preserve the proprietary title of a theft victim until six years following the first provable good faith purchase. But precursor statutes, such as the Limitation Act 1939, did not provide equivalent protection for theft victims and, as a result, before the 1980 Act came into force, title could be lost six years from the first conversion (the theft itself).[18] But that is no longer the case.

Another way in which title can be acquired from an involuntary owner would be according to the laws of a foreign jurisdiction. This is because many legal systems do not share the *nemo dat quod non habet* rule, which is found only in common law jurisdictions such as England and Wales, Ireland, the United States, Australia, Canada (apart from Québec), India and other former colonies of the UK. Continental European legal systems offer greater protection for good faith purchasers and good faith possessors, as a way of ensuring greater certainty in commercial transactions (this also holds true in the many other countries inspired by Continental models). In Italy, for example, a good faith purchaser by contract immediately acquires full title to movable property, even if that property had been stolen.[19] Japan has similar protection for the good faith purchaser.[20] In Germany, a good faith purchaser at a public auction acquires immediate title.[21] Certain countries impose slight delays in the protection provided for good faith possessors (eg three years in France), but on the whole offer substantially more protection than do common law countries.[22] This means that a good faith purchase in certain jurisdictions can bestow title upon the purchaser, as indeed can good faith possession in certain instances.

What is more, English courts will usually apply the conflict of law rule known as *lex situs* when determining whether title has been acquired according to a foreign system of law. If the original owner of property is trying to recover it, even before an English court, this will prove difficult if the prior good faith purchase had occurred in a civil law jurisdiction. For example, in *Winkworth v Christie Manson and Woods*, the plaintiff sought to recover a collection of netsuke (collectible Japanese figurines) that had been stolen from his home in England and then reappeared several years later for sale through Christie's auction house in London.[23] Unbeknownst to him, following the theft the pieces had been transported to Italy where they were sold to a good faith purchaser. The good faith purchaser then brought them back to England and consigned them for auction. Because Italy gives title to such purchasers, the English plaintiff was unable to show a persisting title; the court concluded that his title had been extinguished at the point of sale in Italy. While there are certain exceptions to the *lex situs* rule, on the whole foreign transactions of this nature will be recognised by English courts (and indeed by courts in most other common law jurisdictions).[24] This is therefore an important way by which title can be lost by one party during a transaction – and gained by another.

The Title Rules Applied

How do these rules relating to title apply in the case of the Parthenon Marbles? First of all, they can offer a better understanding of whether title does indeed rest with the Trustees, as the Trustees themselves claim, or whether it might conceivably lie elsewhere. We know the position of the UK Government and the British Museum, namely that the Marbles were legally acquired by Elgin under the 'appropriate laws of the time'.[25] And we know from chapter three that a series of documents obtained from the Ottoman authorities did appear to grant Elgin and his men permission to remove the Marbles, at least insofar as Ottoman law was concerned, though the documents of course said nothing about title. Antiquities legislation in the Ottoman Empire would only be introduced much later, in 1869: prior to this, the extent to which title could be acquired flowed directly from the permission granted by the Sultan's Court at Constantinople.[26]

On the English territory, the Marbles would have been considered chattels.[27] As we have seen, title validly acquired in a foreign jurisdiction will usually be recognised under English law (as in *Winkworth*). This is through the operation of *lex situs*. But while *lex situs* goes back to the late nineteenth century, earlier courts would have been more likely to rely upon the *lex domicilii*, by which they would have applied the law of the owner's domicile.[28] When the Marbles arrived in London, Elgin's title could have been recognised as flowing from his acquisition under the rules of the Ottoman Empire (*lex situs*), which is the approach the Select Committee seemed to have taken in 1816, without referring to the principle as such. Or it could have been assessed under the law of Elgin's place of domicile (*lex domicilii*), which would have been Scotland (the location of Broomhall), though this may have been complicated by the amount of time he had spent as a diplomat (1799–1803), his house arrest in France (1803–1806) and the location of the Marbles in London at the time.

A more logical approach might be to consider the possessory rule discussed above. When chattels enter the jurisdiction, as we saw, English law offers a presumption favouring the possessor. Possessory title is not proprietary title, but serves as title nonetheless, displaced only by one with superior title, such as the true owner. Failing such a displacement, English law would continue to protect the possessor. Were the argument to have been made at the time that title had remained with the Ottoman Sultan, the clear rebuttal would have been that no Ottoman representative had presented himself in the English jurisdiction to challenge Elgin's title. As such, possessory title would have been the best possible title in England.

But the Trustees of the British Museum do not need to rely on Elgin's possessory title. They soon acquired their own source of title under an Act of Parliament. The clearest indication under English law that the Trustees obtained title to the collection of Lord Elgin, including the Marbles, has nothing to do with the title Elgin had himself obtained. What mattered was that title to the collection was vested in the Trustees by the Act of Parliament passed on 1 July 1816, which made its intent manifestly clear in its title: *An Act to vest the Elgin Collection of ancient Marbles and Sculptures in the Trustees of the British Museum for the Use of the Public.*

The House of Commons had voted, Royal Assent was given and the Act came into effect. Within England, statutory vesting is strong enough to defeat possessory title, and can defeat even an executed deed of gift. In the nineteenth-century parliamentary system, Parliament was supreme and able to legislate as it saw fit. As Jean-Louis de Lolme famously wrote in 1771, Parliament 'can do everything but make a woman a man and a man a woman'.[29] The 1816 Act therefore made it clear that the Trustees were bestowed with title under English law. And this title has persisted, uninterrupted since that first enactment, under the British Museum Act 1963. So that would seem to resolve the matter – subject to the 'volatility of title' (to which we will return).

The British Museum Act 1963

With title come statutory obligations. While trustees of national institutions in the UK have legal title to their collections, they do not enjoy the rights of regular owners of property. In fact, the British Museum is established according to the structure of a trust whereby legal title is held by the Trustees and the beneficiaries are the members of the public. When the Museum was first established by Act of Parliament in 1753, the Trustees were vested with title in the collection, but were given duties to maintain and preserve the collection 'for publick use to all posterity'.[30] This way the Trustees would not be at liberty to sell, trade or give away important parts of the collection. The model of the statutory trust was then used for other national institutions established in Britain during the nineteenth century.[31]

Under the British Museum Act 1963 (see Figure 6), the Trustees are required to keep the collection 'within the authorised repositories of the Museum' and to make objects available for 'inspection by members of the public' when required, as 'far as appears to them to be practicable'.[32] They will not be able to 'dispose' of any object vested in them,[33] with certain narrow exceptions to this general rule. Disposal here refers to selling, exchanging, giving away or otherwise disposing of an object.[34] The exceptions provided under the 1963 Act are at section 5(1):

a)   If the object is a duplicate;
b)   If the object appears to pre-date 1850 and is of printed matter and a copy is already held by the Trustees;
c)   If, in the opinion of the Trustees, the object is 'unfit to be retained in the collections' and can be disposed of 'without detriment to the interests of students';
d)   In order to destroy or otherwise dispose of an object that has 'become useless' due to damage, physical deterioration or infestation.[35]

In addition, the Trustees are able to transfer an object to the Natural History Museum or to those other UK national institutions listed in Schedule 5 of the Museums and Galleries Act 1992.[36]

British Museum Act 1963

CHAPTER 24

Figure 6 Detail of the British Museum Act 1963, which is the current governing legislation of the British Museum collection and its Trustees

Two further exceptions have since been added by Parliament. The first came through the Human Tissue Act 2004 which, amongst other matters, allowed the boards/trustees of listed national institutions (including the British Museum) to transfer from their collections human remains less than 1,000 years of age.[37] The principal purpose here was to permit the repatriation of remains to overseas claimant communities. The second came through the Holocaust (Return of Cultural Objects) Act 2009, which allowed the boards/trustees of listed national institutions (also including the British Museum) to transfer from their collections objects looted during the Nazi period, if the transfer has been recommended by the Spoliation Advisory Panel and approved by the Secretary of State.[38]

Thus, although the Trustees of the British Museum have legal title to the collection, they remain severely limited by legislation in terms of what they can do with it. This explains the repeated statements that, even if they wanted to, the Trustees would be unable to return the Marbles permanently to Greece without a change in their governing statute.[39]

There may be an argument that under the section 5(1)(c) exception for objects considered 'unfit', the Trustees would be able to dispose of the Marbles and deliver them to Greece. This, however, seems unlikely. As can be seen from the Explanatory Memorandum that accompanied the enactment of the exception in 1963, while discretion would be generally reserved to the Trustees under this exception, the types of objects that were referred to were forgeries or those wrongly identified.[40] The Museum's current De-accession Policy (2018) refers to objects 'no longer useful or relevant to the Museum's purpose' the retention of which does not benefit scholars or the general public.[41] Arguments have been made (including by the present author) that certain objects in the collection – for example, the 11 sacred tabots of the Ethiopian Church kept in storage and for which access is reserved only to Ethiopian priests – would fit within such an exception, since they appear manifestly unfit for a museum collection and could be removed without causing detriment to the interests of students.[42] But few other objects would meet this threshold. The only recorded instance in which the exception was used was in 1975 when a 'relic of cannibalism' was judged to be unfit and was exchanged with the country of Fiji for a collection of prehistoric shards.[43] The argument would be impossible to maintain for major collections such as the Parthenon Marbles, to which many members of the public (including students) have a significant attachment. And, in any event, the 'unfit' exception can be used only if the Trustees themselves wish to return objects. There is no indication that they would ever want to use this exception for the Marbles. As such, the argument remains largely academic.

Another ground under which the Trustees might be able to return an object would be if title to it had never vested in them in the first place. This would occur in situations where an object was acquired from parties who did not have proprietary title themselves, according to the *nemo dat quod non habet* principle. In such rare circumstances, it may be possible to challenge the Trustees' title to such an object. It would have to be shown that there was no basis upon which title had been acquired. For instance, if the Museum acquires an object and it is then discovered that the object had been stolen from its true owner, the owner would be able to bring a claim in the tort of conversion, provided it fell within the Limitation Act 1980 (see above). In such situations, it is almost certain that the Museum would return the object prior to the issuance of a claim.[44] In fact, this is what happened after the British Museum acquired a group of miniature bronze shields as part of the 'Salisbury Hoard' in 1989. After further provenance research by the curator, it transpired that these had been stolen from a landowner in Wiltshire and, in 1995, the Museum agreed to transfer them back to the landowner. The decision was made in recognition of the legal claim the landowner could have brought, and out of a desire to avoid costly and reputation-damaging litigation. The Museum clearly recognised that the items would not be covered by the statutory restriction in the British Museum Act 1963 and so could proceed with their disposal from the collection.[45] Guidance in the museum sector would certainly encourage such an outcome.[46]

Today of course the Museum would not knowingly acquire material that had been stolen, looted or illegally exported in the first place. This is set out in the British Museum's Acquisitions Policy (2018), whereby objects will be acquired only if they are 'legally available' and where there is no reasonable cause to believe they were 'wrongfully taken' from a lawful owner, looted from an archaeological site or museum, or wrongfully exported or imported.[47] The objects must also have a documented legal history, where applicable, which extends back before 14 November 1970 (the date of the UNESCO Convention on the Means of Prohibiting and Preventing the Illicit Import, Export and Transfer of Ownership of Cultural Property),[48] an approach in keeping with 2005 guidance from the Department for Culture, Media and Sport,[49] as well as the ethical norms set out in the applicable Codes of Ethics (like the ICOM Code of Ethics we saw in chapter three).[50] If through accident or oversight the Museum acquires property today that turns out to have been stolen, looted or illegally exported, it would have an ethical obligation to return it according to such standards.[51] Whether the Trustees could do so legally would depend on their use of one of the exceptions to the statutory restriction mentioned above.

The Trustees are protected from legal claims under English law by both the vesting provision of the 1963 statute (which affirms the vesting from previous statutes like the 1816 Act) and by the six-year limitation period. We know that under the Limitation Act 1980, even in cases of theft, the title of the original owner is extinguished six years after the first good faith purchase.[52] And under predecessor Acts title was extinguished six years after the theft itself. Either way, Trustee title to old acquisitions appears secure, at least under English law. We will soon consider the international angle, both in this chapter and then in chapter seven, which may add another layer of complexity. But first let us turn to the more immediate question of morality.

Morality Considered

We already began to look at the question of morality at the end of chapter three. In that chapter, I showed that the manner of acquisition of the Marbles, while legal at the time, was nevertheless problematic according to the ethics of today.[53] We know that ethics cannot serve to force a prescriptive outcome. But what happens when decision-makers *want* to respond to an ethical challenge by taking action? What happens where the Trustees in this instance feel a moral compulsion for returning an object from the collection? Can they follow their conscience? Or will the return be barred by the usual legal restrictions? This matter has indeed arisen in the past and has become especially relevant today owing to a forthcoming change in law. Let us begin with the past example.

Around the year 2000 it came to light that four drawings from the British Museum's collection had been looted by the Nazis in 1939 from a Jewish man, Dr Arthur Feldmann, in Brno, Czechoslovakia. The Museum had acquired the pieces in the late 1940s: three by purchase in 1946 and one by bequest in 1949 from a former Keeper of Prints and Drawings. Upon receiving a request for the drawings to be returned to Feldmann's heirs in 2002, the Trustees were unsure how to proceed. At the time, the Holocaust (Return of Cultural Objects) Act 2009 had not been enacted and the British Museum Act 1963 only included relevant exceptions for duplicates, unfit objects and useless objects. The Trustees sought the approval of the Attorney General to allow restitution based on an equitable rule from charity law: the principle of the 'ex gratia payment', derived from the 1970 case of *Re Snowden*,[54] under which charity trustees can seek approval from the Attorney General or the court to make a payment (or any other application of property) if they are under a 'moral obligation' to do so. The Attorney General then sought clarification from the High Court, which led to the decision in *Attorney General v Trustees of the British Museum*.[55] The court in this case refused the action: where there is a clear statutory restriction on disposing of assets, as in the British Museum Act 1963, a principle of charity law cannot be used to override this. As such, the Trustees were unable to restitute the drawings.[56] This legal obstacle would not be remedied until four years later with the passage of the Holocaust (Return of Cultural Objects) Act 2009 discussed above. However, the exception introduced by this statute was limited to objects lost or stolen during the Nazi period in Europe and did not apply to collection objects more generally.

The decision in *Attorney General v Trustees of the British Museum* served to reinforce what already appeared to be a watertight restriction. While the court had recognised the possibility that the Trustees could return objects that had not been properly vested in them (as had happened with the Salisbury Hoard), it specified that the Trustees would not be able to waive the protection of the limitation period in relation to title: they were bound to retain objects vested in them as part of the collection, even if that title derived from the operation of the Limitation Act 1980.[57] Interestingly, the Trustees did not attempt to argue that disposal might be possible under the 'unfit' exception, perhaps to avoid the exception being used with respect to more controversial returns (the fear of the so-called 'slippery slope'), so this point was not raised before the court. All parties had instead asked that the court operate under the assumption that the claimants did not have a claim at law or in equity, though the point was never in fact admitted by the claimants themselves.[58]

The case began to attract some criticism over the years. The view from the charity sector was that the ex gratia principle was important, even if it was used only on rare occasions, and should not be subject to statutory restrictions.[59] The *Snowden* power had in fact become more entrenched for charity trustees over the years. Having been codified in the Charities Act 1993, it was then reaffirmed at section 106 of the Charities Act 2011, which gave authority to the Charity Commission of England and Wales, together with the Attorney General, to authorise such applications of property. When the Law Commission examined the point in its 2017 report, *Technical Issues in Charity Law*, it questioned the practical result of the decision in *Attorney General v Trustees of the British Museum*, suggesting that the ex gratia power of section 106 should be made available to trustees of charities established by statute (which included national institutions such as the British Museum), even when the statute imposed restrictions on disposing of property.[60] The recommendations of the Law Commission were eventually taken up by Parliament, which enacted the Charities Act 2022, a statute that received Royal Assent on 24 February 2022. The new Act included a provision to amend section 106, giving trustees the ability to make ex gratia applications of charity property with authorisation from the Charity Commission, Attorney General or the court, regardless of existing statutory restrictions.[61]

The question of the 'moral obligation' in such situations therefore becomes crucial. How is it to be assessed? For its part, the Charity Commission had been overseeing ex gratia applications for many years and had published guidance on the matter, much of which echoes the statements of the court in *Snowden*. For instance, the power to authorise should 'not be exercised lightly or on slender grounds but only in cases where it can be fairly said that if the charity were an individual it would be morally wrong of him to refuse to make the payment'.[62] In assessing an application, the Commission needs to ensure that there are reasonable grounds for the trustees to believe they would be acting immorally by refusing to make the payment or transfer.[63] More specifically, when museum trustees decide upon the morality of returning a collection object, they can find support within a number of codes and guidance documents that are well-known within the museum sector, including the ICOM Code of Ethics and the Museums Association Code of Ethics (the British Museum, for example, subscribes to both). More recently, Arts Council England has published guidance for museums making decisions in this area called *Restitution and Repatriation: A Practical Guide for*

Museums in England (2022), which lists factors to be considered when making a decision on an ethical basis.[64] There is therefore guidance to support trustees in coming to a morally-sound decision in these matters. In fact, the Charity Commission authorised in 2022 restitutions of Benin Bronzes from the collections of both Cambridge University and the Horniman Museum and Gardens under section 106, demonstrating an institutional familiarity with the required thresholds and the ability to apply them to cases of restitution.[65]

It was originally intended that the relevant provisions of the Charities Act 2022, ss 15 and 16, would be brought into force by the Secretary of State for Digital, Culture, Media and Sport in the autumn of 2022. But when the full implications of the Act became clear, the UK Government decided to delay the implementation date.[66] Although the provisions had been proposed by the Law Commission, studied by a parliamentary committee and voted on by both Houses of Parliament, the knock-on effect for national museums had not been fully understood. In a statement read out in the House of Lords on 13 October 2022, the Government representative, Lord Kamall, said that the Government needed to further understand the implications of this change for national museums and other charities before it could be brought into force. At the time of writing, it remains to be seen how this investigation will proceed and what the outcome may be. The Secretary of State may seek to postpone the commencement indefinitely, although this could be difficult without returning the matter to Parliament, as the public duties required of government ministers with respect to Acts duly passed by Parliament are considerable.[67]

If the provision is brought into force, however, it is unlikely to have a direct impact on the decision of the British Museum Trustees in the case of the Marbles. While it would open up the possibility of returning objects on moral grounds, the power cannot be exercised 'lightly or on slender grounds' and would be used only in the rarest of cases: perhaps, for example, in relation to the Ethiopian tabots, but almost certainly not for major collection objects such as the Marbles. It would be difficult to imagine a Board of Trustees, at present or in the foreseeable future, ever feeling itself under a moral obligation in this regard. Even the current Chair George Osborne, who has shown himself open to striking a deal with Greece, has made it clear that the Marbles would still remain legal appendages to the Museum. This is demonstrated through statements such as 'dismantling the collection must not become the careless act of a single generation' and so forth.

But what the change might offer is a subtle shifting of positions on this and other restitution claims. No longer would it be possible to use the somewhat tired argument that restitution is impossible because the British Museum Act 1963 prohibits it. First of all, we know this is strictly not true, as exceptions currently exist for duplicates and unfit objects. The Museum's traditional positioning in these matters has tended to force claimants into a corner: it comes across as rigid and categorical, prompting the other party to take an equally rigid and categorical position. And more importantly, the position seems to have been adopted internally as well. The statutory restriction has allowed the Trustees to avoid questioning themselves about the moral grounds on which they hold certain controversial items, including the Marbles. This has allowed them to grow rather soft over the years, atrophied and untested on some of the more important questions of the day. The new ex gratia power would put wind in their sails, it is hoped, by requiring them to re-examine and put forward a morally defensible position, one suited to today's ethical landscape, rather than simply relying on a legislative enactment that was made 60 years ago. By this token, the debate could move forward, even if only incrementally.

The Volatility of Title

One complicating feature in all this is that title, when considered internationally, can also become unstable. While its status may be settled under English law, title would not necessarily be guaranteed outside the UK territory. Title is not as universal as we may assume. By the principle of *lex situs*, courts in England (and indeed most common law jurisdictions) will generally recognise title acquired elsewhere, but even this rule has its exceptions. These exceptions were referred to by the English judge in *Winkworth* and include situations where the goods were transiting through a foreign jurisdiction, where the relevant transaction had not been entered into in good faith, where the foreign rule is contrary to English public policy or where a statute in the court's jurisdiction prevents the foreign law from being applied.[68] When it comes to recognising title obtained abroad, English courts have shown themselves willing to disregard foreign laws if their application would lead to a result contrary to English public policy (*City of Gotha*)[69] or where they are considered to be in gross violation of international law (*Kuwait Airways*).[70] US courts have also shown themselves able to disregard title acquired in a foreign jurisdiction if it would not have been so acquired under US rules: this has been especially true in relation to artwork misappropriated during the Nazi era and then later acquired according to the laws of a European state.[71] Title to chattels is not necessarily preserved across space and time: it can change, sometimes depending on the jurisdiction and the particular law to be applied. The point here is that title is by its very nature volatile.

When it comes to the Marbles, there is of course no risk that the Trustees' title would ever be disregarded by an English court. However, the same could not be said of a court in a foreign jurisdiction, including Greece. How such a court would treat the matter might depend on its own particular conflict of law rules and its own limitation periods. While it may be likely that such a court would recognise the Trustees' title, this is in no way guaranteed. Of course, the Trustees do hold title, vested by an Act of Parliament, but that title extends only to British shores. There is no such thing as 'international title': that is, title that is automatically guaranteed in all countries around the world; rather, title is a nationally-derived right.[72] This might help to explain the British Museum's long-established hesitations about lending the Marbles to Greece, for fear that they might then be subject to a potentially unknown foreign legal regime, without some form of acknowledgment provided by Greece that Greece recognises title held by the Trustees.

This brings us squarely to the question of the title acknowledgement that the Museum has traditionally required of Greece prior to contemplating any loan of the Marbles. This requirement has been affirmed on numerous occasions and has also formed part of the 'Trustees' Statement' about the Marbles, a statement that continues to appear on the Museum's website as follows:

> The simple precondition required by the Trustees before they will consider whether or not to lend an object is that the borrowing institution acknowledges the British Museum's ownership of the object ... The Trustees' policy and their willingness to consider loans to Athens has been made clear to the Greek government, but successive Greek governments have refused to consider borrowing or to acknowledge the Trustees' ownership of the Parthenon sculptures in their care. This has made any meaningful discussion on the issue virtually impossible.[73]

If current negotiations do move forward, how will this precondition be treated? Is it fair for the British Museum to continue to demand it prior to lending the Marbles to Greece?

The insistence on such a precondition would seem rather harsh. It is not specifically required under the British Museum Act 1963, which only requires that the Trustees 'have regard to the interests of students and other persons visiting the Museum', to the 'physical condition and degree of rarity' of the object in question and to any 'risks to which it is likely to be exposed.'[74] According to the Museum's own Loans Policy, the Trustees will lend in circumstances 'when the perceived risk to the object is considered reasonable' and when the borrower 'guarantees that the object will be returned to the museum at the end of the loan period', with no specific mention of acknowledging title.[75] Nor do the standard loan forms used by the Museum include a clause with such a requirement.[76] In museum loan contracts around the world, such a precondition would be highly anomalous, as it is not usually the borrower who is required to acknowledge title, but the lender.[77] So the insistence on the precondition in relation only to the Marbles seems unfair, as a potentially discriminatory measure that only targets one prospective borrower.

What is more, we now know that title can change based on the jurisdiction – it is essentially volatile. Precisely what title would the Trustees like acknowledged? Title broadly speaking, which as we know is impossible? Title under English or UK law? Or title under Greek law?

It does appear now that the Museum has begun to distance itself from the precondition. As recently reported, the usual statement about the precondition has now been softened by the Museum's press department.[78] Osborne himself has stated that he did not want to 'force the Greeks to accept things that they find impossible.'[79] Though the 'Trustees' Statement' on the Museum website has not changed – this has remained static for many years – the main 'Parthenon Sculptures' page now states that the Trustees 'will consider any loan request for any part of the collection (subject to all our normal loan conditions)', without mention of the precondition (the precondition seems to have been dropped in early 2022). Perhaps this is a sign that discussions are indeed moving forward.

As a way for the parties to reach a compromise on the point – and if an acknowledgement is still required by the Trustees – then if anything the acknowledgement should be limited in scope. This would flow neatly from the fact that title, as we know, is by its nature nationally derived. As such, Greece might be able to acknowledge the title of the Trustees, but only under English or UK law. This would avoid the thorny (and politically troublesome, at least in Greece) question of whether Elgin himself had obtained title from the Ottomans. It could instead be limited to a recognition that an Act of Parliament settled English title in 1816. Likewise, the British Museum would need to recognise that to impose any broader scope within the acknowledgement would create a theoretically impossible task for Greece. Perhaps on this small point there is room for some agreement, which might allow for greater cooperation between the parties on other matters.

Immunity from Seizure

Such a solution would be unlikely, however, to assuage the fears that the Trustees might have in the event of a long-term loan to Greece. Would the objects ever return? What guarantees could be sought from Greece that they would? At the hearing of the Select Committee for Culture, Media and Sport in 2000, the Chair of Trustees of the British Museum stressed this worry on two grounds:

> [T]here could be political reasons why it would be impossible for them to come back. There could also be legal reasons. There could be cases in the Greek courts which would hold them there indefinitely, so I think the Trustees would take the view that it would not be feasible to send them to Greece.[80]

Back then, this was enough to forestall the hopes of a long-term loan. But now, if loans or related arrangements are to become part of the future relationship, how would those fears be allayed?

There are practical options for preventing worst-case scenarios. One of these would be if Greece lent choice items from its national collections while the Marbles were in Athens, a proposal suggested by Mitsotakis that is apparently part of the current negotiations.[81] A reciprocal loan to the British Museum would serve as a type of collateral, ensuring that everything returns at the end of the agreed period – referred to by commentators, perhaps tactlessly, as 'the cultural version of a hostage swap' or words to that effect.[82]

Another way the Marbles might be protected is through the principle of sovereign immunity, whereby state property is generally secure against seizure or confiscation in a foreign jurisdiction. While it is likely that the principle alone would not protect property held by the Trustees (not strictly speaking 'state owned'), it could nevertheless be extended were Greece to pass a broader law providing immunity for cultural objects on loan. The British Museum's Loans Policy refers to guarantees of immunity as what is usually expected of borrowers in any event, a commonplace in the museum world.[83] Greece, presumably, would be able to comply with this. The British Museum has also felt confident enough lending to Greek museums in the past.[84] So in many ways the groundwork is already there. A number of countries have specific immunity laws for cultural objects on loan, so there is a plethora of models that Greece could choose from.[85] In fact, the UK itself has one of the best immunity laws for protecting cultural objects on loan, found in Part 6 of the Tribunals, Courts and Enforcement Act 2007.

An example of how these work in practice – and one that involved the British Museum itself – may be instructive. In 2004, the British Museum lent to Museum Victoria in Australia a number of Aboriginal artefacts, including three nineteenth-century bark paintings and a ceremonial representation of an emu. At the time, Australia did not have specific immunity from seizure for cultural objects on loan. During the loan, these items were seized pursuant to an emergency declaration by an Inspector under Australia's Aboriginal and Torres Strait Islander Heritage Protection Act 1984 on the basis that they could not leave Australia until their status had been negotiated with the relevant Aboriginal communities.[86] While the declaration was eventually overturned by the Australian Federal Court and the objects returned to the British Museum, the matter took a full year to resolve, much to the chagrin of the British Museum's Trustees. Australia later passed immunity-from-seizure legislation, the Protection of Cultural Objects on Loan Act 2013, which guaranteed immunity for cultural objects on loan from international sources like those ones. With the Act in place, the Trustees felt comfortable lending a number of Aboriginal artefacts from the British Museum to the *Encounters* exhibition at the National Museum of Australia in 2015, including one of the same bark paintings that had earlier been seized under the Inspector's orders. These artefacts were safe from seizure during the loan and were promptly returned to the British Museum at the end of the exhibition.[87] This illustrates the effectiveness of such laws, while also demonstrating the Trustees' reliance upon them in the past when deciding to lend abroad, despite the risks.

If there were ever problems securing the return of objects sent to Greece, reliance could also be placed on the Trade and Cooperation Agreement signed by the UK and the EU on 30 December 2020 to accompany the UK's withdrawal from the EU. Article 21 (GOODS) of Part II/Title 1 of this Agreement requires the UK and EU parties to the Agreement to 'cooperate in facilitating the return of cultural property illicitly removed from the territory of a Party', which can extend to property 'not returned at the end of a period of lawful temporary removal' (such as an unreturned loan).[88] Thus any problems arising out of the long-term arrangements could be escalated to the EU-UK level, which could help to provide the necessary impetus to prompt a return where necessary.

If additional support were needed, it might be found in the form of the UNIDROIT Convention on Stolen or Illegally Exported Cultural Objects (1995). This Convention allows contracting States to request from the court or competent authorities of another contracting State the return of illegally exported cultural objects, including temporarily exported objects not returned in accordance with the terms of an export permit (Article 5).[89] Greece is already party to the Convention.[90] The UK is not, but the Report from the Select Committee for Culture, Media and Sport had recommended its adoption in 2000, a recommendation supported by the British Museum at the time.[91] Were the UK to join, the Museum would be afforded this added layer of legal protection regarding any risk that the Marbles would not be returned at the end of the loan period. This would involve the British Museum taking a stand, once again, to promote the adoption of an important international convention. It could be a positive turn, allowing the Museum to help emphasise its (very real) commitment to the fight against the contemporary trade in illicit cultural objects, something that is often forgotten in the debate over the Marbles.[92]

If the UNIDROIT Convention were ratified by the UK, it would also improve the UK's standing abroad, allowing the country to celebrate its status as the first important art-market State to do so. Such a ratification would no doubt have an impact on other art-market States (such as Switzerland, Germany, Japan and the United States), which could be an entirely positive step in helping to root out the illicit trade in antiquities. It would also provide that extra layer of protection, should one be needed, for the Marbles during a long-term loan to Greece.

Loan, Bailment, Usufruct

If there is to be a resolution of the Marbles dispute, it appears inevitable that it will be on the basis of a compromise. If a permanent and immediate return appears impossible, so too does a simple maintenance of the status quo. Some third way needs to be envisaged. And this appears to be what the parties have been discussing of late. If current reports are to be believed, the British Museum might be willing to offer upwards of a third of the Marbles to Greece, including a significant stretch of frieze and metopes, for a period of 10 years, possibly 20.[93] If such an arrangement succeeds, and the objects are returned, then more would be sent to Athens in a second tranche. This model would then be replicated according to a 'ratchet' mechanism whereby a growing number would be sent: at any given time there would always be some British Museum Marbles on public display in Greece. These would of course be mere transfers of possession, and temporary ones at that, with (English) title remaining vested in the Trustees. How then could this be squared with the Greek Prime Minister's statement in 2021 that he 'will not accept a loan'?

There may be two answers to this. First, Mitsotakis is a shrewd negotiator with professional experience in the private sector. Public statements during his UK visit may have been intended as an instigation, a newsworthy catchphrase to get the ball rolling. It may also have been used to score political points back home, showing that he could be tough in the face of a more powerful ally, but not in a way that would jeopardise his country's more pressing financial and diplomatic interests. Since we know that, during the visit, he met with Osborne in secret to discuss a way forward on the Marbles, his public statements do not necessarily reveal his underlying strategy, which appears to include an openness to compromise.

The second answer is that the parties may be able to skirt the impolitic 'loan' term if there is to be an agreement. The Victoria & Albert Museum, when facing a similar challenge in relation to an object from its collection that it sent back to Turkey in 2022 employed in the agreement the term 'renewable cultural partnership'. This related to the small 'Eros Head', which had been in the collection since 1883, but which was part of a larger sarcophagus from Sidamaria, Turkey held at the Istanbul National Museum.[94] Some might call it a euphemism, others an unconvincing compromise, but nomenclature can be quite important in this area. It is perhaps an approach that could work for the Marbles, seeing as the British Museum is already using the term 'Parthenon Partnership'.

If a legal vehicle is nevertheless needed, a term such as 'bailment' might be considered worthy. Bailments are familiar in common law jurisdictions such as England. They arise when one party voluntarily transfers possession of chattels to another for a period of time while retaining title. The recipient (bailee) owes a duty of reasonable care to the owner (bailor), but can otherwise enjoy the use of the chattels.[95] Interestingly one of the duties of the bailee is to refrain from denying the bailor's title. Bailment forms its own branch of law, outside both contract and tort, while sharing features with each: it forms an agreement that can be amended by written terms, while it also imposes a duty of care on the bailee. This is of course a common law principle, certainly available to the Trustees, but would it be acceptable in Greece? Thankfully a similar principle exists in civil law. In fact, 'bailment' at common law found its inspiration in Roman Law, which of course is the origin of Continental legal systems.[96] Greece has the principle of χρησιδάνειο ('chrisidaneio'), involving a free transfer of possession for the recipient's use and enjoyment within a set period of time.[97] There will of course be subtle differences with 'bailment', but the two principles are not dissimilar. An alternative might be the principle under which the Salinas Museum in Palermo initially transferred a frieze fragment to the Acropolis Museum in early 2022, as a 'deposit *sine die*' (that is, a transfer of possession without a specified end date).[98]

There are other possibilities that can be explored as well. The Trustees might be familiar with terms such as 'life interest' or 'limited interest', often used in the context of land. As we saw earlier, legal dismemberments can be contemplated for chattels as well. While a life interest may not be appropriate in these circumstances, something short of this could perhaps be envisaged: a retention by the Trustees of their base title, but a transfer of the benefits associated with the use, enjoyment and auxiliary financial benefits (such as ticket revenue) to the recipient. Greek lawyers would perhaps be familiar with the term επικαρπία ('epikarpia'), otherwise known as 'usufruct', a principle common to all civil law jurisdictions. Its structure allows the owner to retain legal title, while allowing the possessor to use and enjoy the property widely, while benefiting from the 'fruits' thereof. In fact, museums in civil law jurisdictions are familiar with using usufructs in relation to works donated by private individuals to their collections (for example, the Louvre and Musée d'Orsay in France).[99] Perhaps there is enough common ground here to build an agreement acceptable to both sides? The delicate term 'loan' would of course be dropped, at least on paper.

None of this is of course meant to resolve the matter on its own. The dispute over the Marbles is about more than legal niceties. It is possible that terminological matters such as these prove unimportant in any deal struck between the parties. As we often see in sophisticated commercial arrangements, contractual terms go into some detail as to the rights and obligations of each party. This would probably be the case here too. Or it might even be that the terminology used – loan, bailment, deposit, usufruct – is not enough. There may be other issues at play here too. This is not, after all, about seeking out tidy solutions to a classroom exercise. This is a 200-year-old conundrum, one invested with all the weight of history, national identity and politics across two countries. If there is to be a solution, it will need to address the larger issues in the dispute as well – otherwise it may fail dramatically.[100]

7

Wellington and International Law

In 1815, the year Lord Elgin first petitioned Parliament for the acquisition of his collection, great change was underway on the Continent. Napoleon had just been defeated by a coalition of armies at Waterloo, ending his ill-fated attempt at regaining power in France and overcoming his adversaries in Europe. While statesmen at the Congress of Vienna had recently settled the boundaries of post-war Europe, the victorious generals, along with their armies, had converged on Paris to begin their occupation of France. In charge of the coalition was Arthur Wellesley, the Duke of Wellington, who led the army that had defeated the French at Waterloo (see Figure 7). In addition to the military and political challenges of that year, Wellington was faced with one particular problem. And it related to art.

Figure 7 Francisco Goya, *The Duke of Wellington*, 1812–1814, was painted during the Peninsular Wars prior to Wellington's involvement in restituting art from Paris (detail)
Source: DeAgostini/Getty Images, DEA / M. CARRIERI / Contributor.

Beginning in the 1790s, French armies had taken artworks from the territories they had conquered, with a stated intention of 'centralising' great works of art in public galleries in Paris.[1] This initially involved the Revolutionary Army confiscating works from churches in the Low Countries and bringing them to Paris, perhaps most famously the *Descent from the Cross* by Rubens taken from Antwerp Cathedral in 1794 and placed in the Louvre. Napoleon continued this tradition, but formalised it: in the peace treaties that he concluded after his victories over the princely states of Italy, and the Vatican, he set out the number of valuable objects to be handed over to France: usually this consisted of 20 works of art and 50 manuscripts, though in the case of the Vatican, it consisted of 100 works of art and 500 manuscripts.[2] In total, it is estimated that over 2,000 artworks were brought to France during the period of French military success, as well as many more manuscripts and other objects.[3]

Following the defeat of Napoleon, the Allies occupying Paris (and Wellington in particular) were confronted with the question of what was to be done with all this 'looted' art, some of which had been on public display at the Louvre for two decades. Many in France were adamant that these artworks should remain, arguing that their initial transfer had occurred pursuant to international treaties and that they had by this time become mainstays of French culture. Notable voices were those of the Louvre's director, Vivant Denon, and the author Stendhal, who argued that restitution would be contrary to international law as a violation of earlier peace treaties.[4]

The matter culminated for Wellington in September 1815 when the Minister of the King of the Netherlands requested his help in recovering works from the Louvre. This was in order to obtain, in Wellington's words, what was the King's 'undoubted property'.[5] Artists, connoisseurs and commentators all agreed, according to Wellington, that the Napoleonic spoils 'ought to be removed to their ancient seat.' Wellington considered it his duty 'to take the necessary measures to obtain what was his right', and that the Allies 'having the contents of the museum justly in their power, could not do otherwise than restore them to the countries from which, contrary to the practice of civilised warfare, they had been torn during the disastrous period of the French revolution and the tyranny of Bonaparte.'[6]

This was part of a more widespread series of restitutions undertaken by the occupying armies at Paris. In addition to the Dutch, the Prussians, Italians and Spanish all began the process of identifying looted pieces and arranging for their return. The Pope sent the renowned sculptor Antonio Canova to Paris to negotiate for the return of the many masterpieces that had been removed from Vatican collections by Napoleon, notably the ancient sculptures of *Laocoön* and the *Apollo Belvedere*, as well as Raphael's celebrated *Transfiguration*.[7] And the Rubens, absent for over 20 years, would soon be reinstalled at Antwerp Cathedral.

While the eventual Treaty of Paris, signed 20 November 1815, was silent on the restitution of treasures, the approach was considered correct and appropriate by the Allied Powers. Accompanying the Duke of Wellington in Paris for the signing was British Foreign Secretary, the Viscount Castlereagh. Castlereagh too had made it clear, in a note to the Allied Ministers of 11 September 1815 and 'placed upon their Protocol', that the claims by the royal sovereigns of Europe for the art of which their 'respective States have been successfully and systematically stripped by [the] Government of France, contrary to every principle of justice, and to the usages of modern warfare' placed a duty on the Allies to 'effectuate what justice and policy require' in returning all the 'spoils'.[8] Why allow France to keep acquisitions, he asked rhetorically, 'which all modern conquerors have invariably respected as inseparable from the country to which they belonged?' All modern conquerors, that is, except Napoleon.

Additionally, Castlereagh set out the position of the British Sovereign (represented by the Prince Regent) that the Allies must at all times refrain from removing any item that had belonged to France prior to the conflict. They were not to use the opportunity, 'either directly or indirectly', to bring into their dominions 'a single article which did not of right, at the period of their conquest, belong either to their respective family collection, or to the countries over which they now actually reign'.[9] This exhortation was followed by the occupying armies, as they thereafter refrained from removing that which had belonged to the French before the conflicts began in the 1790s.[10] This was no mere victors' justice; it was a higher form of justice, one imposed as a principled remedy for breaches of an international order. To Stendhal, and no doubt to many others in France, this was an illogical calculus, since Napoleon's takings had been permissible by treaty, while the Allies had no such instrument by which to justify their actions.[11]

Of course, not all looted works were returned. Denon, the Director of the Louvre, had been sending pieces to minor museums around France since 1801 and accelerated the process in order to conceal them from Allied troops.[12] His agents were also able to convince the Allies that Veronese's immense *Wedding Feast at Cana*, taken by the French from the San Giorgio Monastery in Venice in 1797, was too large and delicate to travel, instead offering in its place a work by Le Brun.[13] While it remains impossible to obtain a precise figure on the proportion of items returned, it was clearly significant. Estimates by Stendhal at the time were that, of more than 2,000 artworks taken, 1,150 were restituted, amounting to about 55 per cent of the original loot.[14] Taking into account the challenges of identifying and recovering all relevant pieces, the success rate was impressive. This was clearly one of history's great episodes of restitution.[15]

The public statements by Wellington and Castlereagh were particularly telling. By deeming Napoleon's actions 'contrary to every principle of justice', they indicated recognition of a practice that had become established over the course of the eighteenth century, namely that works of great artistic value, as well as religious relics, should not be removed in times of war, regardless of the pretext (such as treaties to the contrary).[16] This practice was to be respected by invading armies and, in the case of breach (or multiple breaches, as with Napoleon), the proper redress would necessarily involve restitution. Castlereagh added in his note to the Allied Ministers that it was impossible to adopt a 'middle line' as a remedy to the evil of spoliation: 'The principle of property regulated by the claims of the territories from whence these works were taken, is the surest and only guide to justice.'[17]

Such a view seemed to accord with a decision two years earlier by Judge Croke of the British Admiralty Court sitting in Nova Scotia in the case of the *Marquis de Somerueles*.[18] In that case an American vessel had been captured by the British during the War of 1812 and its cargo, which included Italian paintings destined for the Philadelphia Academy of Arts, was seized. The Court held that objects of artistic value were 'part of the common heritage of all mankind and thus protected from seizure during war' and ordered that they be returned to their American owner: the 'arts and sciences are admitted amongst all civilised nations as forming an exception to the severe rights of warfare, and as entitled to favour and protection.'[19] Clearly the principle was evident that works of art were not to be treated as prizes of war, and were deserving of protection at all times.

The irony of course is that while Wellington and Castlereagh were advancing this principle in Paris, across the Channel Elgin's collection would soon be acquired by vote of Parliament, bringing the Parthenon Marbles into the holdings of the British Museum. The apparent contradiction was barely noticed at the time. Elgin's former secretary William Richard Hamilton, who had overseen much of the administration of the removal of the Marbles between 1801 and 1804, was by 1815 British Under-Secretary for Foreign Affairs operating in Paris, reporting back to London about the actions that were being taken to restore works of art to their original sovereigns. When the Prime Minister had earlier asked whether the British Museum might be able to acquire works from Paris, Hamilton's response was categorical, combining a righteous idealism with an acute sense of how it would be played against them: 'It would throw an odium upon our exertions to restore stolen goods, and those French who are the most exasperated against the general measures of restitution already make use of this argument against our pretended disinterested exertion in the cause of justice.'[20] And the great German writer Goethe, who had supported the Prussians in their attempts to retrieve art from Paris, would also show great admiration for the British Museum in having acquired the Marbles from Lord Elgin.[21]

Despite this inconsistency, the returns of 1815 marked an important yardstick in the development of international practice for the protection of works of art during conflict. While the episode did not result in a complete restitution of art, it indicated a custom recognised by the Sovereigns of Europe and their ministerial delegations in Paris. 'The restitution of plundered art in 1815,' according to international legal expert James Crawford (a former Judge of the International Court of Justice), 'marked a change in attitude and laid the foundations for the development of international cultural heritage law.'[22] The imperfect nature of the returns did not appear to undermine the guiding principle of the Allies, as retention in France was usually the result of subterfuge or practical difficulties in locating and returning works. Throughout 1815 the Allies, to use the words of Castlereagh, avoided the middle line: it was the principle of recovering foreign sovereign property that was the surest guide to justice.

The Nineteenth Century Law of Nations

International legal norms can be established by agreement, such as treaty or convention, as well as by the custom of States, what is known today as customary international law.[23] Where a custom exists, it can form a legal rule binding on States, despite the lack of any formal agreement committing it to writing. In order to prove today the existence of a rule derived from custom, one must advance evidence of a consistent and generalised State practice along with an *opinio juris*, a belief among States that such practice derives from a legal obligation.[24] It is not enough for States to act in a consistent or generalised pattern – they must do so through a belief that they are obliged to act in such a way. Such customary rules become important during times of war, especially in relation to aspects of a conflict that are not provided for in international agreements or, if they are, where parties to the conflict have not signed the relevant instruments.[25] Where an obligation arises through customary international law, States in most instances remain bound to follow it and any active disregard would be considered a breach of international law.

The definition of a 'custom' in international law has changed over the past 200 years. The 'law of nations', as it was known during the eighteenth and nineteenth centuries, related to the established usages of 'civilized nations', the term employed by jurists at the time to denote the practices of European States as between themselves (and eventually other western States such as the United States).[26] But the law of nations went beyond usages, encompassing general principles of natural law as well.[27] The pioneer of international law, Hugo Grotius, was the first to establish the approach in the seventeenth century, followed by others later on, whereby the positive laws of war were set out, followed by the accepted usages of States and other moderating influences on behaviour.[28] Both Grotius and his eighteenth century follower Emer de Vattel set out in writing that temples, public buildings and works of art should be spared during the conduct of war as an example of moderation. For Grotius, this would have been due to the influence of the natural law; for de Vattel a century and a half later, usages established by States in the intervening period would come to confirm this view.[29]

Seeking to apply the law of nations to the words and actions of 1815 is a two-part enterprise. First, it must be discerned whether the activity of the Allies in recovering (most of) their spoliated art was part of the accepted usages of the time. This is a matter of fact, but it would appear that the returns were clear and generalised enough across the States represented in Paris: the Netherlands, Prussia, Brunswick, Bavaria, Austria, Spain, the Vatican, Austria, Tuscany, Modena, Parma and others. And, despite the imperfections of the project, it did result in the majority of art being returned – and certainly all of the works considered of primary importance to each State.[30] While it could be argued that Napoleon's earlier looting established its own 'usage', this was seen at the time as a breach of existing norms rather than the confirmation of any countervailing practice. It therefore appears, on balance, as though the returns served as a remedy for the breach of an

established practice, namely to refrain from removing artworks during or immediately following a war.

Secondly, it must also be established that the practice accorded with what
today we would call an *opinio juris* – but more likely at the time was to be understood as according with natural law.[31] 'By mid-1815,' according to one scholar,
'there was broad agreement that the French confiscations of cultural objects
were contrary to contemporary rules of law and that objects could not remain
in Parisian collections.'[32] The statements by Wellington (describing spoliations
as 'contrary to the practice of civilised warfare') and Castlereagh (as 'contrary
to every principle of justice, and to the usages of modern warfare') indicate as
much. The restraint shown by the fact that works originating with France were
not seized by the Allies demonstrates that they held themselves to be bound
by the same principles to which they held the French. In this respect, we can
bring to mind the statement relayed by Castlereagh from the Prince Regent and
the exhortations of Under-Secretary Hamilton. This approached what might be
called a rule of law – moderation imposed by the dictates of reason and natural
law – rather than the exigencies of military power. This seems to form evidence
of an established practice at the time, as well as a belief among many of the State
representatives that the practice accorded with their notion of justice.[33]

During the nineteenth century, however, legal scholars were not unanimous as
to whether the returns of 1815 reflected a rule of international law. The Prussian
official and law professor Johann Ludwig Klüber (involved also at the Congress
of Vienna) would write confidently in 1819 that artistic and literary works, along
with public monuments and private property, were ordinarily neither destroyed
nor mistreated during war, citing in support the returns of 1815.[34] And later, the
British jurist Travers Twiss was sympathetic to the returns, though reporting
'disagreement' amongst fellow commentators as to whether they could be generalised beyond the particular context of Napoleon's defeat.[35] While one of the leading
texts, *Wheaton's Elements of International Law*, was initially equivocal on the point,
in the 1866 edition editor Richard Henry Dana included, in reference to 1815,
his own well-reasoned argument in favour of accepting the custom of preserving
works of art in public collections, writing of his ardent hope that 'such works will
be ever treated as out of the category of trophies of war'. Dana explained emotively
in 1866 (he had served as US Attorney during the recently concluded US Civil
War) that to 'strip a conquered belligerent, whose sovereignty we recognize and
permit to continue, of works of art – the instructors and civilizers, as well as the
just pride of the nation – simply to transfer those advantages to ourselves, clear
of all political question of indemnity or security, and of the avowed objects and
purposes of the war, is a course which the enlightened and liberal civilization of
modern times ought to denounce.'[36]

So, whether or not such a practice or rule had truly begun to solidify by 1815,
it was certainly more firmly entrenched by the end of the century. While armed
conflicts in Europe continued to inflict damage on cultural and religious sites,
there are few – if any – reported instances in the nineteenth century of systematic

removals of artworks by European Powers against one another.[37] Indeed by 1874, the project of an International Declaration Concerning the Laws and Customs of War had been drafted at Brussels by representatives of 15 European States. Though the 'Declaration' was not formally binding, it did make clear that pillage and the confiscation of artworks should be forbidden in war.[38] Similarly, the Institute of International Law in the *Oxford Manual* of 1880, which would serve as a guide to troops on the ground, prohibited pillage and the seizure from, inter alia, institutions devoted to arts and science, as well as reprisals.[39] While neither instrument was binding, together they indicated a custom that had clearly been accepted by this stage. In the words of the *Oxford Manual*, a breach of such norms would violate 'the principles of justice which guide the public conscience', even if not the express provisions of any binding treaty. By 1899 such customs would be codified in Regulations to the Hague Convention (II) with Respect to the Laws and Customs of War on Land. The Regulations set out, in particular, clear rules that both pillage and the seizure of works of art were to be forbidden: Article 47 prohibited pillage while Article 56 prohibited seizure of (as well as destruction and intentional damage to) 'works of art or science', and required that such action be 'made the subject of proceedings' (implying the punishment of perpetrators).[40] These rules applied at the time only to conflicts between State signatories (51 in total, including all major powers of Europe).[41] Therefore, as the nineteenth century progressed, the custom amongst European States of respecting one another's works of art became increasingly entrenched until finally it was codified by the century's conclusion.

Law of Nations and Marbles

Could any usage or custom of international law have applied to the removal of the Parthenon Marbles from Athens? It might be argued that, as Ambassador, Lord Elgin's activities could have engaged the responsibility of Great Britain under international law. Several witnesses in Athens at the time of the removal admitted to the House of Commons Select Committee in 1816 that the advantage secured by Elgin in obtaining Ottoman permission resulted from his position as Ambassador, and the Select Committee's Report seemed to accept this premise.[42] The letter from the Kaimacam of July 1801 referred to Elgin as an ambassador ('our sincere Friend his Excellency Lord Elgin, Ambassador Extraordinary from the Court of England'), indicating that it was in this capacity that Ottoman approval was bestowed.[43] Added to this was the fact that many of the shipments of sculptures that left Piraeus beginning in 1801 were taken or accompanied by HMS naval vessels.[44] Under international law, it is widely accepted that the actions of an ambassador can trigger the responsibility of the State he represents, even if his actions are ultra vires his usual duties.[45] In any event, Parliament's vote to acquire the collection for the British Museum, and the subsequent Act of 1816, could themselves be evidence of State adoption of Elgin's activities, another avenue by which State responsibility might be imputed.[46]

Were this so, what 'internationally wrongful act' might Great Britain have committed? As explained, it can be argued that the words and actions of the Allies in Paris evidenced a norm of custom or natural law at the time. But could this apply beyond times of strict military conflict? There is logic in the supposition: rules which apply in times of war ipso facto apply in times of peace. But that premise is nowhere reflected in the international events of the time. While usages could develop through the peaceful relations between States (rights of passage, sovereign immunity and so forth),[47] this would have required consistent and generalised State practice as well as a recognition by States that this practice accorded with a binding principle. Unfortunately, neither was evident at the time in relation to the acquisition of antiquities, even if those acquisitions were made by agents of one State upon the territory of another. Viscount Castlereagh had indicated in his 1815 note that Napoleon's actions were 'contrary to every principle of justice', but he was implying a breach of a rule of war (the spoliation of a conqueror). It would be difficult to infer anything broader. As a result, the contrast between the two positions taken by Great Britain – that of 1815, the other of 1816 – while revealing an inconsistency of principle, if not hypocrisy, would appear to have no bearing on the legal status of the removal of the Parthenon Marbles under international law.

International Law Today

Despite this, the situation today might nevertheless give rise to obligations under international law. The focus in this instance would not relate to the status of the removals in the early nineteenth century, but rather to the continued retention by the UK as a current and persisting violation of international law. It might be possible to find today a principle – a norm – of international law that could have a bearing on the matter, but it would have to be located amongst a plethora of legal sources.

If a claim under international law were to be brought today, it would be done before the International Court of Justice (ICJ) in the Hague. The Court was established in the period immediately following the Second World War in Europe and has a broad jurisdiction to deal with claims between States. The Statute of the ICJ, which dates from June 1945, sets out the rules which the Court will apply in determining the international responsibility of States. These rules derive from:

a.   international conventions, whether general or particular, establishing rules expressly recognized by the contesting states;
b.   international custom, as evidence of a general practice accepted as law;
c.   the general principles of law recognized by civilized nations;

d.   [...] judicial decisions and the teachings of the most highly qualified publicists of the various nations, as subsidiary means for the determination of rules of law.[48]

The question to ask is whether a relevant norm rooted in these sources could bring about the State responsibility of the UK in relation to the Parthenon Marbles – and if so, could it include as a remedy restitution to Greece?[49]

Instructively, in 1937, one of the leading jurists of the time (and future judge of the International Court of Justice) Charles de Visscher considered the legal principle around preserving monuments of great importance for humanity, finding that such a principle lent itself to the argument for the return of the Marbles to Greece. 'Despite the reasons given by Lord Elgin to justify his action,' he wrote in his treatise of that year, 'it was severely judged even in England. It is very doubtful however whether the arguments put forth can actually justify the irreparable damage resulting from his action. The fact is that the principle of the unity and integrity of a monument of such extraordinary and historic value clearly outweighs any other consideration here.'[50]

Unity and integrity: here de Visscher introduces an argument that stems from the loss suffered by the monument itself, by which logic the continued harm caused to the Parthenon could itself constitute the wrongful act. International law today clearly recognises the importance of sites of great importance. This is set out in UNESCO's 1972 Convention Concerning the Protection of the World Cultural and Natural Heritage (World Heritage Convention), which places obligations on the State on whose territory a property of 'outstanding universal value' is located to ensure its identification, protection, conservation, presentation and transmission to future generations.[51] Under the Operational Guidelines to the Convention, all properties on the list must satisfy the conditions of 'integrity', with the term defined as 'a measure of the wholeness and intactness' of the property, taking into account 'all elements necessary to express its Outstanding Universal Value' and the extent to which it is 'of adequate size to ensure the complete representation of the features and processes which convey the property's significance.'[52] Both Greece and the UK are party to this Convention (along with 192 other States, an impressive number for an international convention) and the Acropolis has been inscribed on the World Heritage List established under the Convention since 1987. The Convention does not simply place obligations on the State where the property is located (in this case Greece), but on other States Parties as well, for they must recognise that 'such heritage constitutes a world heritage for whose protection it is the duty of the international community as a whole to co-operate.'[53] These other States must also undertake to give their help in the identification, protection, conservation and presentation of inscribed sites if so requested by the relevant State.[54] Might this give rise to a duty on the UK as signatory to co-operate and provide assistance in relation to the Acropolis?

Other international instruments further emphasise the value of integrity of monuments and the necessity of international cooperation. In addition to the World Heritage Convention are the set of international 'Charters' drafted by the world's leading conservation professionals, the first of which was signed in Athens in 1931 which affirmed the importance of preserving the authenticity of historic buildings.[55] The most effective and long-lasting of these has been the Venice Charter for the Conservation and Restoration of Monuments and Sites of 1964 which set out that monuments had to be maintained on a permanent basis and that items of sculpture 'which form an integral part of a monument may only be removed from it if this is the sole means of ensuring their preservation'.[56] The Charter also enshrined in practice the fittingly Greek term of *anastylosis*: the 'reassembling of existing but dismembered parts' of monuments.[57] At the time of the Venice Charter, the International Council on Monuments and Sites (ICOMOS) was founded, which continues to serve as a professional organisation that provides support for the conservation and protection of monuments and sites around the world. ICOMOS has many times reaffirmed the value of integrity for cultural monuments, especially in relation to the Acropolis and Greece's ongoing claim relating to the Marbles.[58] In addition, the European Convention for the Protection of the Archaeological Heritage of Europe, to which both Greece and the UK are party (along with 48 other States), reaffirms the importance for States Parties of protecting the architectural heritage 'as a source of the European collective memory and as an instrument for historical and scientific study'.[59]

Not only is there recognition of the importance of protecting and promoting cultural monuments under international law, but the same principles can be found in domestic legal systems as well. As discussed in chapter five, Greece has been protecting archaeological sites through legislation since 1834.[60] In its current legislation, Law 3028 of 2002, monuments are given broad protections, including in relation to accessibility, enhancement and the promotion of public awareness.[61] The UK, for its part, has had legislation protecting ancient monuments since the Ancient Monuments Protection Act 1882. In the current UK law, the Ancient Monuments and Archaeological Areas Act 1979, any works done to 'scheduled' monuments, including removals or repairs, are strictly forbidden, subject to written authorisation from the Secretary of State, and anyone who executes such works without authorisation is guilty of an offence under the Act.[62] The vast majority of States have similar legislation protecting cultural monuments: in fact having or enacting such laws is an expected corollary of accession to the World Heritage Convention.[63] The rules found in domestic legal systems therefore appear to validate a universally-accepted principle that the integrity of cultural monuments must at all times be respected, protected and maintained. This could perhaps serve as evidence of a norm of international law derived from the 'general principles of law recognised by civilised nations', one of the sources listed in the Statute of the International Court of Justice.

A Case before the International Court of Justice?

An argument could conceivably be advanced that, if such a principle were flagrantly violated, the presumptive remedy might be restitution. Under international law, however, such a remedy may be difficult to obtain. As we know, the body to decide such matters would be the ICJ. According to its Statute, the Court applies the sources of international law referred to above.[64] It has jurisdiction over cases directly referred to it by the parties involved, where such jurisdiction is provided for in a treaty or convention, or where the parties have already accepted the compulsory jurisdiction of the ICJ.[65] However, remedies are difficult to obtain from the Court – and difficult to enforce. The process is far less predictable than before domestic courts, where a remedy for legal breach is usually set out by domestic law. This is not the case under international law, where judicial outcomes based on concepts as fluid as international custom or the principles of civilised nations are impossible to prescribe.

Where international conventions are in place, restitution can be achieved in favour of States of origin, though only in narrow circumstances. The 1970 UNESCO Convention on the Means of Prohibiting and Preventing the Illicit Import, Export and Transfer of Ownership of Cultural Property (1970 UNESCO Convention), to which both Greece and the UK are party, does allow States of origin to claim back stolen property, but only for a limited subset of designated cultural property. A State can request the return of cultural property that had been stolen from a museum, monument or similar institution and that had been listed on the inventory of such an institution after the coming into force of the Convention in the States concerned (which, in any event could not precede 24 April 1972, when the Convention itself came into force).[66] And, though Parties to the Convention must undertake to 'admit actions for recovery of lost or stolen items of cultural property brought by or on behalf of the rightful owners', this applies only insofar as it is 'consistent with the laws of each State',[67] meaning that domestic law need not be amended to facilitate restitution claims.[68] Lastly, the Convention provides that States Parties can conclude special agreements regarding the restitution of cultural property removed *before* the Convention's entry into force, but this is not obligatory.[69]

Nor are other international instruments of any assistance in providing for mandatory restitution in matters such as this. The 1995 UNIDROIT Convention on Stolen or Illegally Exported Cultural Objects, which was drafted partially with a view to filling the gaps left by the 1970 UNESCO Convention, has been acceded to by Greece, but not the UK.[70] This Convention does provide a mechanism by which the domestic courts of States Parties could be utilised by other States Parties to seek the restitution of stolen cultural objects or, in certain circumstances, the return of illegally exported cultural objects.[71] Such claims, however, must relate to cultural objects stolen or exported after the Convention came into force in the relevant State Party, which in any event could not predate 1 July 1998, when the Convention itself came into force.

The First Protocol to the 1954 Hague Convention for the Protection of Cultural Property in the Event of Armed Conflict (to which both Greece and the UK are party) provides for restitution as between Contracting States, but only in relation to cultural property removed from occupied territories following an armed conflict; and it too is non-retroactive.[72] The Trade and Cooperation Agreement between the UK and the European Union of 30 December 2020, which did include a provision for facilitating the return of illicitly removed cultural property, limits this to property removed from the territory of either the EU or the UK on or after 1 January 1993.[73]

With such limitations, would the ICJ ever consider a case involving the Parthenon Marbles and, if so, provide restitution as a remedy? In the one instance when the ICJ has dealt with a particular heritage site, the case of *The Temple of Preah Vihear (Cambodia v Thailand)* of 1962, the Court did order restitution. The case involved the Temple of Preah Vihear which sits on territory at the frontier between Cambodia and Thailand. There was a dispute between the two countries as to which had sovereignty over the temple and the surrounding land. After an exhaustive examination of the history of the site and how it had been accessed and mapped over time, the Court concluded that the temple fell within the sovereign territory of Cambodia. It ordered that Thailand remove the troops that had been occupying the site since 1954 and, additionally, ordered that Thailand return any 'sculptures, stelae, fragments of monuments, sandstone model and ancient pottery' that may have been removed by Thai authorities from the temple (it was never proved before the ICJ whether such removals had actually taken place). Nevertheless, the Court made a powerful statement in favour of return more broadly: cultural restitution was considered by the Court to be 'implicit in, and consequential on, the claim of sovereignty itself', demonstrating an important – if all-too-briefly stated – link between sovereignty and the movable property associated with a religious site.

There are some, like Geoffrey Robertson KC, who have said that such an argument should be made in relation to the Parthenon Marbles.[74] In his book *Who Owns History?*, Robertson contends that a custom of international law appears to have 'crystallised' today whereby States are under an obligation to return looted property of historical significance to States of origin, saying that 'analogous conventions, state practice, principles shared by civilised nations and decisions of domestic courts cohere to point in that direction.'[75] He explains that an *opinio juris* exists that underpins such a custom.

Robertson argues for one of two approaches: either for an international convention to be drafted that would codify this custom or alternatively (possibly as a prelude to such a convention) that the matter be taken up by the ICJ in order to confirm the existence of the custom.[76] Since the UK accepts the compulsory jurisdiction of the ICJ only for claims relating to disputes arising after 1 January 1987 in relation to situations or facts subsequent to that date,[77] an advisory opinion would need to be sought instead. As Robertson explains, the ICJ is empowered to give such advisory opinions at the request of any body authorised to do so under the UN Charter, which includes the UN General Assembly and agencies such as UNESCO.[78]

In this respect, it may be propitious that the UN General Assembly has already voted overwhelmingly to approve resolutions calling on States and UN bodies to work together to 'address the issue of return or restitution of cultural property to the countries of origin and to provide appropriate support accordingly', including most recently in December 2021.[79] Through such resolutions, the General Assembly has also invited States to apply the Operational Guidelines of the 1970 Convention, which specifically encourage parties to seek a 'mutually acceptable agreement' for dealing with cases where cultural property was imported *before* the Convention entered into force and to do so 'in accordance with the spirit and the principles of the Convention'.[80] And UNESCO's Intergovernmental Committee for Promoting the Return of Cultural Property to its Countries of Origin or its Restitution in Case of Illicit Appropriation more recently reproached the UK for its failure to engage with Greece through mediation over the Parthenon Marbles, recognising that the 'obligation to return the Parthenon Sculptures lies squarely on the United Kingdom Government' and calling on the UK to reconsider its position.[81]

If the relevant bodies were convinced of the merits of seeking an advisory opinion on the Parthenon Marbles, and if the ICJ agreed to give such an opinion, there might remain some difficulties with the substantive recognition sought. In Robertson's opinion, the international custom that the Court might recognise is very broadly construed. It would apply, according to him, to property of historical significance that had been 'looted'.[82] But defining the term 'loot' might be difficult: it invariably depends on the circumstances of the original taking. Categorising the removal of the Parthenon Marbles as 'looting' may prove legally challenging, as we saw in chapter three. In order to fit the Marbles within a specific definition, then, that definition would necessarily have to become elastic, so as to include historical removals that may have been lawful at the time but that are today considered unethical. Yet the broader the definition, the less legally workable it becomes. It could extend to items that might not have been contemplated in the first place. If, on the other hand, 'looting' were limited to instances of violent removal or outright theft from previous owners – a definition that would attract greater international consensus – then it might not attach to the Marbles in the first place. So there are inevitable, possibly insurmountable, challenges in making such an argument before the ICJ.

The Unity and Integrity of Monuments

Were an advisory opinion to be sought from the ICJ, a more modest option would be to obtain a determination on a less contentious premise. An argument could be sculpted around the universal value of cultural monuments, and the importance of the 'unity and integrity' of such monuments, to use de Visscher's words from 1937. These have been recognised broadly around the world, as exemplified in the World Heritage Convention and its Operational Guidelines, in the Athens and Venice Charters, in the constitution and other policy statements of ICOMOS, and in the domestic laws of almost all States. The wide acceptance of the principle, clearly recognised and adopted by 'civilized nations', could perhaps offer a greater chance of success.

That said, it is unlikely that such an opinion would include mandatory orders against the UK – and certainly not in an advisory opinion. Rather it would be a judicial pronouncement the content of which would consist of statements supporting the above assertions: clarifying in legal language what the broader world already accepts about the importance of the unity and integrity of cultural monuments of great importance. And while it would not be directly enforceable, it would go some way towards confirming the value of the Parthenon and its sculptures as a complete work. Though the structure has been beset by alterations, attacks and removals throughout its long and storied history, it may be appropriate to reunify (even imperfectly) what architectural sculptures do remain.

Restitution advocates may not be satisfied with such an opinion. But it would be the only international consensus on which the ICJ could safely pronounce. And it might serve a rather different purpose: as the basis upon which the parties in the dispute could come together in order to forge a more appropriate partnership, the focus of which would not be on each party's desired outcome, but on the best interests of the monument – and its sculptural scheme – as a whole. This could lend great heft to the notion of a 'Parthenon Partnership'.

8

The View from Athens

Under a large pine lit by hanging lanterns outside the Natural History Museum in Kifissia, I am sitting at a table with several local Greeks talking about the Parthenon. Kifissia is a leafy suburb of Athens and its broad sidewalks and colourful mansions look more California than Attica; in fact, before the financial crisis hit, the area had been called the 'Greek Beverley Hills' and it still maintains much of that lustre today. It is also a perfect setting in which to hear the Greek perspective on the Parthenon Marbles. Not far away is the looming shadow of Mount Pentelikos, where I began the journey in chapter one. Assembled around the table are five Greek professionals with informed opinions about Greek heritage and identity.

First there is Katerina Vagia, a lawyer who studied and worked for many years in the UK, and who until recently resided with her husband and son on the other side of Penteli. Katerina is of the opinion that the Marbles are vital symbols of Greek identity, especially at times of financial and political upheaval. Next to her sits Elena Lampousis, a nutrition scientist and Yale University graduate, who says the Parthenon has always represented freedom, both democratic freedom and the national freedom of the Greek State. Elena's husband, Stratos Lampousis, is here too. A psychiatrist by profession, he is also a font of Greek historical knowledge. He believes that his country's focus on recovering the Marbles helps show the world that Greece has long been dispossessed of a major part of its cultural heritage. There is also Zoe Adrianopoulou, younger than the others, who is about to set off for a Masters degree in political science at the London School of Economics. She has a particular interest in how heritage in Greece impacts the country's minority communities. The context of the evening is relaxed and convivial, and we are about to have dinner.[1]

Ancient heritage is central to modern Greek identity, I am told. As a student, one begins with courses on Greek mythology at the age of eight. After that comes ancient Greek history, which is then re-introduced in greater depth in high school and then repeated again prior to university.[2] One ends up covering topics such as ancient Athenian democracy no fewer than three times before the age of 18. All students must also learn the Ancient Greek language and this begins at the age of 12, first with grammar and syntax, followed by readings of classical authors like Homer, Herodotus and Euripides.[3] This makes Greece the only country that requires universal instruction in the ancient language at school, something that would have been commonplace across Europe (and indeed in Britain) a century ago.[4]

Their explanations offer a convincing response to certain statements that have been made in the past questioning the link between Ancient Greece and the modern nation state. In truth, such accusations over the years have always been a little unsavoury. Back in 1891, an English journal editor, James Knowles, had written dismissively of 'the mixed little population which now lives upon the ruins of ancient Greece' and the same sort of scepticism has been displayed many times since, though with perhaps greater civility.[5] As recently as 2004, a commentary in *The Guardian* surmised that 'it would be ridiculous to try and claim that Fred Bloggs of Chester-le-Street was a direct descendant of the Celts, or that George W Bush was of the Sioux, and it is equally ridiculous to try to claim that the modern Athenian carries the blood of Pericles and of fifth century Athenians in his veins'.[6] The point is made that the Greeks no longer worship the same gods, and the intervening centuries have brought shifts in population throughout and between Greece and the territories of present-day Turkey, Bulgaria, Romania and the Balkans. These arguments are usually put forward by those who hold the view that the Marbles retain significance for all of humanity, not just for Greece, and that the public good is served by their maintenance in an encyclopaedic institution like the British Museum.[7]

I am told here that such arguments clearly ignore many of the obvious links that have indeed persisted. In addition to the teaching of mythology and Ancient Greek, the alphabet and much of the language remain the same. Official names such as Ελλάδα ('Ellada', the modern name for Greece) and Αθήνα ('Athena', the modern name for Athens) would have been instantly recognisable to the ancients. Recent genetic testing has also compared the DNA of modern Greeks with that found in human remains from ancient Mycenaean grave pits, and the populations have indeed remained ethnically consistent over the past 3,000 years.[8] In fact, the Greeks at our table are affronted by any argument to the contrary. For them, there is no question that they are the cultural heirs (if not the direct descendants) of the ancients 'Hellenes'.

This seems to align with what others in Greece have said about the connection, including those speaking in an official capacity. When I talked to Elena Korka from the Ministry of Culture and Sport earlier that day, in a little office at the back of the Ministry filled with books on archaeology, she was categorical: 'All these people saying we have no connection with our past. That's totally impossible. In every land, the gene survives.' For Korka, there is a physical, perhaps even mystical connection between people and place: 'The earth, the ground, the environment, every little pebble, speaks to them,' she says. 'It springs out of the earth. It is your backyard and you may not tend to it in a hospital-like way, having everything nice and sterile and clean, but it is nevertheless your backyard.'[9]

Much earlier, in 1930, Greek diplomat and renowned bibliophile Ioannis Gennadios had powerfully evoked the connection between Greek identity and the loss of archaeological heritage, as expressed through the myths that had developed around that sense of loss. After describing the oft-told story of the Caryatids on the Acropolis supposedly mourning their 'sister' imprisoned in the town below, he asked, 'what man with a heart has not been moved to tears reading about that most poetic of Athenian traditions, equal to the most beautiful myths of ancient Greece?' The story inspired in him a romantic strain, out of which came an attack on those who had robbed Greece of its heritage, which for him included Lord Elgin:

> Only a people that preserve its nationhood vigorously and trustily, a people with an inborn dignity and self-awareness, only a genuinely Hellenic spirit could ever formulate such a marvellous expression of its anguish ... Myths! Yes. But they are the creations of nobler hearts, the offspring of stronger intellects, and the enchanting songs of more authentic Hellenes than the venal practices of our modern antiquity thieves.[10]

One gets the sense that this connection between the Greeks of today and the ancients, and indeed between the Greeks and the land upon which they live, while it might be justified through science and culture, is also about the feeling itself. In fact, when contemporary Greeks speak on this point it reveals certain elements of the national psyche that are difficult to transcribe. Is that a problem? Perhaps not. The point in all this is that a link between the distant past and the generation of the present can indeed persist even without an unbroken line of descent – and this can be interpreted in multiple ways. The question might instead focus on what the past means to people *today*.

The Ministry of Culture

The talk at dinner now turns from these more general themes to the Parthenon itself. Again, my companions are unanimous in their view of the importance of the structure. 'The Parthenon is central to Greek identity,' says Zoe. 'In particular, to our cultural heritage,' adds Stratos. The monument, they point out, has been a symbol of freedom and democracy throughout Greek history. During the twentieth century, it was from the Acropolis that the young Konstantinos Koukidis was said to have taken his own life rather than hoist the Nazi Swastika up the flagpole in 1941, plunging to his death wrapped in the flag of Greece, an event later commemorated by a monument at the base of the hill; from here too that the liberation of Greece from German occupation was declared in 1944; and from here that the end of the dictatorship of the military Junta that ruled Greece from 1967 to 1974 was proclaimed.[11]

It is understandable, then, that Melina Mercouri, who herself had gone into exile during the rule of the Junta, made such an impact with her pleas for the Marbles in the 1980s.[12] Her larger-than-life face was beaming out at me that afternoon as I waited for the metro at the Akropoli station, about to begin my journey from central Athens to Kifissia. A photograph of her waving in front of the Parthenon, taken in the early 1980s, has been enlarged and placed on permanent billboards on either side of the platform, near two long reproductions of the Parthenon's frieze procession (see Figure 8). Mercouri's term as Culture Minister began a mere seven years after the fall of the military dictatorship and so the campaign for the return most certainly was important for Greeks as a sign that the pieces of democracy were at last being reassembled.

Figure 8 The platform of the Akropoli Metro station in Athens, located a short distance from the Acropolis Museum, features replicas of the North frieze of the Parthenon along the walls
Source: © Alexander Herman (with thanks to Urban Rail Transport S.A., Greece).

It is incredible how the personality of 'Melina' still looms over the Marbles debate. I am told by my companions that no other culture minister would dare let the matter drop. In fact, Mercouri remains almost universally admired. Our little group in Kifissia, who might argue between themselves about whether a socialist or capitalist party was best suited to lead contemporary Greece, are unanimous in their praise for the former minister. Her favourite drinking establishment in the Plaka neighbourhood has even been preserved mausoleum-like and re-baptised *Melina's*, with images from her films covering the walls and a candle-lit memorial along one side. Above the window near the entrance is a quote from the late politician about the Marbles, next to a reproduction of the frieze. It states simply: 'They belong here.'

As we learned in chapter five, Mercouri served an eventful eight years in her first stint as Culture Minister.[13] For her it was a fitting role; a labour of love – quite different from some of the other politicians in Greece who have used the position as a stepping-stone to other, more prominent portfolios. In fact, in Greece since Mercouri's tenure three culture ministers have gone on to become Deputy Prime Minister, three have become Foreign Minister and four have even served as Prime Minister.[14] In no other country is the culture portfolio so promising in its prospects, and thus so intrinsically political. Added to this is the keen interest displayed towards the Marbles by Prime Ministers over the years, including most recently Kyriakos Mitsotakis.

The Culture Ministry remains, thanks to Mercouri, intrinsically linked to the Marbles cause. The Minister at the time of my visit even told me that the restitution claim was one that no government would ever abandon: 'From Melina on,' she said, 'we continue serving this claim. We will never give up. It's an issue for all the civilised world.'[15] There is, in addition, a Hellenic Advisory Committee for the Parthenon Sculptures, which consists of a representative from the Ministry of Foreign Affairs, the Director of the Acropolis Museum and the President of the Melina Mercouri Foundation, and this committee advises the Culture Ministry on developments on the matter and strategies for resolution.[16] But one thing is clear: the position of the Greek Government remains entirely consistent across the various government departments. And because the Ministry sets policy for public museums in Greece, it remains uniform down to the museum level as well.

The current Minister, Lina Mendoni, was appointed by Mitsotakis in July 2019. She certainly knows the brief well. Unlike others who have occupied the position, Mendoni is not a career politician. She is a civil servant who has worked in the Ministry for most of her career: coincidentally, she was one of the three Greek representatives who had appeared before the UK's House of Commons Select Committee back in 2000, accompanying Foreign Minister Papandreou and Mercouri's widower Jules Dassin.[17] Since assuming her current role, she has been very vocal on the matter, making numerous public statements demanding repatriation and painting the UK Government and the British Museum in a negative light.[18] This might seem counterproductive, if there are indeed high-level talks taking place in the context of a 'Parthenon Partnership'. But she has persisted, perhaps because to her the matter is so deeply ingrained. She has referred to Elgin's use of 'illicit and inequitable means' as a 'blatant act of serial theft'[19] and, most recently, has said that Greece would not 'recognise the British Museum's jurisdiction, possession and ownership of the Sculptures.'[20]

Through the Minister it has been made clear that the position of Greece remains that of the reunification of the entire sculptural scheme. In many regards it is similar to the position expounded by Mercouri in the 1980s, with one notable difference. While the earlier position called for the return of all pieces taken off the Acropolis, the current position seems to relate only to the sculptures from the Parthenon.[21] Along the way, the Caryatid, Athena Nike frieze and other architectural members seem to have been left out. It may be that the position has narrowed over time – or that it is a reflection of the sentiment already noted earlier: that the Parthenon, even more than its neighbouring monuments, has become the identifying symbol of pride and identity for modern Greece.[22]

How different things would appear to be in the UK, where culture (and its safeguarding) has traditionally been a more fragmented affair. Not only is the cultural portfolio in the UK divided between UK-wide ministers and the devolved nations, but the administration of the national collections is managed by bodies at arm's length from Government. As we have seen, a separate board of trustees runs each national institution, managing their collections on the basis of trust principles and according to the statutory controls in their governing legislation.[23] Short of proposing legislative changes, there is little the UK Government can actually do to dictate or alter positions taken by the museums (provided that these are done in accordance with the museums' own governing legislation), even if the government of the day might disagree with these. The water has been muddied somewhat of late, with noteworthy interference by government on cultural issues for what appear to be political reasons.[24] But this is presumably an aberration that will correct itself in the long run.

The traditional framework applies to the British Museum and has been adduced whenever the UK Government has been brought into the Marbles debate. This was part of the official response in 1984 to Greece's first claim: that the matter was one for the Trustees, and that an Act of Parliament would be needed to override the legislative restrictions.[25] In response to UNESCO's mediation request in 2013, a public letter from the Chairman of Trustees reiterated the Museum's operational independence from government: 'The British Museum, as you know, is not a government body, and the collections do not belong to the British Government. The Trustees of the British Museum hold them not only for the British people, but for the benefit of the world public, present and future …'.

This decentralised system was exemplified by the loan of the River God to Russia in late 2014. The move caught everyone, including UK Government authorities, by surprise. This was because it had been undertaken while Government policy was firmly seeking to punish Russia for its invasion of Crimea.[26] It was a 'moderate shambles', according to Boris Johnson, writing then as Mayor of London and Member of Parliament in *The Telegraph*, 'in which the trustees of a national museum have taken a decision, at the urging of their flamboyant and enterprising director, which simply does not cohere with British foreign policy.' Yet he went on to say that 'the decision, therefore, is all the more glorious – and all the more correct.'[27] As much as the move may have been questioned at the time, Johnson had a point. It would have been inconceivable for a national museum in Greece at the time to orchestrate a similar loan of a major collection item without the involvement of the Culture Ministry. In countries like Greece – and the list includes cultural heavyweights such as France, Italy and indeed Russia – cultural matters are centralised, bureaucratic and dictated by national policy.

One of the reasons why, in the past, the dispute over the Parthenon Marbles never moved closer to resolution might become apparent. Culture in Britain has traditionally been a matter in which government should play a very limited role, while in Greece it is quite the opposite. When it comes to negotiating around the Marbles this caused an inevitable disconnect. In Britain, the matter should be museum-to-museum; in Greece it is state-to-state. In Britain, the sculptures are pieces in a museum collection; in Greece they are symbols of national identity. Prior to 2022, whenever discussions on the issue took place, they had led nowhere. It was perhaps because the institutional disconnect was entrenched before the talks had even begun. Around the table sat the British Museum Director, the Chair of Trustees – and the Greek Minister of Culture. Naturally, they would be speaking different languages.

Museums are often making arrangements with one another, organising loans and joint exhibitions or negotiating transport and insurance. This is usually done by experts: the curators who know the material and the registrars who know the documentation. Politicians may be good at setting policy, but when it comes to the subject matter itself, they appear somewhat out of their depth. This is one drawback to making the reunification of the Parthenon sculptures an affair of state in Greece. As governments come and go, so too does the momentum for resolving the dispute, and with it any sustained willingness to seek out creative solutions.

Now, of course, things seem to have progressed. There has been a recent series of high-level talks which appear to be moving forward. Chair of Trustees George Osborne has said he thinks there is a 'deal to be done', while Greek sources have claimed that negotiations are 90 per cent complete.[28] With all the accumulated baggage of the past, will they be able to reach an agreement? The fact that the Museum itself is speaking of a 'Parthenon Partnership' is positive. But the institutional disconnects do remain.

In the past, the involvement of politicians ultimately doomed the discussions. Now the politicians are everywhere: although Mendoni is not herself a traditional political figure, the direct involvement of Mitsotakis has certainly given the matter a political air. And on the British Museum side it is not Director Hartwig Fisher, a curator by training, who is taking the lead, but the former politician Osborne. Inevitably this is an issue that attracts the politically minded at both ends, those predisposed to staking a claim, defending a position or (potentially here) pursuing that most elusive of resolutions, something that can be seen as scoring political points. Will they end up undermining what will likely have to be a very delicate arrangement between the two museums?

Invasion and Heritage

Back in Kifissia, my Greek interlocutors are asking me why the British Museum is so intent on keeping the Marbles when, in their view, they are so clearly associated with the cultural heritage of another country. When they ask, they are not bitter or particularly incensed, but are genuinely curious about the motivations for holding on to such pieces. It is as though they know very well what the Marbles represent to Greece, but would like to understand exactly how the Marbles are valued as artefacts in a foreign museum. Why, when it would be so easy to make amends for a past offence, would a museum with so many items in its stores not consider returning this one set of objects so important to the Greek people? The refusal mystifies them.

With great respect for my hosts, I try to explain the British Museum's position, that its Trustees are strictly governed by an Act of Parliament which prevents largescale disposals of objects, even for the purposes of restitution, and that, in any event, the Museum sees the Marbles as essential parts of the story that it seeks to tell, which is the history of human civilisation. If it removes the Parthenon sculptures, then that history becomes incomplete.

My companions show only a modicum of sympathy for this position. 'It's fine for a place like the British Museum to call itself a "universal museum"', says Elena. 'But what about countries that never had the chance to build a world museum? In Greece, we don't have the major pieces from other countries. We don't have the Van Goghs. All we have is what's ours, so we should be able to hold onto it.' She has a point. Of the great museums of Athens – and there are many – not one of them is committed to creating an encyclopaedic collection of western artefacts akin to the British Museum.[29] They are instead concerned with collecting and displaying the artefacts that tell the long history of Greek lands – from Cycladic figures, Minoan vases and Classical sculpture to Byzantine icons and modern Greek painting.

There is a feeling too that those in control at the British Museum are lacking in sympathy for what could be considered the long Greek plight. To the Greeks, the Parthenon has long symbolised the freedom of the people and a resistance to tyranny in all its forms: it was built on the ruins of the older temples destroyed by 'barbaric' Persians when the city was sacked in 480 BCE; it was used as the place to proclaim the new Kingdom of Greece in 1832; as mentioned, it was used as a symbol of liberation from the Nazis and the Junta. The fact that essential pieces of the monument remain in another country causes offence to that great symbol, as though their absence denotes that the Liberation remains incomplete, as if the Greeks can only make this symbol of national freedom complete once the sculptures are returned.

The word 'occupation' comes up a great deal in the discussion. There is no question amongst those present that rule by the Ottomans for 350 years was an *occupation*, regardless of the legal niceties in the term.[30] This is, after all, how history is taught in Greece, with that period known as the Τουρκοκρατία ('Turkokratia'), the rule by the Turks.[31] As Stratos says, recollecting how the period was generally portrayed when he was younger, 'the Turks were seen as brutal, taking away Greek children to make them Muslim warriors to fight against Christians and also making it difficult for Greeks to be educated and to worship.'[32] If the rest of western civilisation emerged from the Dark Ages during the Renaissance, in Greece this perhaps happened only in 1821. The continued control by the Ottomans of Greek-speaking and ethnically Greek territory in Macedonia and Crete into the twentieth century served only as a reminder of the threat from the outside. The current stalemate in Cyprus continues to do this. Like the ancient Athenians who erected images of battles between Greeks and foreigners on the Parthenon, there is a continual reminder never to become complacent: the fragile democracy remains under siege.

'When has Britain ever been occupied?' I am asked, somewhat rhetorically by Stratos. 'Or even invaded?' Julius Caesar comes to mind, as does William the Conqueror, but certainly nothing since 1066. It is true, there is no visceral memory, at least amongst the English population, of being invaded and ruled by foreigners (putting aside certain sentiments in Wales, Scotland and Northern Ireland); in fact, the people pride themselves on this. The pronounced feeling among my friends is that the memory of being dominated by an alien power makes a population particularly attached to material elements of culture removed during that period of foreign rule, even if not taken by the rulers themselves.

Britain of course never occupied Greece and, as such, the claim for restitution is less clearcut. As we have seen, there is a growing consensus amongst former colonial powers to return selected cultural artefacts to the peoples they had once dominated, usually premised on the ethical reasoning of addressing past wrongs. France is doing this for Benin and Senegal, Belgium for the Democratic Republic of Congo and Germany for Namibia, while Italy has done it in the past for both Libya and Ethiopia.[33] Important objects such as the Benin Bronzes have even been returned from certain institutions in the UK, although the British Museum has of course remained impervious to such demands.[34] Important exceptions remain, of course, but the moral case for return has become almost overwhelming in the post-colonial context. Examples like the Parthenon Marbles, where objects were taken not by the occupiers but by a third party, are perhaps more ambiguous because the objects were not taken under direct threat of military force by Britain.

The point here is less about the circumstances of the original removal and more about the vulnerability felt by modern Greeks, especially when it comes to threats from the outside, and the traditional inability of those on the British Museum side to show much empathy. Recent debates in Greek society, all of them eliciting enormous passions, often relate to similar worries over historical heritage. The construction of a new mosque in Athens, for instance, has been hugely controversial for many years.[35] While mosques have been allowed in northern parts of the country, the Muslim community in Athens had been prevented from building one, forced instead to worship inside makeshift spaces, usually in private apartment blocks. This might strike outsiders as surprising, even unconscionable, for an EU Member State and a State Party to the European Convention on Human Rights, which protects freedom of conscience and religion at Article 9. In November 2020, an official mosque was finally opened in Athens, but it was tightly controlled by the government: it was not even allowed to include a minaret.[36]

The tough stance on mosques may be seen not only as a manifestation of strength, a conclusion too easily drawn by foreigners, but rather as an indication of vulnerability. 'The symbol of a mosque,' Stratos tells me over dinner, 'is not in itself a problem for Greeks. The issue is that it represents so much more, including the history of domination by the Ottomans for over 300 years. Mosques in those days were built by the conquerors and continue to be seen as such.' It is true, few Greek towns that survived the Ottoman period were without their mosque (Athens originally had several), but after independence these were quickly converted into churches, assembly halls, concert halls and even, in the case of the little mosque on the Acropolis, storage depots for excavated antiquities.[37]

Perhaps it is difficult for citizens of other western nations to understand this quintessentially Greek predicament. Without having been under the control of a foreign power, it is arguably easier to be open to minority faiths today. In Britain, there are no stories of glorious revolutions against 'tyrants in Turkish garb', or any reasonable fears that an alien culture could one day overtake the dominant western civilisation. And it is true that the English themselves have never felt the yoke of foreign tyranny over the past millennium. This may help to explain English confidence on cultural matters – or at least a perceived confidence from the Greek perspective. As we shall see below, the position of the British Museum in relation to the Marbles has less to do with confidence than with its own particular sense of institutional vulnerability, though not the type that comes from foreign occupation.

There is another point to be made about Greek heritage as it relates to the Marbles. Although the pieces were removed some 200 years ago, the feeling of attachment remains acute today. This is clear both at senior levels of government, as we have seen, but also in the population more broadly. As we already saw in the introduction, recent polls have shown a huge majority support return (as much as 93 per cent in one instance).[38] The group at the table might form something of a microcosm, if not of the population as a whole, at least of professionals from Athens. And, in fact, throughout my trip I did not meet with anyone who, when prompted to discuss ancient heritage, was not familiar with the Marbles debate and did not, when asked, indicate a conviction that they should be returned. The taxi driver mentioned in chapter one, who drove my friend and me up the slopes of Mount Pentelikos, is a perfect example.

When we think about it, this is remarkable. The sentiment about the Marbles involves a very particular form of attachment to property that is effectively missing, a heritage constructed around absence. In his remarkable book *The Nation and its Ruins*, Yannis Hamilakis has explained how a yearning to reassemble a fragmented monument evokes the larger project to unify the national territory of Greece:

> It is the dismemberment of the imagined once unified national body, it is the dismemberment of the whole, be it the national territory of Hellenism, or the corpus of the ancient Greek material heritage … if these artefacts were not fragmented, mutilated bodies and human figures, if they were not so violently separated from their home, their place of birth, their relatives, they would not have aroused such passions, such feelings and emotions.[39]

That sort of missing heritage creates its own momentum. The aftermath of the Marbles' removal caused (or at least coincided with) the strict antiquities law of the Kingdom of Greece in 1834, the first comprehensive national law of its kind anywhere in the world.[40] By retaining public ownership of discovered antiquities from that point onwards, and severely limiting their export, the country and its museums were forever enriched. One wonders if this would have happened without a palpable sense of loss spurring the young country on.

Another consequence of loss can be seen in the construction of the Acropolis Museum. Not only was the intention of the Museum, in the words of one former Prime Minister, to 'add new and very strong arguments' in favour of restitution, but the Museum has since become a display space for absence. After its opening, large gaps were left to represent the missing Marbles and, even today, the Caryatids from the Erechtheion are shown without their missing 'sister' (the one whose abduction so moved the diplomat Gennadios back in 1930), with only two footmarks in the location where she would otherwise have been.

But beyond this, the long and fruitless pleas for restitution might have helped provide the necessary motivation to construct a building like this. The opening of the Museum was a reflection of that strength of feeling. Seeing the Acropolis Museum in all its glory today, and knowing exactly the economic pains that Greece suffered shortly after its completion, is enough to leave one marvelling at the ambition of the project. It also leaves one a little uncomfortable at the thought that millions were spent on a museum when public finances were collapsing. But perhaps that commitment – that extravagance – is a testament to the Greeks' attachment to their ancient past. It produced an edifice that is at once both glorious and immeasurably sad.

One Final Suggestion

While the palpable sense of foreign rule may be alien to most in Britain, there can nevertheless be a sense of cultural loss. Let us consider the Bayeux Tapestry: an object of great cultural and historical value for Britain kept permanently outside the country. An interesting nineteenth-century reproduction does exist in the UK, meticulously displayed at the Reading Museum, but it is largely overlooked today. In Kifissia, I go so far as to mention the comparison. My companions look bemused. It came as my belated response to a question about cultural heritage in the UK. How can the British really sympathise when they have never experienced the same separation from an essential artefact of their own history? Are there any such objects which still reside outside Britain?

The Tapestry, actually an embroidery, is 70 metres long and tells the story of William the Conqueror, his claim to the English throne and the defeat of his Anglo-Saxon competitor at the Battle of Hastings in 1066. Though the point is not entirely settled, the tapestry appears to have been woven in Kent, England in the late eleventh century. Schoolchildren in England are taught about the tapestry and know very well the evocative images it depicts, including the famous one of Anglo-Saxon King Harold with an arrow in his eye.[41]

And yet the original tapestry does not reside in England, but in the town of Bayeux, France, from which it derives its name. As an item that is far more important to British than French history, its placement in France may appear counter-intuitive. Perhaps the considerable vintage of the item or its long-ago placement at Bayeux is enough to convince reasonable people in Britain that it can remain there undisturbed. Perhaps Britain is confident enough in its great stores of cultural holdings not to concern itself with an old embroidery from the Continent.

But the reverse has proven true. In early 2018, on a visit to his counterpart Theresa May, French President Emanuel Macron tabled a proposal that caused a stir in Britain. His suggestion was simple, familiarly so, and involved sending the Bayeux Tapestry on a long-term loan to the UK. His stated intention in doing so was to 'commemorate the shared cultural history' of the two countries.[42] The response in Britain was unanimous. Cultural luminaries, the conservative press and Tory MPs all celebrated the prospect of bringing this great record of British history 'back' to Albion's shores. 'President Macron's offer to loan the Bayeux Tapestry to the UK is a diplomatic masterstroke,' wrote Peter Frankopan in the *Evening Standard* just after the announcement. 'Even the most ardent Brexiteer can recognise the gesture of a European leader extending the hand of friendship at a time of discord and difficulty.' An early contender to receive the tapestry was the British Museum. Bookmaker Ladbrokes had the institution's odds at 1:1, ahead of Westminster Abbey and Canterbury Cathedral. Director Hartwig Fischer announced that the institution would be 'honoured and delighted' to borrow the work. The loan, he said, was 'a gesture of extraordinary generosity and proof of the deep ties' that link France and Britain.[43] Others mentioned that it might put the Museum in the mood to loan out the Rosetta Stone – even the Parthenon Marbles – using Macron's arrangement as a model.[44]

Although nothing has come of the proposed loan, the reaction demonstrates just how much cultural items with a particular attachment to a nation's history can mean, and this principle perhaps stands true universally. Every country has the potential to rejoice at the chance to reconnect with a piece of its long-lost cultural heritage. Even Britannia.

It is sometimes said that, in order to reach an amicable settlement, parties to a dispute must learn to see the matter from the other's perspective. But this does not seem to have occurred much in the Parthenon Marbles debate. Instead for many years we have witnessed quite the opposite: what is known as positional bargaining.[45] Each side holding a position and attacking the other side's logic, while doggedly clinging to its own. 'I am right and you are wrong – and if you don't believe me today, I will find new ways to convince you tomorrow.' This has been the continual refrain from both sides for so long.

But if Macron's Bayeux gambit teaches us anything, it is that the two sides may have more in common than was originally thought. The English may not have been occupied by a foreign power, but they are keenly aware of (and indeed sensitive to) their own history, as well as the cultural products that came out of it. They would like to see the Bayeux Tapestry on display at the British Museum, even if for a limited period of time, because it would help reveal a missing chapter of that history. It would give them the ability to study up close those famous sequences of Norman embroidery. Parents would take children. Strangers would come and compare notes. The nation would rejoice.

Macron of course never offered a permanent transfer of the Tapestry. He made clear that the loan would only last while renovation work was underway at the Bayeux Museum and that, when the museum reopened, the tapestry would need to go back. But the offer itself was enough to provide an insight into the British psyche. The cultural exchange envisioned by Macron offered a reminder – this perhaps was his true 'masterstroke' – of what unites countries, whether it be a shared system of values, an appreciation of artistry and aesthetics or a common history. And the success of such an exchange would occur precisely because it avoided all-or-nothing outcomes. It would be predicated first and foremost on establishing a relationship between the parties and eschewing the extreme outcomes: outright return or status quo. In such situations, it is the middle ground that is often most fertile.

At last we have finished dinner in Kifissia and are sipping from glasses of pine-tinged mastika, a drink that can be harvested only from a particular type of tree on the Greek island of Chios, near the coast of Turkey. I bring up the question of a possible solution to the Parthenon saga. Perhaps the two sides could meet halfway: by way of a long-term loan, something along the lines of Macron's proposal for the Bayeux Tapestry, the suggestions of Venizelos in the early 2000s or indeed the more recent 'Parthenon Partnership' being discussed between the parties today? The nuance is that it would be a loan of *some* of the pieces, as a first step to begin to mend the relationship? Would it not be beneficial for the Greeks to see, for instance, the pediment sculptures back together or several uninterrupted sequences of the frieze, even if only for a finite period?

I am very careful when suggesting this. I know for instance that for Greek politicians asking for a loan from the British Museum was tantamount to political – and cultural – suicide. Melina Mercouri never spoke of a loan and the Greek position, as expressed most recently by the Prime Minister, expressly rejected such an arrangement: the claim is for full restitution of the Parthenon Marbles from the UK. But what do my Greek interlocutors think?

My companions are at first hesitant. They agree that something is better than nothing and that it might be symbolically useful for Greece, after all that it has been through of late, to see at least some of these long sought-after pieces temporarily returned to Athens. On the idea of striking a deal with the British Museum, Stratos becomes reflective. 'We want – and always will want – what is ours,' he begins, then stops himself, as though readjusting the automatic response that comes with reciting the national dictum. He continues in a softer tone, 'But a compromise may be possible, yes … It's like the goddess Demeter. She lost her daughter Persephone to Hades, the underworld, and as a result refused to allow crops and fruit to grow. To bring her daughter back to the world, an agreement had to be made. She was allowed by Hades to see her daughter again, but only for three months of the year. And because Persephone represented the harvest, she brought with her a period of agricultural richness. So Demeter was able to see her daughter once a year. That was the compromise. And everyone else received the harvest as a result.'

It seems even the gods of old had done well on negotiation. And the indirect result was that all of us in the end could benefit.

9

Inside the British Museum

Stepping behind the scenes at the British Museum is an eye-opening experience. In comparison with the cavernous and often crowded galleries open to the public, the staff areas offer a very different kind of atmosphere. They consist of a warren of passageways lit by modest light fixtures with fire doors in inopportune places; they are full of framed posters from past exhibitions hanging from faded walls. Parts of these back areas are visibly Victorian, while others are more modern, with narrow staircases haphazardly connecting the two. Employees bump into one another and hold impromptu meetings in the hall or steal away to dusty, under-lit meeting rooms. The place has a disorderly charm.

I have had the good fortune to go behind the scenes on several occasions. One experience worth mentioning occurred before the pandemic. My organisation, the Institute of Art and Law, had been contracted to provide in-house training to the collections and exhibition staff at the Museum. The training was to consist of instruction on the laws and ethical norms that apply to the museum sector, covering topics such as contract law, governance, treasure and deaccession, as well as restitution and repatriation.[1]

The training began on a day of heavy rain in late September. My colleague and I were brought soaking wet into the museum through the security checkpoint at the eastern end of the main entrance (see Figure 9). We were led through a series of interconnected corridors that seemed impossible to retrace. We eventually entered the modern wing at the back of the Museum, part of the World Conservation and Exhibition Centre, a £135 million extension completed in 2014.[2] This particular area had been built to provide the Museum, at long last, with a large, dedicated exhibition gallery and a space that would allow for the conservation of the Museum's many holdings. In fact, one of the main areas was now being used to store exhibition models that looked like set designs for the theatre. Workspace for regular employees was relegated to the top floor, where an open-plan office area was shared with several glassed-in meeting rooms along the edges.

During the training, I was struck by two things. First, the *esprit de corps* amongst the staff. It is widely known that, below Director and senior management levels, pay at the Museum is extremely modest: less than that of civil

Figure 9 The staff entrance to the British Museum on a rainy day, hidden behind the Ionic columns of the building's imperious façade

Source: © Alexander Herman, 2023.

servants with comparable levels of education and even less than that offered by some of the other museums in London.[3] Nevertheless, the employees we inter-acted with all seemed excited and proud to be working at the Museum. I even had the impression that a number of them would have gladly made whatever sacrifice was necessary to better the state of the Museum. They were constantly enquiring, with us and between each other, about how to improve the stand-ards at the institution, how to bring in major loans for exhibitions and how best to conserve, update and care for the collection in their custody. Within the staff canteen (a large space in the mid-twentieth century part of the Museum where we dined during the training), I watched colleagues from across different departments share tables, exchanging ideas and insight into best practice, some of which they had gleaned from our course. I even caught a glimpse of the Museum's Director, Hartwig Fischer, having lunch with what looked to be a member of the security personnel, intently engaged in conversation. In many ways, everyone here operated at the same level. I wondered how many other museums – or indeed what other workplace – would display such openness and comradery.

The second noticeable feature was the fact that the Museum itself was in a state of disrepair. During the rainstorm that accompanied our first visit, one could see water leaking from the ceiling in several rooms. An entire area of the canteen had to be cordoned off because the water coming through the skylight had accumulated on the floor below, making it unsafe for walking. Apparently, the basement of the new conservation space – the one dating from 2014 – was flooding, putting the artefacts there in danger of water damage. As the storm continued throughout the day, there was a muted sense of embarrassment amongst staff. There was, however, no panic. It was as though, on days like this, such a situation was merely a matter of course.

I remember thinking: is this institution really the cause of so much hand-wringing, the seat of some great maleficent power? In discussions about the Parthenon Marbles, it is often assumed that the British Museum is the menacing Goliath, with Greece playing the role of David. And in the past, the Museum may have exuded a slightly irksome degree of self-assurance whenever the restitution issue arose.[4] The solidarity I witnessed amongst staff, as commendable as it was, could very easily be mistaken from the outside as a kind of institutional arrogance. But this may be limited to appearances. The source of that apparent arrogance – like the source of the solidarity underpinning it – might not relate to any sense of strength, but rather to a vulnerability that extends throughout the institution. In fact, during the time I spent in the canteen, nobody mentioned the cordoned-off area at all, as though the situation was entirely commonplace, or perhaps that doing so might be taken as a sign of weakness, like giving up a point by the home team.

The cracks, however, are beginning to appear in public. The Ancient Greece galleries have revealed many of the same problems that I noted backstage. Around the time of my visit, the skylight in the Duveen Gallery had been photographed showing leakage and discolouration.[5] Later, during the pandemic, the Gallery was closed to the public due to the rise in accumulated moisture following a major downpour in July 2021. A photograph came out in the press showing the Gallery's door to the outside wedged open and another with a large floor fan operating at its centre.[6] These makeshift attempts at removing the moisture in the air and protecting the sculptures incurred the ridicule of many on the pro-restitution side, including the Greek authorities. The Greek Culture Minister, Lina Mendoni, issued a statement following the release of the images, saying it helped strengthen the 'legal, ongoing and non-negotiable request from Greece for the reunification of the sculptures.'[7] During the pandemic, the

Duveen Gallery was closed for an entire year: five months due to government-mandated lockdown, two months for related maintenance work and the rest because neighbouring rooms in the Museum were continuing to experience problems of rainwater ingress.[8]

The contrast with the Acropolis Museum could not be starker. Despite the many delays in construction, the museum in Athens now appears largely flawless, even to the discerning visitor. More than a decade after its June 2009 opening, the structure remains sound despite its unique location over an active archaeological site, which is open to experts and members of the public alike. The concrete pillars and glass walls are still in excellent condition and, even during the public financing fallout and the COVID-19 pandemic, there was no indication that the sculptures were in any danger. When visiting the museum, I have always noticed the solicitousness of staff, from front of house personnel to the cleaners diligently wiping down display cases to remove traces of fingerprints left by visiting schoolchildren. I have often asked myself rhetorically how this museum could be portrayed as the long-suffering victim of some infamous abuse.

The Acropolis Museum has been consistently supported by the Greek State, even during the major crises of the recent past. Meanwhile, the British Museum does not seem to have been treated by its own government with similar largesse. This is certainly clear in respect of maintenance. In the period 2016/17 to 2020/21, the British Museum requested a total of £48.4 million from the Department for Digital, Culture, Media and Sport (DCMS) for core capital bids, but was allocated less than half of this (£21.3 million).[9] Only with the onset and continuation of the pandemic was funding brought close to necessary levels, but it remains to be seen whether this will be sufficient going forward, especially considering the decline in paying visitor numbers.[10] The two museums are of course operating in different leagues: the Acropolis Museum is dedicated to one particular site, while the British Museum is meant to be the 'universal museum' with only a handful of global competitors: the Louvre, the Metropolitan Museum, the Vatican and a couple of others.

Compared to these international institutions, though, the British Museum lags behind in most, if not all, revenue streams.[11] It has not made a major purchase of a Greek or Roman antiquity in the past decade.[12] In 2022, the Museum revealed that it needed £1 billion to follow through with a masterplan that seeks to overhaul its extensive global collections.[13] This money would go towards renovating and reinventing the existing collection space and displays, hiring new staff and contributing to an ever-growing loans programme. The Chair of Trustees, George Osborne, has promised to oversee the fundraising initiative necessary to achieve this grand objective.[14] Meanwhile, as the vast majority of the Museum's holdings are not on public display (only 1 per cent of its 8 million objects is ever on display),[15] new storage and research facilities are needed: one is currently being built near Reading at a cost of £64 million, to be called the 'Archaeological Research

Collection', consuming much of the recent capital investment funding received from government.[16]

The truth is rarely admitted. The British Museum has seen its public funding (grant-in-aid revenue) stagnate, this despite the inevitable expansion of museum activities, the increase in price of cultural items worthy of acquisition and overall inflation.[17] On top of this, the Museum is unable to charge entrance fees to its permanent collection. As we saw in chapter four, the guarantee of free entry dates back to the establishment of the Museum through the British Museum Act 1753 (providing that 'free Access' to the collections be given 'to all studious and curious Persons'),[18] but it was re-affirmed as government policy, and expanded to all national institutions, in 2001.[19] The goal of free accessibility is admirable, but, when paired with a freeze in public funding for the very institutions meant to provide that access, financial sustainability very easily becomes untenable.

The Museum's particular position in British society seems to make it difficult for successive Directors and Trustees to adequately broach the matter with those controlling the funding, namely the Secretary of State for Culture, Media and Sport, along with the DCMS.[20] This may relate partly to the institution's legal independence. As the government does not have direct authority over the day-to-day activities of the Museum it can more easily shirk responsibility in relation to provision of necessary grant-in-aid. This is one of the downsides to the decentralised infrastructure operating in the UK: it facilitates institutional independence and initiative, but also makes reliance on allotments unpredictable. This is compounded by the fact that to ask for money (let alone to beg for it) may have long been considered somewhat unbecoming of British Museum management, especially when it involved operating expenses.[21]

There may be another reason to explain the penury of the institution at the hands of government. Ever since the first official claim for the Marbles in 1983, the UK Government has taken the side of the Trustees and refused to table legislation that would allow (let alone force) the Trustees to return the pieces to Greece.[22] This has been the position, whichever party has been in power in Westminster.[23] This staunch approach manifested itself most recently in Boris Johnson's statement of 2021, Liz Truss's statement of 2022 and Rishi Sunak's statement of 2023, all reiterating the government's longstanding policy on the matter.[24]

But what is the cost of such political support? Of course there are reputational impacts both for the Museum and the UK as a whole: it gives the appearance that the Museum Trustees are operating hand-in-glove with government; it has led to critical statements in the media and at public forums by world leaders, celebrities and scholars;[25] even UNESCO's Intergovernmental Committee for Promoting the Return of Cultural Property has censured the UK for evading its international responsibility in the matter, a responsibility the Committee feels belongs to the State.[26] But in addition to these are the more insidious financial consequences for the Museum. There is always going to be limited political capital afforded to museums in the corridors of power. Every time a Prime Minister or a Secretary of State stands up to defend the Museum's position on restitution, some of that capital is inevitably lost. Sadly, it is far easier for government to rehearse the age-old arguments for keeping the Marbles, rather than marshal the resources necessary to ensure that the Museum is well maintained and that its staff is cared for and fairly remunerated.[27] In some instances, one might even wonder if those in government who speak on behalf of the British Museum really have the institution's best interests at heart – or whether they are using it as an easy way to score political points. In the long run, the involvement of politicians in the debate costs the Museum dearly, in more ways than one.

The Enlightenment Strikes Back

Before he died in 2020, I had the good fortune of having a long and revealing conversation with Dr Ian Jenkins, the long-time senior curator in the Museum's Greek and Roman Department and unrivalled British expert on the Marbles. Not only had he authored or edited half-a-dozen books on the Parthenon and its famous sculptures,[28] but his voice was often used in the media and at conferences to make the moral argument in favour of the British Museum. From the interview, I immediately got the sense that, after 40 years studying and writing on the topic, he remained enchanted and enthralled by the pieces. He therefore seemed the right person to provide the Museum's perspective on the matter.

His office was small, one amongst several along a hallway accessed through an unassuming door off the Museum's Greek and Roman wing. There was a cave-like view out to Great Russell Street where one could see the crowds on their way to the Museum's main entrance. Books on ancient art and architecture were everywhere, falling it seemed from the shelves and piled high on the long desk. I specifically recall his dark eyebrows and broom-like moustache. He started politely, and before long began to methodically set out the Museum's position on the Marbles. While it was an account he had no doubt given many times before,[29] it retained its freshness, and he seemed very much to believe in what he was saying.

Of prime importance to his position was the view that the British Museum was first and foremost an institution of the Enlightenment, one intended to instruct and generally improve the lot of mankind. 'The Museum in the nineteenth century was a place where it was thought you could trace the progress of civilisation,' he said. 'And that was a major Whig battle cry.' The Whig political party had firmly believed in education as a means of bettering society, an education that included regular visits to the British Museum as a way of experiencing the progression of the ancient world from its primitive origins to classical Greece and beyond.[30] But this consisted of more than simply arranging the objects in chronological order: 'it had a moral purpose, which was to create the energy in order for society to take its lesson from the past and improve the lot of ordinary people, so they could share in the material progress of humankind.'[31]

The Marbles fit perfectly within this conception. According to Jenkins, Elgin and Lusieri genuinely believed they were acting 'on behalf of the Enlightenment and civilisation' by removing the Marbles from the Acropolis and preserving them from Turkish vandalism. He offered a tangible example with Block XXX of the north frieze, drawn as an entire block in Athens by English traveller William Pars in 1765, but by the time of Lusieri's arrival in 1801 it had been reduced to a few fragments.[32] These fragments were taken away and are now at the British Museum, in a display case in the southside room off the Duveen Gallery.

Of course, Jenkins made no mention of the damage Lusieri caused in removing the pieces,[33] but it was almost as though he took this as common knowledge: anyone familiar with the debate might be assumed to know the arguments in favour of restitution; his purpose was to offer an unadulterated counterargument. He wanted to show that the Marbles were clearly better off for having been removed and placed in the British Museum in the early nineteenth century, not the opposite.

With their arrival at the Museum, the Marbles became 'embedded' in the story of the Enlightenment. The Museum treated them at the time as 'the most important material productions of man, the most beautiful, the most elevated'. Because of that history, Jenkins told me, it was difficult for the Museum to 'surrender the moral right' by saying they did not belong in the collection, when they 'clearly did belong here'. To ignore this fact was to renege on the Whig promise of progress through education. It was this point that those favouring return always got wrong: 'Restitutionists tend to resent the Enlightenment, to deny the Enlightenment,' he said. 'And it has become slightly fashionable to say that the Enlightenment was one big excuse for holding onto other people's patrimony.' He felt very strongly about this, that his institution had not been afforded the respect it deserved for pursuing an invaluable public mission for more than 200 years. What he resented most was the other side's refusal to accept 'the obvious history': the tendency to try instead to create a 'selective' history, choosing to paint Elgin as a black-hearted villain and the Museum as a 'mausoleum'. This was an unfair taint on the great institution – and on the dignity of the people who continued to work there. 'If you work in this institution,' he told me, confirming much of what I had seen in the staff quarters, 'you can take it for granted that there is sincerity here. There is not one *big lie*.'

His views on the Museum's role were of course similar to those of his erstwhile Director, Neil MacGregor. But they also echoed the position of the legal scholar John Henry Merryman. In a seminal article from 1985, 'Thinking about the Elgin Marbles', Professor Merryman had explained that, putting aside the legal argument for return (which he claimed was weak), the morality of the case still favoured retention by the British Museum.[34] This was because the principal justification for restitution, the notion of 'cultural nationalism', was an improper basis for the allocation of cultural property. Nationalism reflected dubious values, according to Merryman, and was founded on sentiment rather than reason. Decisions about where to hold cultural property should instead be based on the principle of 'cultural internationalism', which reflects the chief concerns of preserving heritage, maintaining its integrity, and distributing it so that it can be accessible to the widest possible public. In the case of the Marbles, Merryman had concluded in his article that these factors favoured retention by the British Museum.[35]

In his interview with me, Jenkins was equally critical of the nationalistic basis for restitution. 'Nationalism is not a pretty sound,' he told me. 'It will always sound shrill and self-interested'. And this was true of Greek nationalism, much as it was for other nations looking to claim back lost artefacts. 'The Greeks must take their place in the civilised world as participants with the rest of us. They can't just pick and choose the bits they want. We all have to own our past.' For Jenkins, the story of the Parthenon should include the full history: not simply focusing on Elgin, but also recognising that 'the Greeks did more damage to the Parthenon than any other nation' when, in the sixth century, Christians hacked off parts of the sculptures in order to ensure the sanctity of the building as a church – a rather unsettling statement when one considers the Venetian attack of 1687 and the Turkish bombardments of the Greek War of Independence.[36]

There is one important difference, though, between Jenkins and Merryman: for Jenkins this went beyond abstract argument; he was directly implicated. While Merryman was an academic staking a position in the battle of ideas, Jenkins directly represented the Museum in a very real dispute. It was therefore understandable how the matter could become personal: 'it *is* rather personal for me', he admitted, 'and what is personal for me is largely museum policy as well'. He had borne the brunt of the restitutionists' arguments for many years and had known many of them personally, which served only to accentuate the affront he felt. This included several past chairs of the British Committee for the Restitution of the Parthenon Marbles (as it was originally known),[37] such as the late Professor John Gould, who had taught Jenkins as an undergraduate at Bristol University.

Jenkins found the actions of such groups petty and beneath the positions many of their members held as scholars. He gave as an example an episode in 2009 when the Committee's then Chair, Professor Anthony Snodgrass of Cambridge University, had publicly condemned a British Museum announcement about the discovery of polychromy traces on the sculptures, calling it a 'diversion' from the opening of the Acropolis Museum, which was occurring that summer. Jenkins was disappointed that a classicist and archaeologist like Snodgrass, instead of rejoicing at the discovery, would try instead to detract from its contribution to the accumulated body of knowledge on classical Greece. Rather than seeking to uncover the truth about the past, Jenkins told me, many of these figures were determined to gain political advantage. And politics, in this context, was a dirty and 'very unsatisfactory world'.

Jenkins was keen to point out the partnerships that do exist between the British Museum and the Acropolis Museum. These are often overlooked in the media, which tends to focus on the more divisive issue of restitution. He mentioned research partnerships, one of which had resulted in the discovery of the polychromy so attacked by Snodgrass;[38] another had involved studies by Dr Vasileia

Manidaki from the Acropolis Restoration Service in the British Museum archives and the presentation of her research at the Museum (she had succeeded in digitally reconstructing many of the pieces split in two by Lusieri).[39] Jenkins mentioned his close friendships with many scholars and museum professionals in Greece, including the then President of the Acropolis Museum Dimitrios Pandermalis. These friendships were of great importance to him and he expressed gratitude that they could persist despite the obvious political divide.

And he mentioned loans. The British Museum is one of the world's biggest lenders, with just under 4,000 collection objects out on loan at any given time.[40] As Jenkins reminded me, the Museum has also made 'considerable loans' to Greek institutions, such as the Museum of Cycladic Art, the Heraklion Museum and the National Archaeological Museum. There have even been more recent loans to the Acropolis Museum.[41] But when it comes to the reverse, the subject becomes sensitive: Greek museums refuse to lend to the British Museum, almost certainly for political reasons. And, for all the outward loans to Greece, the British Museum never asks for anything in return. In practice it does not even *request* loans from Greek museums. Both features – the Greek refusal and the British Museum's self-imposed embargo – are highly unusual within the larger context of the global lending network. 'We don't ask,' Jenkins told me, 'because we know what the answer would be.'

This appears to be yet another sad consequence of the dispute over the Marbles. Until they are returned, the Culture Ministry in Greece will (apparently) reject loan requests coming from the British Museum – and the British Museum, possibly out of a sense of pride, never bothers to ask. The result is that the Museum loses out on what could very easily be essential pieces of classical art for use in exhibitions. For example, Jenkins had curated the 2015 exhibition at the Museum, *Defining Beauty: The Human Body in Ancient Greek Art*, which had loans from Italy, Germany and Croatia, but not a single object from a Greek museum. This must have been disappointing, especially for the curator, seeing how so many of the great remaining works of archaic and classical sculpture are indeed kept in Greece, held in the collections of prominent institutions there. But until there is a resolution, this uncomfortable status quo will persist, another knock-on effect of the age-old disagreement over the Parthenon Marbles.

The Discreet Nationalism of the British

There is a point to add on the issue of nationalism. Like Merryman and MacGregor before him, Jenkins had said that restituting the Marbles would be tantamount to giving in to nationalist sentiment, whereas retaining them at an international institution helped to reinforce a more tolerant, pluralist world view. As Jenkins said about his museum: 'it is a place where all cultures are shown, but none is privileged, where all religions are represented but none is preached.' In Athens, the

Marbles could only be displayed within the national narrative; in London, they were part of the world's story.

When my interview with Jenkins concluded – more than two hours after it began – he kindly accompanied me back down to the public galleries of the Museum, through the inevitable conjunction of hallways and back stairwells described earlier. Before parting, he turned to me and said, 'I have spent four decades researching in the archives of this institution. And not once have I seen mention of the words *Empire* or *Imperial*. They were simply not part of the story being told at this museum.' His point, once again, was that the Whig museum cared not for power or political domination; it was instead a place of scholarship and of learning. The British Museum did not seek to justify, or even underpin, the British Empire. It was independent of the nation in which it stood and existed beyond the realm of politics.[42] To hear it from him in this way was quite revealing.

But to see the theme of nationalism operating solely on one side of the debate may be to overlook its considerable impact on the Marbles' place within the British establishment. When the pieces arrived at the Museum, they were not only evocations of a broader European Enlightenment, but they also played a role in their country of adoption. 'If Greek claims for return were later to be characterised as nationalist,' writes one scholar, 'there can be little doubt that the British position was equally imbued with a sense of national pride and identity formation.'[43] They formed an essential part of a national museum, one that continues to fly the Union Flag above its entrance. They inspired the arts and culture of nineteenth century Britain, from the poems of Keats to the sculptures of Westmacott. And, perhaps more subtly, they reflected the effectiveness and reliability of British institutions. Elgin's motives and actions, as controversial as they might have been, were thoroughly investigated and publicly debated in Parliament.[44] The acquisition passed through the processes of parliamentary democracy: the petition, the Select Committee hearing, the report, the debate, the vote and, finally, the Act of Parliament.[45] These processes reflect attributes that many in Britain would consider quintessentially British: accessibility, debate, diligence, fairness, transparency and so forth. Had the Marbles been an unqualified gift from Elgin, without question or scrutiny, they might have held less meaning for the country as a whole. Instead, the Marbles became part of the wider political culture of the nation, and arguably remain part of that today.

In this way, the *Britishness* of the Marbles reminds us that nationalism often underlies the arguments in favour of retention as well. Despite the considered opinions of Jenkins, Merryman and MacGregor, retention is not some unqualified triumph of internationalism over nationalism; in the case of the Marbles, it reflects that which is institutionally and ethically British as well. As Jenkins told me, to simply repatriate the Marbles would be to ignore (to undermine) the role of the Museum in collecting, safeguarding and caring for the pieces over all these years. Was there not something rather British in his view? An impetuous return would be wrong because, put simply, it would be *unfair*, an outcome that ignored the interests of one entire side of the equation. Britain, after all, was a country of balance, of debate, of piecemeal change, of slow and considered movement. Such is true of British law, from the development of the common law to constitutional conventions and the 'unwritten' constitution. How could such an institution ever countenance the return of an entire collection in one fell swoop?

But nationalist inclinations might also help to reveal what both sides hold in common. That is, they both hold these objects to be important parts of a heritage, and as such, the objects reflect a certain view of the past: for Greece, the golden age of Pericles, Phidias and Athenian democracy; for Britain, the parliamentary tradition and the principles of education and progress. These periods were historical – Greece of the fifth century BCE, Britain of the nineteenth century – but they continue to persist as symbols that retain their potency today. They serve as goals towards which each nation aspires, and as motivations for improvement as well. This way of using the past to inspire the present seems to reflect the very notion of cultural heritage – even if that heritage is constructed somewhat differently within each place.

The UK's attachment to its heritage can be seen in the way it protects and preserves that heritage on its territory. The Ancient Monuments and Archaeological Areas Act 1979, referred to in chapter seven, provides a strict scheme for protecting scheduled monuments and archaeological sites, while the Planning (Listed Buildings and Conservation Areas) Act 1990 ensures that removals from, and works undertaken on, 'listed' buildings of special architectural or historic interest, even in private ownership, proceed only with consent from public authorities.[46] Certain objects found in the ground that are over 300 years of age automatically become vested in the Crown, according to the Treasure Act 1996. The UK also places significant export controls on works of art and objects of cultural interest: export licences can be 'deferred' for up to one year to allow UK entities the opportunity to acquire a work from an exporter – and thus to 'save it for the nation', according to the language frequently employed by the Secretary of State and the DCMS.[47] This system has led to many artworks being retained by the UK: not only works by British artists such as Turner, Reynolds and Constable, but also a preponderance of works by non-British artists as well, such as Raphael, Canova and Manet.[48]

This could at first smack of hypocrisy. It may seem at the very least ironic that the UK would bemoan and combat the departure of cultural objects considered 'British' treasures (as broadly as that category might be construed), while fighting to retain treasures of foreign origin like the Marbles within UK institutions. But it also demonstrates that the UK cares deeply about its own past, imposing rules in order to retain cultural property considered of national importance. The strict laws providing for monument and building preservation, for the vesting of treasure in the Crown, and those controlling exports, reflect a particular sentiment about the past, namely that the past can – and in some cases must – be held onto tightly, lest it slip away. We learned this about Greece in chapter eight, but now we see it with the UK too.

Both countries have a proud history and, in many respects, continue to contemplate the loss of empires: if the Greeks look back on Classical Athens or the rule of Alexander the Great, the British do so onto an empire that in many ways reached its apex in the Victorian period, not long after the Parthenon Marbles had become the keystone of a national collection. Neither empire remains; and so, in a sense, their cultural emanations have become the new battleground. This might explain why, when it comes to the Marbles, the interests appear irreconcilable. But it can also help to show on what grounds a possible reconciliation could occur.

10

Resolving the Dispute

So where does this leave us? Will the parties ever be able to abandon their accumulated baggage and resolve the world's longest-standing cultural dispute? There has been much talk over the past year of a potential deal to be struck, one that might involve a significant portion of the Marbles being lent to the Acropolis Museum for a certain number of years, in exchange for major loans from Greece to the British Museum, an arrangement that could be further 'ratcheted up', if successful, for subsequent periods of time.[1] The British Museum is now referring to a 'Parthenon Partnership', implying that it is willing to move beyond the obstinacy of the past. And a third-party association called the Parthenon Project, consisting of public figures of considerable import, is actively promoting a 'win-win' solution that would appear to benefit both sides. But will all of this be enough to bring the matter to a close?

Disputes as complex and enduring as this one rarely lend themselves to simple solutions. In fact, the more intricately woven the arguments have been on either side, the less likely it is that an object-centred proposal will suffice. Can the parties afford to paper over or ignore all of their other differences? Dominic Spenser Underhill, a solicitor and international arbitrator with 30 years' of experience working out solutions to seemingly intractable commercial problems, explained this in a recent lecture he gave in London. He said that one of the principal reasons why this particular dispute had persisted for so long was that 'entire forests of moral principles have grown up on either side of it.'[2] For this reason the moral values alleged on either side would be extremely difficult to reconcile. A comprehensive solution would have to address these differences. Otherwise, any future agreement would stand on very shaky ground.

In order to see whether a full resolution of the Marbles dispute is possible, we would be wise to measure it against one of the leading frameworks for understanding the resolution of disputes more broadly. The framework offers a method of understanding the causes of conflict in a dispute such as this, as well as a way of finding opportunities for the parties to move forward. Out of these causes, as we will see, come the tools that the parties can use to carve out creative solutions – as ways of resolving different aspects of the dispute, or at least effectively placing them to one side. Let us consider the approach.

Understanding the Causes of Conflict

Christopher Moore has spent many years as a professional mediator resolving conflicts and examining the different forms they can take, from disputes between co-workers or neighbours to larger geo-political disputes embroiling world leaders on the international stage. His theoretical contribution to the study of dispute resolution has come in the form of *The Mediation Process: Practical Strategies for Resolving Conflict*, the first edition of which was published in 1986.[3] He approaches conflict by seeking to understand the underlying causes or drivers of disputes and by offering effective strategies for resolving each of them. According to Moore's original typology, known as the 'Circle of Conflict', there are five types of conflict: data conflicts, interest conflicts, structural conflicts, value conflicts and relationship conflicts.[4] Minor or more limited disagreements might involve one or two of these, while longstanding, complex disputes (like ours) will usually involve all of them operating in concert. Each type of conflict will have its own unique causes and so, to better understand the nature of the Parthenon Marbles dispute, it is important to investigate each according to Moore's system. By doing so, we can then pass on to the next part of the framework, which will allow us to examine the methods of resolution.[5]

Let us begin Moore's Circle of Conflict with 'data conflicts'. Data conflicts arise when parties interpret existing information differently, or when there is a lack of information or the presence of misinformation in a dispute. An illustration might be when two students argue over a topic they know little about, or indeed when each thinks they understand the matter better than the other. Data conflicts may also arise when parties hold differing views as to what may be most relevant in a dispute. This could occur, for instance, when two scientists disagree as to how best to interpret the same set of lab results.

Next are 'interest conflicts'. Interest conflicts arise when the interests at issue appear to be irreconcilable. This could occur when two hunters compete for the same bird or when two dog trainers compete for the prize of 'best in show'. In such cases there is a finite resource but a desire on each side to monopolise it for themselves. There are other aspects of such conflicts that relate more to the procedures available to the parties and their willingness to resort to them.[6] This can also arise when the parties have different understandings of the best process to resolve the dispute: an employee, for example, might hope to settle a workplace grievance before a public tribunal, while the employer may wish for the matter to be settled privately.

Then come 'structural conflicts'. Structural conflicts are usually more ingrained than data or interest conflicts because they relate to matters that go beyond the particular dispute at hand. So, for example, there may be unequal decision-making powers between the parties, such as when the manager of a business fires a young employee. Or else there may be an unequal control of resources, such as when a company decides to clearcut a forest on its own land to build a shopping mall, despite the opposition of nearby residents. Or it could occur when two parties appear structurally at odds with one another, such as when a government minister goes up against a mob of protestors, or vice-versa, or when the parties are marred in a bureaucracy that will not allow them to speak directly to one another.

Next we have 'value conflicts'. Like structural conflicts, their causes are deeply rooted, but this is often due to a disconnect in the underlying philosophy or ideology of the parties. In a word, the *values* that each side promotes are incommensurable. Accepting one side's argument could mean fundamentally denying the validity of the other's. Or, more problematically, it could involve values that might be difficult to address or satisfy in any resolution. This can occur when, for example, an evolutionary biologist and a Christian fundamentalist debate the origins of life on earth.

Lastly come 'relationship conflicts'. These conflicts often reflect the manner in which a dispute or disagreement is being aired. They can be spurred on by strong emotions held by the parties, by the (possibly mistaken) views held by one party about the other, by attitudes that might be uncooperative or even malicious, or by a lack of communication between the parties. As a result, such conflicts are less reflective of the substance of a dispute or of structural limitations and more about the approach the parties have taken towards one another. An example might occur where one party has resorted to calling the other names, or treating them in a manifestly derogatory way, or when both parties simply begin speaking across one another.

Moore's typology is remarkably well-suited for better understanding the Marbles dispute. As the dispute has persisted for so long, it has indeed become marked by each of these types of conflicts: they have accreted over time, hardening the dispute and making it less open to resolution, in contrast to other, relatively 'young' controversies that might attract the fresh energies of the actors caught up in them. Across the long history of our dispute nearly every conceivable course of action has been tried, or at least suggested, without any solution so far manifesting itself. In the past, we have seen attempts by Greek Ministers of Culture and British Parliamentarians, by journalists and campaigners, but none has been successful.[7] It is only by properly understanding the complexities of the dispute that we can begin to identify the potential avenues of redress. Let us consider Moore's conflict types in relation to the Marbles.

Beginning with data conflicts, we know that both the Greeks and the British Museum have interpreted identical or similar facts in vastly different ways. From the outset, the portrayal of Lord Elgin has been the source of conflict: on the one hand, he was a saviour trying to rescue works of art for posterity; on the other, he was a thief employing guile and influence to acquire assets from an occupying power.[8] Conflicting views also exist with respect to the removal itself: on the one hand, a legitimate act supported by Ottoman approval; on the other, an act both unlawful and immoral. It is not for lack of information that discussions around these points have traditionally gone nowhere; it is instead the result of incompatible readings of what is largely the same information. The protracted nature of the dispute has allowed each party the opportunity to further solidify an interpretation that best suits its own argument, and to reject interpretations to the contrary.

The interest conflict has also been apparent since the beginning of the dispute, with each side seeking to monopolise what is effectively a finite resource. The Marbles are articles of property, which, as a collection, can in principle be possessed only by one side at the expense of the other. And there is a longstanding disagreement about title as well: while suggestions have been made to put ownership aside, the fact remains that it still needs to be satisfactorily resolved.[9] Taking into account the attitudes of each side, the interests remain manifestly oppositional: the Greek Prime Minister states that the Marbles must be returned outright, while the Trustees continue to assert their lawful ownership.

A structural conflict is evident here as well. One side has control of the disputed resource, while the other side does not. There is a major disconnect between the parties too: a museum (with its trustees, managers and curators) on the one hand and a government (with its ministers and bureaucrats) on the other. Past attempts at negotiation have led nowhere partly because of this institutional dissonance. When the parties did meet, they appeared to be speaking different languages.[10]

The disconnect is further revealed in the value conflict. For Greeks, recovering the Marbles is a step towards reuniting an essential part of the nation's cultural heritage.[11] For the British Museum, keeping the Marbles means maintaining a cornerstone of its collection, while relinquishing them would be a renunciation of its very *raison d'être*.[12] The conflict can therefore appear ideological, with national heritage and the unity of monuments on the one side, and international access and the integrity of museum collections on the other.

And, finally, a relationship conflict is evident as well. There are numerous examples of ill-thought-out and, at times, petulant statements from both sides. But the relationship has been damaged even more in the subtle, passive aggressive nature of the exchanges over the years. One of the quintessential examples of this has been the way in which both sides have addressed each other in the past: not directly, but through statements made in the press. In this way, they were speaking across one another. We continue to read public statements that fail to take the other side's view into account. On the UK side, this is evident from the series of comments made on the matter by recent Prime Ministers and Secretaries of State.[13] And, from the Greek side, this would include the recent statement from the Minister of Culture that Greece will not 'recognise the British Museum's jurisdiction, possession and ownership of the Sculptures, as they are the product of theft'.[14] None of these political statements serves as a particularly welcome invitation to further cooperation. In fact, they tend to make matters far worse.

Opportunities for Collaboration

For each type of conflict within the Circle of Conflict, Moore suggests a particu-lar way of bringing about resolution. This can be through specific 'interventions', which are meant for mediators (like Moore himself) to use when attempting to bridge the seemingly unbridgeable divide that separates parties in a dispute, but they are also apparent earlier, within the composition of the conflict itself. In this earlier form, they are referred to simply as 'opportunities for collaboration' and as such can be acted upon by the parties, in some cases without the need of a third-party mediator.[15] Each type of conflict therefore includes its own potential for resolution, even if such resolution can at times be difficult to ascertain.

For data conflicts, opportunity for collaboration might exist where parties can agree on determining how to assess the relevant information, which particu-lar information can be agreed upon, and (where necessary) seeking an outside opinion on disputed information to break a deadlock. For interest conflicts, opportunity might arise where parties are able to negotiate around those interests, rather than arguing over positions (avoiding what is known as 'positional bargain-ing', a counterproductive form of negotiation that almost always fails to achieve resolution),[16] and where they can identify how such interests can be shared. For structural conflicts, it might involve ensuring that the roles of the parties are clearly set out, taking into account any differences in power and access, and that a fair process is put in place so as to give the parties a feeling that, regardless of their status, they are being listened to and afforded a meaningful opportunity to express themselves. For value conflicts, collaboration might involve putting aside views based on different value systems, or limiting them in some way, and seeking out broader values that all sides can agree on. For relationship conflicts, an opportunity might involve setting up a procedure with clear rules (or a joint communications strategy) as a way of streamlining the relationship and avoid-ing miscommunication and hurtful allegations, ensuring that counterproductive behaviour cannot repeat itself. [17]

When it comes to the Marbles, a way forward may become discernible if we are able to divide the dispute into its component parts. We know of the data conflict over each side's interpretation of past events. A solution to this problem could involve an agreed statement setting out those parts of the history that *can* be agreed upon.[18] This would have to be done carefully, and possibly with the involve-ment of a third-party expert. Parties in legal disputes are often able to provide a 'joint statement of facts', usually drafted by legal counsel, which at a minimum provides the basis for an understanding of some of the evidence involved. This then allows the judge to focus on applying the legal rules to the accepted facts, as well as resolving any remaining facts still in dispute. In our case, it would serve a somewhat different purpose, ensuring that the history recounted by both sides going forward remains relatively neutral and avoids the antagonisms of the past.[19] It can also serve, at its best, as a joint enterprise by which the parties might be able to begin mending a frayed relationship: a project in which they can both be invested.

If the existing interest conflict has been caused by incompatible desires involving a finite resource, then an opportunity for collaboration can be found in the sharing of that resource – or indeed in the expansion of the resource itself. This appears to be what is being contemplated at present, namely in the proposed arrangement that would involve the long-term transfer of possession of some the Marbles complete with reciprocal loans of objects from Greece to the British Museum.[20] Of course identifying the shared interests in all this will become essential, but resolution also depends upon how the arrangement is carried out. We have already seen how the question of ownership could be addressed.[21] It needs, above all, to reflect the specific interests of each party and to set out how those interests would be advanced through a deal. As outlined above, this could involve a joint statement to help clarify the mutual benefits obtained by each party out of the settlement.[22] Otherwise it may prove difficult for the parties to convince their respective stakeholders (such as staff, funders and members of the public) that they have derived a meaningful outcome.

The structural conflict is evident in the institutional disconnects that exist between the two sides. These might be assuaged by establishing a fair and neutral procedure that could be used as a framework for continuing negotiations. Such a procedure would need to be drafted in an objective way such that one party is not seen as gaining an unfair advantage, while offering a forum in which both parties can engage meaningfully and express themselves. Procedures of this nature are already envisaged in sector guidance such as *Restitution and Repatriation: A Practical Guide for Museums in England*, published by Arts Council England in 2022, which sets out a procedure for museums to follow, while emphasising the importance of transparency, collaboration and fairness throughout negotiations.[23] In the present context, this may be difficult to imagine, since the Greek Prime Minister and the Chair of Trustees have already embarked upon secret negotiations. The potential problem with negotiations of this nature is that they remain opaque and do not follow objective, sector-approved guidelines. They also rely upon the personalities involved. Should the actors change – for instance, if a new Chair is appointed or another Prime Minister elected – the negotiations are likely to break down, much as they have in the past.[24] Instead, a more suitable approach might involve the use of a negotiating procedure based on objective criteria (eg a forum which is fair and neutral for both sides), a greater degree of transparency (eg periodic press releases providing updates on negotiations) and a sustainable format that could withstand the vicissitudes of any change in leadership on either side.

The deep-seated value conflict, reflecting an opposition between the values of repatriating part of a nation's cultural heritage and the values of the universal museum, might be more difficult to address. One attempt might see the parties seeking to establish broader goals that each could agree to, reflecting such universally held 'museum values' as public accessibility, the value of curation and the bonds between museums and communities of origin – all of which are adhered to by the British Museum and the Acropolis Museum through the Code of Ethics of the International Council of Museums.[25] We have also seen some of what Greece and the UK do share in regard to their relationship with the past and their over-riding interest in preserving heritage in the present.[26] Perhaps this could form the basis of a more elaborate statement of shared values between the parties and, ulti-mately, of a greater sense of mutual understanding.

Beyond such general points of agreement, it may also prove important for each party to accept, at the very least, the *validity* of the other's position, even if fully acceding to it remains difficult. The arbitrator Dominic Spenser Underhill (mentioned at the beginning of this chapter) has referred to something of this nature in relation to negotiations between parties with adverse positions. He has said that there is a 'moral obligation for each party in a negotiation to try to under-stand what the other side is trying to say' – and there would be no exception in our case.[27] Statements of mutual respect for values espoused by the other side may be of particular use here: for Greece to recognise the value of universal museums and for the British Museum to recognise the centrality of the Parthenon to the cultural heritage of Greece. Neither statement needs be to be exclusionary: that is, accept-ing one does not exclude the other. Such statements are in fact common in legal disputes, and usually circulate extensively as 'without prejudice' drafts before the parties can agree to them.[28]

When it comes to the relationship conflict, this has been exacerbated over the years by unwise statements made by both parties and by their occasional use of combative tones. In such situations, one solution might involve ensuring that such mistakes are avoided going forward and that, with time (it is hoped), the long-term damage inflicted can be healed. There are different options here. The parties might think, in the first instance, of how to improve communication between their institutions and of considering the use of joint press releases, perhaps even placing an embargo on speaking to the press without having first consulted the other side. Later, as a way of rebuilding the relationship, energies could be marshalled towards common goals such as joint exhibitions between the museums. The research and data-sharing partnerships of the past would be worth extending in this respect, as a way for the parties to broaden their working relationship.[29] None of this sounds particularly grand or newsworthy, but without it, an agreement on the Marbles becomes far less tenable. How, after all, could a comprehensive and potentially long-lasting agreement be achieved without a strong foundation of professional familiarity and trust between institutions?

These of course remain suggestions. It is up to the parties themselves to investigate whether each can be taken further. While collaboration might not be possible on all heads, it seems unlikely that a valid agreement on the Marbles could succeed without some level of understanding on most of the other points discussed. Complicated disputes, after all, require more than superficial solutions; they require solutions that are themselves complex and multifaceted, broad and all-encompassing, responsive and supple. This dispute, if anything, is about far more than a collection of stones: it is about what that collection represents to each side, the historical baggage that each side brings to the discussion, the differing interpretations of the relevant history, the differing language used to describe the matter, the structure of the legal entities involved – in a sense it is about all the different types of conflict in Moore's Circle of Conflict.

Mediation

While we may see opportunities for direct collaboration between the parties, is it also possible for sustained involvement from the outside as well? Some may think that too much emphasis on mutual discussion and collaboration between the parties would allow them to grow slack. In some ways, this could provide the British Museum with a way out: to continue discussing the matter indefinitely, without taking any meaningful action. To alleviate situations such as this, Moore's framework suggests the possibility of 'interventions' from third parties: for instance, a mediator who can use particular techniques to assist the parties in resolving the various conflicts at issue. But is there room for such a role in this dispute?

In the past, Greece has sought the assistance of UNESCO, which as an international agency, might seem a logical forum to address such issues. A claim was brought to UNESCO's Intergovernmental Committee for Promoting the Return of Cultural Property to its Countries of Origin or its Restitution in case of Illicit Appropriation (the Intergovernmental Committee) in 1984, but the UK refused to engage in the process and has maintained this position ever since.[30] A request was also made in 2013 by Greece for UNESCO's assistance in mediating the dispute through its mediation rules, but this too was rejected by both the UK Government and the Trustees in 2015. One might think that these refusals are further examples of the intransigence of the British side – and perhaps in part they are. But it is important to ask whether UNESCO procedures are indeed appropriate for resolving a dispute as notorious and complex as this one.

The Intergovernmental Committee was established in 1978, in the wake of the 1970 Convention on the Means of Prohibiting the Illicit Import, Export and Transfer of Ownership of Cultural Property, and part of its purpose was to hear claims for the return and restitution of cultural property brought outside the strict terms of the Convention. At the time of Greece's claim in 1984, however, the Committee had procedures dating from 1981 that were largely untested: no successful claim had been brought through the system at the time; even now, 40 years later, only three successful outcomes have directly resulted from the procedure.[31] Similarly, the UNESCO mediation procedure, established in 2010, was still relatively new when Greece brought its request for UNESCO's assistance in mediation; it has still not been used to this day. While UNESCO itself is a valuable and integral part of the international order, there is a lack of evidence showing that these specific procedures would be appropriate for resolving the multi-layered Marbles dispute (then as now).

When it comes to the use of third-party assistance, the relevant third party must first possess legitimacy in the eyes of the parties before a dispute can realistically be referred to it. Such legitimacy cannot be assumed: it must be earned over time. In his work *Legitimacy Through Procedure*, the philosopher Niklas Luhmann refers to three composites of legitimacy for a body tasked with decisional or advisory authority in resolving a dispute: that body must consist of members of good repute, it must have independently-drafted rules and it must engender the trust of the broader society.[32] Examples of bodies that fit this model are sundry, even in the cultural heritage field.[33] But it can be questioned whether the two UNESCO forums, referred to above, have earned the necessary legitimacy to offer an appropriate venue for dispute resolution. As such, no single body appears to exist that could offer useful mediation for the many issues at play.

This does not mean, however, that the present situation should remain without resolution. As we have seen, there are layers of conflict between the parties that remain largely unresolved. The lack of a forum does not allow the British Museum and the UK Government to ignore the many points of conflict that still require resolution. Ignoring the considerable moral volatility associated with keeping the Parthenon Marbles is ethically problematic, seeing as it ignores well-established ethical principles in the museum sector.[34] Past inaction has also been reprimanded by international and foreign bodies – UNESCO's General Assembly and its Intergovernmental Committee, the International Council of Museums, the International Council of Monuments and Sites, the European Parliament, the New Zealand Parliament, the Legislative Council of the South Australian Parliament, the World Hellenic Inter-Parliamentary Association, the Greek Orthodox Archdiocese of Great Britain[35] – and this will probably continue to be the case. Numerous world leaders have voiced support for the Greek campaign. A majority of the British population, according to polls mentioned in the introduction, believes the Marbles should be returned.[36] Clearly the status quo has become ethically indefensible; further engagement is required. But how far should this extend?

A Win-Win 'Solution'?

Simply because no third party exists to offer mediation or another form of dispute resolution does not mean that outside intervention remains impossible. Instead, third-party interventions will be (as in the past) more sporadic and piecemeal in nature, involving stakeholders advancing the discussion in targeted ways at different points in the process.[37] There are of course advocacy groups seeking the outright return of the Marbles (such as the British Committee for the Reunification of the Parthenon Marbles).[38] While none has succeeded in its aims, each has certainly managed to hold the British Museum's feet to the fire over the years, helping to ensure, with their sustained focus on this one central issue, that the matter never falls too far from the limelight.

More recently we have seen one particular body occupy a large part of the 'interventionist' space: the Parthenon Project. Its suggestion of a 'win-win' solution is indeed enticing, and might appear to align with some of the proposals being considered in the current negotiations by the British Museum, such as a long-term loan of the Marbles, in exchange for a rotating series of loans of Greek objects to the British Museum. But the full contents of such a 'solution' have yet to manifest themselves. In fact, this group is not the first to seek to 'mediate' the dispute from the outside. In 2010, the founder of the airline EasyJet, Sir Stelios Haji-Ioannou, who is of Greek-Cypriot origin but has spent many years in the UK as a student and businessman, tried to resolve matters. He had suggested an arrangement that would involve reciprocal loans between the British Museum and the Acropolis Museum of something in the range of 10 to 20 of the Marbles, all the while putting aside the question of title. But his creative initiative never progressed once the financial crisis took hold in Greece.[39]

In many ways the appeal of 'win-win' is in its very imprecision. But at a certain point, specific details would need to be advanced. Were Greece able to offer loans of major antiquities to the British Museum, this would undoubtedly be of some value to the borrowing institution,[40] especially in the context of the effective moratorium on loans discussed in chapter nine. Greek law now allows its museums to lend out antiquities on a long-term basis, something that was historically forbidden.[41] But what specific pieces might be included in this arrangement? Without precision on the content of the loans (or even a guarantee in principle) it might be difficult for British Museum staff to get particularly enthusiastic about this, or indeed to make plans around it. It might instead be more beneficial to align the offer with existing museum priorities: for instance, the Museum's forthcoming exhibition schedule (major exhibitions are usually planned three years in advance), the refurbishment of its Greek and Roman Galleries and the larger goals of its major renovation project.[42]

More importantly, 'win-win' might not adequately address most of the simmering conflicts we saw above. It certainly satisfies the 'interest conflict', by allowing the parties to bargain based on potential shared interests, always a step up from positional bargaining, which we know is a problem. But what of the other types of conflict? There remain significant conflicts around data, structures, relationships and values. For 'win-win' to succeed, it would need to directly address these other conflicts as well. Failing this, a proposal may be hard to justify – and may lack the legitimacy needed to stand the test of time.

Many have sought to offer solutions to the dispute, but so far not one has hit the target. Unless important lessons are learned from the dispute as a whole – and unless mutual respect is demonstrated throughout by the parties – it is difficult to see how any arrangement can be effective. Even if a deal is struck through the machinations of the Chair of Trustees and the Greek Government, it will not necessarily end the long-running saga; rather it will be the beginning of a new and promising, though ultimately uncertain, chapter in the history of the Marbles. With this in mind, the relationship between the two museums will have to be strong at the outset and the agreement carefully drafted and implemented. If the proposed solution is built around a transfer of possession (whether termed as a loan or one of the other concepts explored in chapter six), then the complexities of such an arrangement will need to be fully considered: this would include the costs and practicalities of transport, insurance coverage, cost liabilities, condition reporting, a forum and system of law for dispute resolution, and immunity from seizure.[43] For a deal to be sustainable in the long run, it will need to be farsighted, clearly-expressed and responsive to the needs of both parties.

One thing I have learned from researching and writing this book is that it has always been easier to suggest solutions than it has been to see them through. That is perhaps why interventions in the past, well-meaning and sensible though they may have been, have ultimately failed. When the history of acquisition and the points of dispute are so notorious, it is tempting to try and offer an answer to the problem, something that will resolve the matter once and for all. Perhaps it may be better instead to approach the issue with a degree of humility, to reflect on the Marbles and their troubled history, and to leave the ultimate question of resolution to the museums themselves. In the end it is not the politicians or the journalists, the campaigners or the academics, the actors or the businessmen who will care for these objects: it is the museum curators and the teams of professionals who support them in their respective institutions. The space should be theirs to occupy.

Preparation for Movement

Over the course of the story we have seen the Parthenon Marbles from a variety of viewpoints. In chapter one, we considered their history as part of the Parthenon, from the glory of classical Athens to the Venetian attack of 1687. In chapter two, we looked at the way in which they were removed by Lord Elgin's men in the early 1800s. Chapter three brought a legal analysis to the question of permission, as well as a consideration of morality. Chapter four considered the arrival of the Marbles in the UK and their importance to Britain. Chapter five looked at the loss suffered in Athens following their departure and the attempts since then to seek their return. Chapter six dealt with the legal considerations around ownership and potential loan agreements going forward. Chapter seven saw the dispute in the context of international law and the long history of restitution. Chapter eight considered the Greek perspective on the matter, while chapter nine looked at the view from the British Museum. Chapter ten has taken all of this together in order to offer an analysis of the dispute and to consider the different features necessary for resolution.

Each part of the story has been included for a particular reason. Some aspects needed to be reaffirmed: the value of the Parthenon today as a symbol of ancient and modern Greece; the importance of the Marbles as architectural sculptures intended as part of a unified whole; the complications of history that allowed the Marbles to leave Athens when they did; the legality of the removal by Elgin's men within the Ottoman system; the troubling morality of that same removal; the debates held in Parliament at the time of the acquisition; the legal and institutional attachment of the British Museum to the pieces; the strength of feeling on the Greek side; and the current attempts at negotiating a deal between the parties. Other aspects had to be added to the conversation: a more nuanced structuralist account of the Marbles' removal and the role of Elgin himself; the status and legal effect of the Kaimacam's 1801 letter; the more recently discovered Ottoman documents of 1802, 1810 and 1811; a fresh look at the impact of Ottoman rule over Athens and the status of bribery; a consideration of the removal in the context of the French restitutions of 1815; the application of rules of international law to the retention by the UK; a number of overlooked episodes in the long history of the Greek campaign for return; the ways in which that campaign plays into important sentiments within modern Greece; the sad state of the British Museum's finances; the ways in which the British Museum loses out by not resolving the Marbles issue; and the possible common ground that may exist between the parties.

After all this, let us end by returning to the sculptures themselves. It can at times be hard to see them amidst the smoke of discord. They remain, in the words of Ian Jenkins, 'the most important material productions of man, the most beautiful, the most elevated'.[44] Amongst all that they offer, one particular image stands out. The scene is from Block XXII of the west frieze, part of the preparation for the cavalcade and the procession that will make its way towards the gods at the east end of the building. Though the sculpture is badly damaged, its composition remains one of 'matchless artistry' according to experts in Greece.[45] It was part of the sequence that remained on the building after Elgin's men left the Acropolis, one of the pieces Fauvel had claimed was 'saved' for posterity by the actions of the French Ambassador.[46] It suffered weathering in the twentieth century from the elements and pollution of Athens. And yet, after its removal from the building in 1993, it was placed in the care of the Acropolis Restoration Service and has been cleansed of much of the encrustation through laser cleaning.[47] It is now on display, with its west frieze neighbours, at the Acropolis Museum.

Like the metope on the cover of this book, it is a scene of action set in stone, but it conveys a more balanced, tranquil air (see Figure 10). In fact, there is relatively little conflict throughout the entire frieze. There will be movement in the procession of horses and Athenians, but the momentum is unidirectional; apart from two or three stubborn beasts, pushing back against their masters, the scene is one of consent and civility. On this particular block, the cavalcade has yet to begin. Three figures stand by a stationary, impatient horse: the creature has its snout in

Figure 10 The scene from Block XXII of the West frieze of the Parthenon, held at the Acropolis Museum in Athens, shows figures preparing for the cavalcade
Source: PRISMA ARCHIVO / Alamy Stock Photo.

an unusual position between its front legs, as though rubbing itself in anticipation. Next to the horse, a boy stands patiently, while his master affixes something to his wrist before he is able to mount the steed. The central figure in the scene, a marshal, stands contrapposto with one hand on his hip and the other giving belated orders to the departed riders on the left. The three figures are in perfect harmony, and yet the scene reveals a pent-up energy; it is like a coil about to be released. There is a sense of expectation in the human figures, and in the horse as well. An itchy muzzle, a loose strap, a call out to companions who have already left: the final touches before the spectacle can truly begin.

In the dispute over the Parthenon Marbles, the hard reality is that this block and others like it are in many ways still missing from the story that is being told at the British Museum. In the great hall of the Duveen Gallery, the galloping cavalcade begins out of nothing – or rather it emerges from the dark gap at the centre of the room, the same entrance through which the visitors come and go. While Block XII does appear as a plaster cast elsewhere, along the wall of one of the explanatory slip-rooms, it is left outside the main narrative, in a display that is awkwardly confined and forced to double back on itself. If the Parthenon frieze can indeed be called a 'symphony in stone' (an analogy eloquently supported by Ian Jenkins in one of the British Museum publications about the frieze), then the display in the Duveen Gallery seems to be missing its first movement.[48] Meanwhile, the Acropolis Museum does possess that movement, but lacks much of the rest of the piece, forced instead to offer pale replicas. Neither institution is therefore capable of living up to its potential.

And so we are left with two meanings for this little scene. Either it will serve as another example of the perpetually frozen dispute: preparation without deliverance, a beginning without end, a forever-deferred start to some great rush of activity. In that way, Block XXII would remain with its scattering of companions, isolated and somewhat forlorn atop the Acropolis Museum. Or else it can appear as intended by the masters of the fifth century: to reflect an anxious pause before everything starts moving forward. That brief time to get things in order before the rush of events takes over. If it will be the latter of these two possibilities then we need to make sure that everything has been properly accounted for. Because what awaits might be more unpredictable – and also more exhilarating – than anything that has ever come before.

NOTES

Introduction: A Matter Still Unresolved

1. The first comes from Tyrone Guthrie, 'The Elgin Marbles' in *Treasures of the British Museum*, (London, Collins, 1971) 72; the second from poet Lord Byron in *English Bards and Scotch Reviewers* (1809) and the third from 19th-century Royal Academician Ozias Humphry, cited in Tiffany Jenkins, *Keeping Their Marbles* (Oxford, Oxford University Press, 2018) 103.

2. The term 'Elgin Marbles' was commonly used in Britain from the time of their arrival, including by the British Museum. According to the 1816 law that vested in the Trustees the objects acquired from Lord Elgin, such objects were to be referred to as 'The Elgin Collection', though this included a great number of other objects amassed by Elgin from across the Ottoman Empire. The British Museum now refers to the pieces from the Parthenon as the 'Parthenon Sculptures'. In fact, through UNESCO, both the UK and Greek delegations had committed themselves in 2010 to refer to them as such: UNESCO meeting, Paris, 21–23 September 2010. The problem with the term 'Parthenon Sculptures', however, is that it could equally apply to those sculptures from the Parthenon that remained in Athens and are currently at the Acropolis Museum, and such a conflation often leads to unnecessary confusion. The problem with 'Elgin Marbles' is that it has largely fallen out of favour and serves as an unnecessary antagonism to one side in the debate. After I had used the term 'Elgin Marbles', a representative of the Greek Government politely informed me that 'for us, Greeks, the term Elgin Marbles is not an accepted denomination': email to the author, 20 Jan 2018.

3. The number consists of 88 significant works of sculpture (56 blocks of frieze, 15 metopes and 17 figures from the pediment, though the last of these could be counted as 15 individual blocks) and three architectural features (a capital, column-drum and crown piece).

4. Four frieze sections from the Temple of Athena Nike, a 'Caryatid' (sculpted female figure) and a column from the Erechtheion, and architectural pieces from the 'Propylaia' gateway.

5. Former Greek Culture Minister Melina Mercouri, speech to the Oxford Union, Oxford, 12 June 1986.

6. Keeper of Greek and Roman Antiquities BF Cook to British Museum Director David Wilson, 22 March 1991, as quoted in Martin Bailey, 'Declassified Documents Reveal Near Return of Elgin Marbles' *The Art Newspaper* (1 February 2000).

7. Greek Prime Minister Kyriakos Mitsotakis appearing on *Good Morning Britain* (ITV, 16 November 2021).

8. 'Reunification of the Parthenon Marbles', Ipsos poll, conducted on behalf of the Marianna Vardinoyannis Foundation, from 13–18 June 2014.

9. The Akropoli Metro station has a set of reproductions of many of the Marbles at the entrance and on the platform.

10. Elena Lampousis in Kifissia, 14 May 2018. See ch 8 for my discussion about the Parthenon with a group of local Greeks in Athens.

11. See pp 125–29.

12. The Conservative MP Damian Green was quoted as saying, 'if it ain't broke, don't fix it': Gordon Rayner, 'Are We About to Lose our Marbles?' *The Telegraph* (19 November 2021).

13. YouGov polls conducted on 15 August 2017, 4 June 2018 and 23 November 2021 each found a clear majority of British respondents thought the Parthenon Marbles belonged in Greece: respectively 55%/56%/59%, said return to Greece, 21%/20%/18% said keep in Britain and 24%/24%/18% said did not know (4000/2600/7700 respondents respectively): yougov.co.uk/(popup:search/parthenon marbles). See also the earlier polls by MORI in 1998 (return favoured by 2 to 1) and *The Economist* poll of British MPs in March 2000 (return favoured 64% to 34%): William G. Stewart, 'The Marbles: Elgin or Parthenon?' (2001) VI *Art Antiquity and Law* 37, 55.

14. Frederic Harrison, 'Give Back the Elgin Marbles' (*The Nineteenth Century*, March 1890) 495–506.

15. See p 69 and Christopher Hitchens, *The Elgin Marbles: Should they be Returned to Greece?* (London, Chatto & Windos, 1987) 75–78.

16. See pp 84–85.

17. 'The Parthenon Sculptures: The Trustees' Statement', British Museum website: www.british-museum.org/about-us/british-museum-story/contested-objects-collection/parthenon-sculptures/parthenon.

18. See eg Tiffany Jenkins (n 1) 240–50; and Noel Malcolm, 'The Elgin Marbles: Keep, Lend or Return? An Analysis' (*Policy Exchange*, 2023).

19. Mary Beard, *The Parthenon* (London, Profile Books, 2002) 21.

20. See Alexander Herman, *Restitution: The Return of Cultural Artefacts* (London, Lund Humphries, 2021).

21. See pp 96–97.

22. Helena Smith, 'Pope Francis Returns Three Fragments of Parthenon to Greece' *The Guardian* (25 March 2023).

23. See pp 82–86 and Herman (n 20) 9–16.

24. Interview on *Leading Britain's Conversation* with Andrew Marr, 15 June 2022.

25. Gareth Harris, 'British Museum Proposes New 'Parthenon Partnership' with Greece in Bid to End Deadlock over Marbles' *The Art Newspaper* (1 August 2022).

26. George Osborne, Speech at the Annual Trustees' Dinner, British Museum, London, 2 November 2022.

Chapter 1
From the Slopes of Mount Pentelikos

1. The visit took place on 14 May 2018 and was organised by Katerina Vagia, a friend in Athens.

2. For a reassessment of the role of labour involved in quarrying, transporting and sculpting the marble for the Acropolis, see Manolis Korres, *Stones of the Parthenon* (Los Angeles, Getty Publications, 2001) 8.

3. Manolis Korres, *From Pentelicon to the Parthenon* (Athens, Melissa Publishing, 1995) 100.

4. 'The Ancient Stone Carrying Road from Pentelikon to the Acropolis Comes to Light' (*Archaeology Matters*, 17 March 2010).

5. The sculptures of the Old Athenian Temple on the Acropolis were made of Parian marble. Sounion was also of Parian marble, as was the Nike of Samothrace and the Venus de Milo.

6. Yannis Hamilakis, 'Nostalgia for the Whole: the Parthenon (or Elgin) Marbles' in Hamilakis (ed), *The Nation and its Ruins: Antiquity, Archaeology and National Imagination in Greece* (Oxford University Press, 2007) 248.

7. Ian Jenkins, *The Parthenon Frieze* (London, British Museum Press, 2019) 14. Three can still be seen more-or-less intact today: Sounion, the Hephaestion and the Parthenon.

8. Joan Breton Connelly, *The Parthenon Enigma* (New York, Vintage Books, 2014) 61–62, 68.

9. The ancient writer Lycurgus recorded the oath: 'Of the shrines burnt and overthrown by the barbarians, I will rebuild none, but I will allow them to remain as a memorial to those who come afterward of the impiety of the barbarians': RE Wycherley, *The Stones of Athens* (Princeton, Princeton University Press, 1978) 106; Connelly (n 8) 82.

10. In the fourth century BCE the term *Parthenon* was first used to denote the whole building. Prior to this, it was known simply as 'the temple': Connelly (n 8) 230.

11. Plutarch, *The Life of Pericles*, 13:1.

12. Korres (n 3).

13. 'Phidias managed everything for him': Plutarch, *The Life of Pericles*, 13:4.

14. See generally Thucydides, *History of the Peloponnesian War* and Plutarch, *The Life of Pericles*.

15. Connelly (n 8) 77–79.

16. See Thucydides' speech recorded in Plutarch, *The Life of Pericles*, 14:1.

17. ibid 12:3–12:4.

18. ibid 12:5; Connelly (n 8) 86.

19. Connelly (n 8) 110–13.

20. The trident held by Poseidon in the pediment would have also evoked the aperture in the roof and the small holes beneath the floor of the nearby Erechtheion, which was said to have been caused by an enormous trident. The inclusion of figures from Eleusis was also fitting when the pilgrimage of the Eleusinian Mysteries began at the base of the Acropolis and would have continued to the city of Eleusis to the west of Athens: Connelly (n 8) 107–109, 112–13.

21. The figure of Dionysus appeared to be looking out towards the southeast slope of the Acropolis, the location of the Theatre of Dionysus, where the great plays of Aeschylus, Sophocles and Euripides would have been first performed. At the other end of the pediment is Aphrodite, who faces the sanctuary of Aphrodite Ourania on the northeast slope: See Connolly (n 8) 33–34 and Dimitrios Pandermalis, *Acropolis Museum Guide* (Athens, Acropolis Museum, 2015) 78. Aphrodite in the frieze was located immediately below the larger version, pointing in the same direction.

22. Ian Jenkins, *The Parthenon Sculptures* (London, British Museum Press, 2019) 40.

23. BF Cook, *The Elgin Marbles* (London, British Museum Press, 1984) 25.

24. Jenkins (n 7) 35–42.

25. This is upon the author's counting, though it is a challenge owing to the parts of the frieze that did not survive and the difficulty, at times, in discerning the layering of horses.

26. See Jenkins (n 7) 35–42; Connolly (n 8); Mary Beard, 'The Latest Scheme for the Parthenon' (*The New York Review of Books*, March 2014).

27. Frank Brommer, *The Sculptures of the Parthenon* (London, Thames & Hudson, 1979) 36.

28. For example, fighting centaurs and lapiths can be seen on the Hephaesteion in the Agora, the Temple of Zeus at Olympia and the Temple of Apollo at Bassai. Athenians fighting Amazonians can be seen at Bassai, while Gods fighting Giants and the Trojan War were both featured on the Siphnian Treasury at Delphi.

29. Pausanias, *Description of Greece*, Book I, 22–25.

30. Wycherley (n 9) 113: 'In a very real sense, it was the work of the Athenian people, not merely because hundreds of them had a hand in building it but because the assembly was ultimately responsible, confirmed appointments and sanctioned and scrutinised the expenditure of every drachma.'

31. For a somewhat critical view of this predilection, see Connolly (n 8) 340–41.

32. AW Lawrence, *Greek Architecture*, 3rd edn (London, Penguin, 1973) 295: 'The Parthenon is the one building in the world which may be assessed as absolutely right' (quoted in Wycherley (n 9) 125). Elena Korka, Director of Antiquities at the Greek Ministry of Culture and Sports, describing the Parthenon in an interview on 14 May 2018: 'It *is* totally perfect. There isn't one person standing in front of it who doesn't feel this. The perfection covers the architecture and sculptural decoration at the same time.'

33. Connolly (n 8) 89–95. As a contrast to the enduring balance of the Parthenon, my colleague Geoffrey Bennett suggests the far less visually perfect Greek temples at Paestum, Italy.

34. Wycherley (n 9) 115.

35. AH Smith, 'Lord Elgin and his Collection' (1916) 36 *Journal of Hellenistic Studies* 77–78.

36. The population of Athens is three million, nearly a third of the ten million in Greece as a whole. For more on the development of modern Greece, see Bruce Clark, *Athens: City of Wisdom* (London, Head of Zeus, 2022).

37. One can compare the Parthenon to the Temple of Aphaea across the Saronic Bay, which is in roughly the same shape and also had beautiful sculptures taken in the early 19th century, now kept in the Glyptothek in Munich. The former, which is at the epicentre of contemporary Greek life, has captured the public imagination, while the latter, which sits above a dusty town on a forlorn island, remains rather unloved.

38. The Acropolis was inscribed on the World Heritage List in 1987: 'The Acropolis of Athens is the most striking and complete ancient Greek monumental complex still existing in our time' (UNESCO, World Heritage List inscription, 1987).

39. As part of the Documenta Festival, 2017. The artist was Marta Minujin, who had made a similar structure in Argentina in 1983 consisting of books banned by the Argentinean dictatorship: 'The Parthenon of Books' *The Guardian* (1 September 2017).

40. Charalambos Bouras, Maria Ioannidou and Ian Jenkins (eds), *Acropolis Restored*, British Museum Research Publication no 187 (London, British Museum Press, 2015) 12, 46, 55.

41. See Korres (n 2), which reconstructs the journey of a single capital that ultimately went unused due to a fissure.

42. For the different explanations of this bio-chemical process, see Evi Papakonstantinou-Ziotis, 'Surface Conservation' in Bouras, Ioannidou and Jenkins (n 40) 57.

43. See ch 8 on the meaning of the Parthenon to modern Greek heritage as it has developed over time.

44. For a history of the Venetian siege, see Molly Mackenzie, *Turkish Athens* (Reading, Ithaca Press, 1992) 17–25; Mary Beard, *The Parthenon* (London, Profile Books, 2002) 76–81; and Clark (n 36) 277–86.

45. Beard (n 44) 52.

46. ibid 76–87.

47. Elena Korka, *Fragments of the Parthenon Sculptures Displayed in Museums Across Europe* (Athens, Greek Ministry of Culture and Sports publication, 2017) 10: 15 cannons were placed on the Hill of the Muses, nine more on the Pnyx and five mortars on the Aeropagus Hill.

48. Mackenzie (n 44) 18–22.

49. Beard (n 44) 80; Mackenzie (n 44) 18–24.

50. Sadly, the rules of war remain somewhat deficient in prohibiting attacks such as this one. After the Second World War, much was done to avoid attacks on cultural heritage sites, most notably the drafting by UNESCO of the 1954 Convention for the Protection of Cultural Property in the Event of Armed Conflict (Hague, 14 May 1954), especially Article 4, and the Convention's two Protocols from 1954 and 1999. Were an attack like that of 1687 to occur today during an armed conflict between States that had ratified the above-mentioned instruments, it would violate the terms of the Convention only if the site had been specifically listed with UNESCO for 'special' or 'enhanced' protection (very few sites have) or if there was no military necessity. For states not party to the Convention, rules of customary law would apply, which impose similar restrictions: see the Rules of the International Committee of the Red Cross on Customary International Humanitarian Law (2007) Rule 38 (and see pp 112-17 for a discussion of customary international law). The intentional direction of attacks against such buildings is also a war crime under the Rome Statute of the International Criminal Court (Rome, 17 July 1998), provided they are not military objectives: Article 8(b)(2)(b)(ix).

51. Mackenzie (n 44) 20–21.

52. Leopold van Ranke (1843), as quoted in Mackenzie (n 44) 22.

53. I would like to thank Bodil Bundgaard Rasmussen, Senior Curator at the National Museum of Denmark (since retired), for sharing this information along with an image of the pieces' display in the late seventeenth century. See also Korka (n 47) 50.

54. Mackenzie (n 44) 35–36.

55. The exact origin of these stories is difficult to locate. Lord Elgin himself reiterated one in his testimony to the Select Committee of the House of Commons in 1816: *Report from the Select Committee of the House of Commons on the Earl of Elgin's Collection of Sculpted Marbles; &c*, Minutes of Evidence (29 February 1816) 41–2.

56. Beard (n 44) 85–86 and Mackenzie (n 44) 70 ff.

Chapter 2
A Story with Neither Hero Nor Villain

1. The term 'noble Earl' was used by the Select Committee of the House of Commons investigating the acquisition of the Marbles in 1816, as well as by Members of Parliament at the time of debating the acquisition; 'dull spoiler' and 'paltry antiquarian' come from Lord Byron in *Childe Harold's Pilgrimage* (1812–1818) Canto II and Notes; 'marble stealer' from poet Horace Smith, as quoted by Melina Mercouri in her speech to the Oxford Union, 12 June 1986.

2. The Ottoman Court in its diplomatic relations was referred to by the Turks and foreigners as the 'Sublime Porte' or 'Porte of Happiness', a reference to the gate through which diplomats were admitted into the imperial palace.

3. William St Clair, *Lord Elgin and the Marbles* (Oxford, Oxford University Press, 1998) 28. See also Dyfri Williams, 'Lord Elgin's *firman*' (2009) *Journal of the History of Collections* 1–28: his major successes were in assisting the expeditionary force in Egypt with equipment and food and in releasing Maltese slaves at Constantinople.

4. For his time in France and his financial troubles, see St Clair (n 3) chs 11 and 23 respectively; for his divorce see Theodore Vrettos, *The Elgin Affair: The True Story of the Greatest Art Theft in History* (New York, Arcade Publishing, 2011) Part Three ('The Trial').

5. St Clair (n 3) 84–85, 177, 259: from 1820 to 1841 he would serve in the House of Lords, but only as a representative Scottish peer.

6. Elgin and his family were on holiday in Belgrade from 15 June to 9 July 1801 when permission was secured on 6 July 1801: Williams (n 3) 16.

7. Letter from Elgin to Lusieri of 26 December 1801, as quoted in AH Smith, 'Lord Elgin and His Collection' (1916) 36 *The Journal of Hellenic Studies*, 206–08.

8. See Smith (n 7) 264–89, showing correspondence between Lusieri and Elgin from 1805 until 1821.

9. These variations of the spelling of names come from Tatiana Poulou, 'Giovanni Battista Lusieri, Lord Elgin's Unknown Agent and his Excavations in Athens', *200 Years: The Parthenon Sculptures in the British Museum: New Contributions to the Issue* (Athens, Society of Friends of the Acropolis, 2016).

10. Lusieri remained behind to complete drawings for Elgin in Constantinople, only arriving in Athens in April 1801.

11. St Clair (n 3) 96–99.

12. See Lord Elgin's testimony before the Select Committee of the House of Commons in 1816, Minutes of Evidence (29 February 1816) 31–33; also see Smith (n 7) 166 and St Clair (n 3) 6.

13. For an ethical assessment of this approach see pp 51-53.

14. Smith (n 7) 179–80.

15. St Clair (n 3) 66.

16. ibid 86: it is likely that the first *firman* arrived too late and the Disdar had already closed the citadel to foreigners by the time it arrived. See also Smith (n 7) 189–91.

17. See in particular the characterisation of Hunt by William G. Stewart in the Institute of Art and Law Annual Lecture, December 2000, as transcribed in 'The Marbles: Elgin or Parthenon' (2001) VI *Art Antiquity and Law* 37.

18. Hunt letter to Elgin, 22 May 1801, as reproduced in Smith (n 7) 186–89.

19. 1 July 1801, as reproduced in Smith (n 7) 190.

20. Lady Elgin wrote in a letter of 6 July 1801, 'Hunt became Mediator explained exactly what E. expected of [Pisani], saying E. insisted upon his translating literally whatever he gave him without Pisani's taking upon himself to alter his orders by way of pleasing the Turks. After a long confab Pisani thanked Hunt for his friendship & promised all that Man could promise': Williams (n 3) 16.

21. *Report from the Select Committee of the House of Commons on the Earl of Elgin's Collection of Sculpted Marbles; &c*, Minutes of Evidence (n 12) 40.

22. St Clair (n 3) 83–84.

23. St Clair (n 3) 87.

24. Williams (n 3) 1. *Contra* St Clair (n 3) 89, who claims it was Pisani.

25. St Clair (n 3) 89; Williams (n 3) 16.

26. St Clair (n 3) describes a return visit, at 92, while Williams (n 3) implies that all had occurred during a single visit, at 18.

27. Hunt's report to Elgin of 31 July 1801, quoted in Williams (n 3) àt 18.

28. Williams (n 3) 17: news would have reached Constantinople after the letter was issued, but Hunt noted the 'rumours' of success at Cairo when he was negotiating with the Voivode. At the end of the month, the Voivode would have heard from Constantinople about Cairo, which would have made him even more generous in relation to the Englishman's demands.

29. St Clair (n 3) 92–93.

30. ibid 91.

31. ibid 94.

32. ibid 95. This is estimated at between £1,500 and £2,000 per item in today's money. Williams (n 3) writes that later, upon Hunt's arrival, it was 340 piastres for the whole year, or approximately £28 at the time. Elgin's letter to Government in 1811 estimates £15,000 total for gifts to Ottoman officials and cost of labour, though this was an estimate because his accounts and papers were probably destroyed in France: *Report from the Select Committee* (n 12) Appendix 5, vii.

33. See *Report from the Select Committee* (n 12), Minutes of Evidence, Examination of Philip Hunt, 141–45. On the legal effect of bribery at the time, see pp 46-48.

34. Williams (n 3) 19.

35. St Clair (n 3) 93.

36. There is some confusion as to which metope went down first: Williams (n 3) 21.

37. Edward Daniel Clarke, as quoted in Christopher Hitchens, *The Elgin Marbles* (London, Chatto & Windus, 1987) 30.

38. Poulou (n 9) above in 'Giovanni Battista Lusieri' (2016), looked at Lusieri's account books in the Elgin archive, noting four houses taken down, for which the owners were paid and re-established elsewhere. There were 10 homes in total on the Acropolis.

39. See the drawing of the block *in situ* by Thomas Hope from the late 1790s: reproduced in Ian Jenkins, *The Parthenon Sculptures in the British Museum* (London, British Museum Press, 2007) 25. See also ch 1.

40. St Clair (n 3) 98.

41. Vasileia Manidaki, 'The Fragmentation of the Parthenon Frieze' in *200 Years: The Parthenon Marbles in the British Museum* (Athens, Society of the Friends of the Acropolis, 2016).

42. See the drawings of the works made at the time by Sir William Gell (1777–1836).

43. St Clair (n 3) 107–108.

44. It is worth noting that in September 1802, Elgin's brig the *Mentor* set sail with 17 cases in tow, containing 14 frieze pieces, including the two sides of the peplos scene. The ship then sunk off the coast of the island of Cerigo (modern day Kythera). Its cargo remained on the seabed until it was rescued by deep sea divers, a salvage operation only complete more than two years later. See Smith (n 7) 231, 241–59. It might be asked what harmful effect the salt water and debris would have had on those particular pieces of frieze.

45. ibid 45, 112.

46. One was confiscated from the aristocrat by the Revolutionaries in France, while another remained with Choiseul-Gouffier. Both are held at the Louvre in Paris today, in room 347. A further metope taken by Fauvel (south metope VI) ended up being seized by British ships under the law of prize and came into the Elgin Collection at the British Museum: see Smith (n 7) 357 ff.

47. St Clair (n 3) 107.

48. ibid ch 11.

49. It was in 1803 that a column from the Erechtheion was removed, along with one of the famous Caryatid figures that held up the portico roof.

50. St Clair (n 3) chs 12, 14, 18.

51. Poulou (n 9) 77.

52. The structuralist or functionalist school of Holocaust historiography is especially renowned, according to which the Holocaust was interpreted as the product of larger structural causes rather than the direct result of words or actions of specific individuals, such as Adolph Hitler. The leading proponents of this school are historians Hans Mommsen, Martin Broszat and Raul Hilberg.

53. See in particular the work of Bruno Latour on 'Actor-Network Theory', a theory he helped develop, especially *Reassembling the Social: An Introduction to Actor-Network Theory* (Oxford, Oxford University Press, 2005).

54. See eg Charles Swallow, *The Sick Man of Europe: Ottoman Empire to Turkish Republic, 1789–1923* (London, Ernest Benn, 1973).

55. See pp 21–22

Chapter 3
A *Firman* by Any Other Name

1. See the research work of Sarian Panahi, Zeynep Aygen and Orhan Sakin: 'No Official Ottoman Document Testifies Lawful Removal of Parthenon Sculptures' (*Archaeology*, 28 February 2019).

2. Dyfri Williams, 'Lord Elgin's *firman*' (2009) *Journal of the History of Collections* 1.

3. In 1962, while St Clair was researching the first edition of *Lord Elgin and the Marbles*: William St Clair, *Lord Elgin and the Marbles* (Oxford, Oxford University Press, 1998) 1.

4. Williams (n 2) 8.

5. Letter to her father of 9 July 1801, as quoted in ibid 16.

6. Vassilis Demetriades, 'Was the Removal of the Marbles Illegal?', Submission of the British Committee for the Restitution of the Parthenon Marbles, Appendix A, House of Commons Select Committee on the Illicit Trade (2000). Though Turkish expert Edhem Eldem seems to forgive these minimal inconsistencies: Edhem Eldem, 'From Blissful Indifference to Anguished Concern: Ottoman Perceptions of Antiquities, 1799–1869' in Zainab Bahrani, Zeynep Çelik and Edhem Eldem (eds), *Scramble for the Past: A Story of Archaeology in the Ottoman Empire, 1753–1914* (Istanbul, SALT, 2011) 285.

7. Bernard Lewis, Charles Pellat and Joseph Schacht (eds), *Encyclopaedia of Islam* (London, Brill, 1965) vol 2, 804 ('ferman').

8. Demetriades (n 6); and Williams (n 2) 11.

9. The role of the Cadi was to apply and enforce Sharia and state law known as 'kanun': *The Encyclopaedia of Islam* (1965) vol 4, 559 ('kanun').

10. *Encyclopaedia of Islam* (n 9) vol 1, 1357 ('buyuruldu').

11. Hunt had mentioned *firmans* in his guidebook for travellers: St Clair (n 3) 72.

12. See ch 2, Hunt's report to Elgin of 31 July 1801: quoted in Williams (n 2) 18.

13. ibid. Note also that Pisani in his 6 July 1801 letter to Elgin referred to it as a 'most complete letter'.

14. Turkish Ottoman scholar Edhem Eldem is at ease in his exhaustive study of the document with calling it a 'firman': Edhem, 'Blissful Indifference to Anguished Concern' (n 6) 284–87.

15. St Clair (n 3) app 1. St Clair sees the author as Pisani, Williams as Dané: (n 2) 1.

16. David Rudenstine had assessed whether the translation was somehow fraudulent, concocted by Hunt at the behest of Lord Elgin, though ultimately concluding that it probably was not, but rather an unsigned draft Pisani had presented to the Porte for consideration: David Rudenstine, 'A Tale of Three Documents: Lord Elgin and the Missing Historic 1801 Ottoman Document' (2001) *Cardozo Law Review* 22, 1853; 'Trophies for the Empire' (2021) *Cardozo Law Review* 39, 436–43. Williams (n 2) 8, rejects this, since the document explicitly states it is a translation and drafts would have been in Ottoman Turkish, not Italian.

17. Eldem, 'Blissful Indifference to Anguished Concern' (n 6) 298.

18. Williams (n 2) 8.

19. ibid translation of the letter and at 11.

20. Demetriades (n 6).

21. See chs 1 and 2.

22. AH Smith, 'Lord Elgin and His Collection' (1916) 36 *The Journal of Hellenic Studies* 192.

23. This is the interpretation favoured by JH Merryman, 'Thinking about the Elgin Marbles' (1985) 83 *Michigan Law Review* 1899.

24. *Report from the Select Committee of the House of Commons on the Earl of Elgin's Collection of Sculpted Marbles; &c*, Minutes of Evidence (29 February 1816) 35–36: when Lord Elgin was asked whether the permission applied to removing items from the walls of the edifice, he responded, 'I was at liberty to remove from the walls; the permission was to remove generally'. But when pressed as to whether statues were specified, he said he did not know.

25. This can be based on a line in the letter which states that there was 'no harm in the aforesaid images and the buildings being viewed' (and indeed Hunt's memorandum sought the liberty to take away sculptures or inscriptions 'which do not interfere with the works or walls of the Citadel'): see Geoffrey Robertson, 'Let's do a Brexit Deal with the Parthenon Marbles' *The Guardian* (4 April 2017); and Jeanette Greenfield, *The Return of Cultural Treasures* (Cambridge, Cambridge University Press, 2007).

26. This point was affirmed in my correspondence with Sibel Özel, Professor of Law at Marmara University, Turkey in 2015.

27. Merryman (n 23) 1899.

28. Harold Nicolson, 'The Byron Curse Echoes Again: Re-emergence of the Elgin Marbles, Taken from Greece in 1800, Awakens an Old Controversy' *New York Times* (27 March 1949).

29. Eldem, 'Blissful Indifference to Anguished Concern' (n 6) 286.

30. *Report from the Select Committee of the House of Commons* (n 24) 35.

31. These episodes are referred to in the writings of Charles Fellows who excavated the Nereid Temple at Xanthus, Ottoman Turkey in the 1840s, after obtaining a letter of permission from the Grand Vizier in Constantinople: Charles Fellows, *Memoirs* (1843) 12.

32. As an American court famously said about this standard a century ago, 'a bare preponderance is sufficient though the scales drop but a feather's weight': *Livanovitch v Livanovitch* (1926) 131 A. 799. For this reference, I would like to thank my colleague Professor Geoffrey Bennett.

33. Elena Korka, 'New Archival Evidence for the Chronicle of the Removal of the Parthenon Marbles by Lord Elgin' in *200 Years – The Parthenon Sculptures in the British Museum: New Contributions to the Issue* (Athens, Society of Friends of the Acropolis, 2016).

34. Merryman (n 23). But see *contra* David Rudenstein, 'Lord Elgin and the Ottomans: The question of permission' (2001–2002) *Cardozo Law Review* 23, 461 ff.

35. Korka (n 33).

36. Elena Korka in my interview with her, 14 May 2018.

37. Korka (n 33).

38. ibid.

39. William St Clair, mentions both 1804 and 1805 actions: (n 3) 136; Tatiana Poulou mentions only the 1805 ban, referring to it as a 'revocation': 'Giovanni Battista Lusieri, Lord Elgin's Unknown Agent and his Excavations in Athens' in *200 Years – The Parthenon Sculptures in the British Museum: New Contributions to the Issue* (Athens, Society of Friends of the Acropolis, 2016) 73.

40. See William St Clair, *Who Saved the Parthenon? A New History of the Acropolis Before, During and After the Revolution* (Open Book Publishing, 2022) 670–72, citing Alessia Zambon, *Aux origines de l'archéologie en Grèce – Fauvel et sa méthode* (Paris, INHA, 2014) 40, quoting a letter from Fauvel: 'Elgin emportrait tout si le maréchal Brune, à qui je fis connaître ce vandalisme, n'avait obtenu un ordre qui l'arrêta, Ce qui se voit encore de sculptures est dû a cet ambassadeur.'

41. See Poulou (n 39) 68, 73, fn 30.

42. Note, however, that the French Ambassador, who had secured the 1805 ban did plan to seize the cases of antiquities in Athens, though this was frustrated by logistical, financial and transport considerations: St Clair (n 40) 672, citing Zambon (n 40) 40–41.

43. Merryman (n 23).

44. St Clair (n 3) 155.

45. ibid 156–60.

46. Edhem, 'Blissful Indifference to Anguished Concern' (n 6) 292–93 (translations provided by Eldem).

47. ibid.

48. See ch 2 and St Clair (n 3) 91–93, citing Hunt's letter to Elgin.

49. St Clair (n 3) 110.

50. Elgin's 1811 letter to Sir Charles Long, offering his collection to the nation in return for expenses, estimated £15,000 for gifts and local workmen: *Report of the Select Committee* (n 24) app 5, *xiii*. A fair assumption would be that at least one-third of this amount was for gifts, while the rest was for material and labour. In a later postscript, Elgin has his 1803–1814 expenditures totalling approximately £5,000, of which about £1,375 is listed for 'presents' (about one-third).

51. St Clair (n 3) 156.

52. Elgin's 1811 letter to Long (n 24) xii.

53. Merryman (n 23) 1902.

54. Williams (n 2). This view has been supported more recently by Sir Noel Malcolm in his policy paper, 'The Elgin Marbles: Keep, Lend or Return? An Analysis' (*Policy Exchange*, 2023) 14–16.

55. Rudenstine (n 34) 466–69. Though Ottoman Turkey did not have an equivalent of Magna Carta on its statute books.

56. St Clair (n 3) (2nd edn) 157, cited in Rudenstine ibid.

57. William St Clair, 'Imperial Appropriations of the Parthenon' in JH Merryman (ed), *Imperialism, Art and Restitution* (Cambridge, Cambridge University Press, 2006) 79.

58. ibid 79–80.

59. *Black's Law Dictionary*, 11th edn (St Paul, Thomson Reuters, 2019).

60. See Articles 15–16 of the United Nations Convention Against Corruption (New York, 9 December 2003), ratified by 189 States.

61. *Encyclopaedia of Islam* (n 9) 451 ('rashwa').

62. Koran (Al Baqara/II, 188), in which the use of property as 'bait' to receive unfair advantages from judges is condemned.

63. In the *Hadith* (reports of the sayings of Mohammad): *Encyclopaedia of Islam* (n 9) 451 ('rashwa').

64. St Clair (n 3) 34.

65. *Report of the Select Committee* (n 24) 39.

66. In the 1670s, for example, two English travellers plied officials in Athens with three *okas* of coffee in order to gain access to the Acropolis: Molly Mackenzie, *Turkish Athens* (Reading, Ithaca Press, 1992) 35–36. Though bribery remained 'strictly forbidden' in Islam: *Encyclopaedia of Islam* (n 9) 451 ('rashwa').

67. Elgin's 1811 letter to Charles Long, *Report of the Select Committee* (n 24) app 1, xii.

68. *Encyclopaedia of Islam* (n 9) 451 ('rashwa').

69. Officials guilty of bribery could be dismissed: ibid.

70. Geoffrey Robertson, *Who Owns History?* (London, Biteback Publishing, 2019) 55 ff.

71. See also the International Council of Museums, conference resolution No. 5, 1983, referring to 'moral rights' to recover items taken during colonial or foreign occupation, in relation to the Parthenon Marbles, and the European Parliament Declaration of 1999, supported by 339 MEPs, referring to 'occupation' in this respect as well: Greenfield (n 25) 68.

72. Speech by Melina Mercouri, Oxford Union debate, 12 June 1986.

73. The Hellenic Ministry of Culture and Sport, *Memorandum on the Parthenon Marbles* (2000), submitted to the UK House of Commons Select Committee on Culture, Media and Sport, refers to

'Ottoman occupation' at 4. This remains the most comprehensive position of the Greek Government and is still linked on the Ministry's website: www.culture.gov.gr/en/parthenonas/.

74. Convention (II) with Respect to the Laws and Customs of War on Land and its annex: Regulations concerning the Laws and Customs of War on Land (The Hague, 29 July 1899) Art 42. This definition was adjusted slightly by the Hague Convention 1907, a version that governs to this day.

75. See generally Eyal Benvenisti, *The International Law of Occupation* (Oxford, Oxford University Press, 2012).

76. Richard Clogg, *The Movement for Greek Independence 1770-1821* (New York, Barnes & Noble, 1976) xiii.

77. St Clair (n 3) 43.

78. Mackenzie (n 66) 18, 34, 54, 105–106; and Patricia Vigderman, *The Real Life of the Parthenon* (Athens, Ohio, Ohio State University Press, 2018) 29. In 1771, the young Michael Paknanas had been accused by the Ottomans of fomenting rebellion during the Orlov Revolt and was executed. He was later canonised by the Greek Orthodox Church as St Michael the New Martyr: Mackenzie (n 66) 45–46.

79. Mackenzie (n 66) 54.

80. David Brewer, *The Greek War of Independence* (New York, Overlook Duckworth, 2011) 20. The full map can be seen on display at the Historical Archives Museum, Idra, Greece. Note also the existence of the *klephts*, who lived outside Ottoman control and would eventually play a pivotal role in the War of Independence.

81. Mackenzie (n 66) 89.

82. Lord Byron, *Childe Harold's Pilgrimage* (1812–1818).

83. Mackenzie (n 66) 99.

84. ibid 95, citing John Hobhouse, *A Journey through Albania* (1813). Note that Hobhouse was less sanguine about their chances of success, considering the servile and apathetic attitude of the higher classes, including the patriarchs: Clogg (n 76) xii.

85. The fledgling Greek administration would not have firm control over the territory until the Battle of Navarino in 1827, when France, Russia and Britain intervened, allowing the Hellenic State to establish itself more firmly that year. The Acropolis would be recaptured by the Ottomans, who would remain until 1833, one year after the establishment of the Kingdom of Greece.

86. Though it did so while remaining neutral until 1827, when France, Russia and Britain signed the Treaty of London which for the first time established commercial relations with Greece (thus recognising its independent status) and gave the Ottoman Empire one month to agree to an armistice, failing which they would intervene, which ultimately happened at Navarino: Brewer (n 80) 251. The retrospective application of a principle of 'occupation' onto the preceding period could arguably be analogous to interpreting episodes taking place in the early part of Nazi rule in Germany (1933-1935) in light of later developments.

87. See Benvenisti (n 75) 55 ff, 244.

88. Peter Stirk, *The Politics of Military Occupation* (Edinburgh, Edinburgh University Press, 2009) 44.

89. See International Court of Justice, Advisory Opinion, *Legal Consequences of the Construction of a Wall in the Occupied Palestinian Territory* (9 July 2004) para 78: the Court accepted the definition of 'occupation' from the 1907 Hague Convention (derived from the 1899 Hague Convention) and, as a result, held that Israel has continued to occupy the disputed areas since 1967.

90. See '800 Years of Myths' *Irish Times* (30 September 2000).

91. See the obligations on occupying powers in relation to: civilians and prisoners of war in the four Geneva Conventions, and three additional protocols; the rules of warfare in the Hague Conventions; the protection of cultural property in the Convention for the Protection of Cultural Property in the Event of Armed Conflict (Hague, 1954) and its two protocols (1954, 1999); and customary norms of international law.

92. Benvenisti (n 75) 7–9.

93. See Ilias Bantekas, 'Land Rights in Nineteenth Century Ottoman State Succession Treaties' (2015) 26 *European Journal of International Law* 375–90, which explains that some principles of Ottoman land law remain important to this day in relation to the ownership of land on Greek islands. The author also notes that Article 5 of the London Protocol of 1830 (where the Great Powers mediated peace between Greece and the Ottomans) required both territories to guarantee full protection of existing property rights to Christians and Muslims. Even 'tassaruf rights', stemming from the Sultan's ownership, were recognised by Greek courts well into the twentieth century: above, 385.

94. The leading views on what is known as normative ethics can be found in Simon Blackburn, *Ethics: A Very Short Introduction*, 2nd edn (Oxford, Oxford University Press, 2021).

95. Examples would include codes of ethics for universities (eg the Code of Ethics of Cambridge University, 2022), codes of ethics for accountants (eg the Code of Ethics of the International Ethics Standards Board of Accountants, 2018), and codes of professional conduct for lawyers (eg Principles and Code of Conduct for solicitors in England and Wales, 2011).

96. International Council of Museum, 'ICOM Code of Ethics for Museums' (2004, rebranded in 2017).

97. ibid Preamble: 'The Code reflects principles generally accepted by the international museum community.'

98. The ICOM Code of Ethics is the best source for such an examination as it is widely followed across the international museum sector. The British Museum, for instance, complies with and follows the ICOM Code: see British Museum, 'Acquisitions of Objects for the Collection' policy (2018), Annex 1.

99. ICOM Code (n 96) 2.2, 2.3.

100. ibid 2.4.

101. ibid 6.5.

102. Derek Fincham has chosen to apply the 'veil of ignorance' test derived from philosopher John Rawls in order to determine whether the actions would be deemed appropriate today: Derek Fincham, 'The Parthenon Sculptures and Cultural Justice' (2013) 23 *Fordham Intellectual Property, Media & Entertainment Law Journal* 943.

103. These can be referred to as limitations of actions, limitation periods or prescription periods. But note that in criminal law (for indictable offences such as murder), international law and human rights law, limitation periods generally do not apply.

104. See also the concept of 'moral title', as developed by Charlotte Woodhead, which is not subject to the same limits as legal title in relation to the passage of time, but which can also offer a wider variety of outcomes: Charlotte Woodhead, 'The Changing Tide of Title to Cultural Heritage Objects in UK Museums' (2015) 22 *International Journal of Cultural Property*, 229.

105. Alexander Herman, *Restitution: The Return of Cultural Artefacts* (London, Lund Humphries, 2021) 83. Such judgement is of course predicated on the fact that our own actions will be subject to the judgement of later generations.

Chapter 4
Albion's Verdict

1. Christopher Hitchens, *The Elgin Marbles: Should They be Returned to Greece?* (London, Chatto & Windus, 1987) 42–43; William St Clair, *Lord Elgin and the Marbles*, 3rd edn (Oxford, Oxford University Press, 1998) 99–100.

2. See *Report from the Select Committee of the House of Commons on the Earl of Elgin's Collection of Sculpted Marbles; &c*, (1816) xiv, reproducing Elgin's 1811 letter to Charles Long, Paymaster General, which quotes this amount.

3. St Clair (n 1) 163.

4. AH Smith, 'Lord Elgin and His Collection' (1916) 36 *The Journal of Hellenic Studies* 255.

5. St Clair (n 1) 179, 219–20.

6. ibid 245–46.

7. Lord Byron, *English Bards and Scotch Reviewers: A Satire* (1809).

8. *Report from the Select Committee* (n 2) 67 (Joseph Nollekins).

9. David Rudenstine, 'A Tale of Three Documents: Lord Elgin and the Missing Historic 1801 Ottoman Document' (2001) 22 *Cardozo Law Review* 1853; David Rudenstine, 'Lord Elgin and the Ottomans: the Question of Permission' (2002) 23 *Cardozo Law Review* 449.

10. *Report from the Select Committee* (n 2) 4–5.

11. ibid 5–7.

12. ibid 7.

13. Quoted in Smith (n 4) 342.

14. St Clair (n 1) 253.

15. See the speeches of Mr Bankes, who had chaired the Select Committee, and Mr Croker: *Hansard*, HC, Vol XXXIV, pp 1027–40 (7 June 1816).

16. Mr Curwen and Lord Milton, ibid; and, earlier, in February 1816, Mr Preston and Mr Brougham: *Hansard*, HC, Vol XXXII, p 824 ff (23 February 1816).

17. *Hansard*, HC, Vol XXXIV, pp 1027–40 (Mr Hammersley).

18. See entry for 'Hammersley, Hugh', in *The History of Parliament* (online), at www.historyofparliamentonline.org/volume/1790-1820/member/hammersley-hugh-1775-1840.

19. A slight irony is that, many years later, the British Museum did send one of the Marbles to Russia as a loan, part of the celebration of the bicentenary anniversary of the Hermitage in 2014. See p 81.

20. C AP XCIX, 26 G 2, c 22.

21. The British Museum Act 1963 removed the Trustee position reserved for the Earl of Elgin: see William G Stewart, 'The Marbles: Elgin or Parthenon?' (2001) VI *Art Antiquity and Law* 54.

22. Smith (n 4) 345–46.

23. Geoffrey Robertson, *Who Owns History?* (London, Biteback, 2019) 88–91; Rudenstine, 'A Tale of Three Documents' (n 9) 1853, 'Lord Elgin and the Ottomans: the Question of Permission' (2002) 23 *Cardozo Law Review* 449, 'Trophies for the Empire' (2021) *Cardozo Law Review* 39; Jules Dassin, *Memorandum on the Parthenon Marbles* (2000) submitted to the UK House of Commons Select Committee on Culture, Media and Sport.

24. See the British Museum website in two places: 'The Parthenon Sculptures' at www.britishmuseum.org/about-us/british-museum-story/contested-objects-collection/parthenon-sculptures, 'The Parthenon Sculptures: The Trustees' statement' at www.britishmuseum.org/about-us/british-museum-story/contested-objects-collection/parthenon-sculptures/parthenon.

25. *Report from the Select Committee* (n 2) 4.

26. Melina Mercouri, Oxford Union Debate, June 1986.

27. See, most recently, Sir Noel Malcolm's policy paper, 'The Elgin Marbles: Keep, Lend or Return? An Analysis' (*Policy Exchange*, 2023) 15–17.

28. *Report from the Select Committee* (n 2) 5; see also the examination of Hunt and Hamilton in the Minutes of Evidence, 54 ff, 140 ff.

29. ibid 131.

30. Quoted in St Clair (n 1) 210.

31. ibid 211. Though note that Hobhouse was not optimistic about the chances of the Greeks having a revolution independent of foreign aid: Richard Clogg, *The Movement for Greek Independence 1770–1821* (New York, Barnes & Noble, 1976) xi; Smith (n 4) 347.

32. Ellis Tinios, *The Art Newspaper* (1 December 2002).

33. ibid. See also Smith (n 4) 345–49, and more recently Malcolm (n 27) 18–21.

34. There is, however, some doubt as to when precisely this would have occurred. The War of Independence itself took a heavy toll on the Parthenon, as the Ottomans removed as many as 520 blocks from the remaining walls of the inner chambers and reincorporated them into fortifications, even extricating the lead joints in others to make bullets: see ch 5 and St Clair (n 1) 315. On the other hand, one piece that remained in Athens is today the best preserved stretch of the east frieze: the left part of Block VI.

35. See Charalambos Bouras, Maria Ioannidou and Ian Jenkins (eds), *Acropolis Restored*, British Museum Research Publication no 187 (London, British Museum Press, 2015).

36. See p 32.

37. Elgin's secretary William Hamilton and, later, the physicist Michael Faraday: St Clair (n 1) 286.

38. William St Clair, 'The Elgin Marbles: Questions of Stewardship and Accountability' (1999) 8 *International Journal of Cultural Property* 391. This took place in 1937 and 1938 at the behest of Lord Duveen but without the knowledge, initially, of museum management. It resulted in the removal of part of the ancient surface of many of the sculptures. When the actions were discovered they were ordered to be stopped. The full details of the episode came to light with the publication of the third edition of St Clair's book, *Lord Elgin and the Marbles*, in 1998 (n 1) ch 24. See also the short documentary entitled *The 'Cleaning' of the Elgin Marbles* by Waldemar Januszczak (ZCZ Films, 2013).

39. See Robertson (n 23) 81–82, 91–95; and St Clair (n 38).

40. Merryman wrote in 2006 about the fallout from that 'unseemly chapter' of the 1930s that to an 'interested foreign observer it might appear that Mr. St Clair has taken care not to underestimate the damage, while Mr. [Ian] Jenkins [of the British Museum] and Professor [John] Boardman, with comparable scrupulosity, are at pains not to overestimate it': JH Merryman, 'Whither the Elgin Marbles' in Merryman (ed), *Imperialism, Art and Restitution* (Cambridge, Cambridge University Press, 2006) 109.

41. The term comes from Article XX of the 1753 Act establishing the British Museum: *An Act for the Purchase of the Museum, etc. and for providing one General Repository for the better Reception and more Convenient Use of the said Collections, etc.* c. 22, Georgii II, A.D. 1753.

42. The Rosetta Stone had yet to be deciphered and Giovanni Belzoni had yet to return from Egypt with the large Pharaonic heads he had acquired (that of Ramses II would come only in 1821).

43. St Clair (n 1) 261.

44. Marjorie Caygill, *The Story of the British Museum* (London, British Museum Press, 2002) 14–16: There were complaints that the early tours rushed the visitors ('so rapidly were we hurried on through the departments', 'hackneyed through the rooms with violence').

45. ibid 16.

46. St Clair (n 1) 264.

47. Such as James Stuart and Nicholas Revett, *The Antiquities of Athens* (1762, 1789, 1794).

48. Mary Beard, *The Parthenon* (London, Profile Books, 2002) 19.

49. John Keats, 'On Seeing the Elgin Marbles' (1817).

50. For more on their impact, see St Clair (n 1) 261–80, and Yannis Hamilakis, *The Nation and its Ruins: Antiquity, Archaeology and National Imagination in Greece* (Oxford, Oxford University Press, 2007) 252.

51. Beard (n 48) 18.

52. In 1803, quoted in St Clair (n 1) 134.

Chapter 5
The History of a Claim

1. The story has been repeated by many, including Christopher Hitchens, William St Clair, Stephen Fry and Geoffrey Robertson: see for example Robert Browning's introduction to Christopher Hitchens, *The Elgin Marbles: Should they be Returned to Greece?* (London, Chatto & Windos, 1987) 24; Geoffrey Robertson, *Who Owns History? Elgin's Loot and the Case for Returning Plundered Treasure* (London, Biteback, 2019) 82; Stephen Fry on the television programme *QI*, S12E07, 23 March 2015. Note the recent analysis of its origins provided by William St Clair, *Who Saved the Parthenon?* (Open Source Books, 2022) 427–28.

2. An 1825 decree preserving antiquities within the archaeological schools, thus allowing them to set up museums, an 1826 decree preserving the monuments of Athens and an 1827 National Assembly resolution to prohibit the sale or export of antiquities: Daphne Voudouri, 'Law and the Politics of the Past: Legal Protection of Cultural Heritage in Greece' (2010) 17 *International Journal of Cultural Property* 548.

3. Edhem Eldem, 'From Blissful Indifference to Anguished Concern: Ottoman Perceptions of Antiquities, 1799–1869' in Zainab Bahrani, Zeynep Çelik and Edhem Eldem (eds), *Scramble for the Past: A Story of Archaeology in the Ottoman Empire, 1753–1914* (Istanbul, SALT, 2011) 298–308.

4. Mary Beard, *The Parthenon* (London, Profile Books, 2002) 101.

5. For this period generally, see Bruce Clark, *Athens: City of Wisdom* (London, Head of Zeus, 2022) 346–61.

6. Voudouri (n 2) 549. See also William St Clair, *Lord Elgin and the Marbles* (Oxford, Oxford University Press, 1998) 319.

7. Voudouri (n 2) 560, fn 11.

8. Lyndel Prott and Patrick O'Keefe, *Law and the Cultural Heritage*, Vol 1 (Abingdon, Professional Books, 1984) 36.

9. Words written in a circular by Governor Ioannis Kapodistrias, Greece's first head of state, who had also founded the museum: Voudouri (n 2) 548–49, 560, fn 10.

10. Drafted by a German, Georg Ludwig von Mauer, it was influenced by a Papal States law of 1820.

11. Prott and O'Keefe (n 8) 36; Voudouri (n 2) 549–57. Though note the existence of Sweden's Royal Placat of 1666.

12. Iakovos Rizos Neroulos: Voudouri (n 2) 547.

13. Alexandros Rizos Ragavis. He also said, 'We are gathering every stone of it as though it were a diamond, every fragment a relic. And erecting one of those machines around it to resurrect it, using the very same scaffolds Lord Elgin employed to take the temple apart. And let Europe, as witness to our deeds, judge whose efforts are nobler': from the *Minutes of the Archaeological Society general meeting of 12 May 1842*, Official Minutes of the Archaeological Society (1846) 157–159, as quoted in George Tolias, 'National Heritage and Greek Revival: Ioannis Gennadios on the Expatriated Antiquities' in

D Damaskos and D Plantzos, *A Singular Antiquity: Archaeology and Hellenic Identity in Twentieth-Century Greece* (Athens, Benaki Museum Publications, 2008) 59–60.

14. Letter by the Secretary for Ecclesiastical Affairs and Public Education of 6/18 July 1836, in General Archives of the State, *Akropolis von Athens* (Athens, Alitheia, 2014) 121.

15. Letter by the Secretary for Ecclesiastical Affairs and Public Education of 27 November / 9 December 1836, in General Archives of the State, *Akropolis von Athens*, ibid 121.

16. See Charles Holte Bracebridge letter to Trustees dated 21 April 1844.

17. Ian Jenkins, 'Acquisition and Supply of Casts of the Parthenon Sculptures by the British Museum, 1835–1939' (1990) in *Annual of British School at Athens* 85. There is a somewhat different account in St Clair (n 6) 333.

18. Frederic Harrison, 'Give Back the Elgin Marbles', *The Nineteenth Century* (1890).

19. City of Athens, Resolution no 1950, 3 December 1890, Archives of the City of Athens.

20. Only three years earlier, a young Harold Nicolson, then working at the Foreign Office, tried (without success) to persuade the Foreign Secretary to use the centenary of Byron's death at Missolonghi during the Greek War of Independence as an opportunity to return, as a start, the column from the Erechtheion: Hitchens (n 1) 73–74.

21. This claim was what prompted Ioannis Gennadios to write his treatise on the Marbles and antiquities looted in Greece, *Lord Elgin and Earlier Antiquarian Invaders in Greece, 1440–1837* (1930), which goes into some detail on the removal of the Marbles, then looks at 75 other examples of looting from the Ottoman period (the survey tellingly ends at the year of the Archaeological Society's founding, implying that at this point the serious looting ceased). Gennadios's proposal for the Marbles was for an incremental return, beginning with the pieces most necessary for the ongoing reconstruction by Nikolas Balanos: see Tolias (n 13).

22. For a detailed account of this episode, see Hitchens (n 1) 75–78.

23. ibid 79–80.

24. The speech text comes from the Melina Mercouri Foundation website, 'UNESCO in Mexico, July 29, 1982' under *Speeches*: www.melinamercourifoundation.com/en/unesco-in-mexico-july-29-1982.

25. Note also the resolution at the ICOM General Assembly in London in 1983, stressing the need to 'fulfil the moral rights of people to recover significant elements of their heritage dispersed as a consequence of colonial or foreign occupation': ICOM, Resolution No 5, 2 August 1983. For more, see Jeanette Greenfield, *The Return of Cultural Treasures*, 3rd edn (Cambridge, Cambridge University Press, 2007) 64.

26. *Hansard*, HC, Vol 38, Col 559–560 (7 March 1983).

27. Footage can be seen on the Melina Mercouri Foundation website: melinamercourifoundation.com/en.

28. Greenfield (n 25) 68.

29. For more, see ibid 70.

30. David Wilson, *The British Museum: A History* (London, British Museum Press, 2002) 322.

31. Footage from the Melina Mercouri website (n 27).

32. The conference was in Basel on 8 April 1982: Martin Bailey, 'Declassified Documents Reveal Near Return of Elgin Marbles' *The Art Newspaper* (1 February 2000).

33. ibid.

34. In January 1999, 339 Members of the European Parliament agreed to 'Written Declaration' 8/98 (non-binding) supporting Greece's cause for the return of the Marbles on the basis that they formed an integral part of European culture and architectural heritage and were removed from Athens during a period of occupation. It called on the UK Government to 'give positive consideration to Greece's request'.

35. Beard (n 4) 178.

36. *Seventh Report of the Select Committee for Culture, Media and Sport*, 18 July 2000.

37. These were then dealt with by subsequent Acts of Parliament: the Human Tissue Act 2004, s 47, and the Holocaust (Return of Cultural Objects) Act 2009, as to which see and pp 92-93.

38. An Advisory Panel on Illicit Trade was established by Howarth in 2000 which recommended instead that the UK accede to the 1970 UNESCO Convention on the Means of Prohibiting and Protecting the Illicit Import, Export and Transfer of Ownership of Cultural Property, which occurred in 2002.

39. Nigel Reynolds, 'British Museum Chief Quits after Two Years' *The Telegraph* (8 September 2001).

40. A formal diplomatic request had been renewed by Greece in January 2002: Anthee Carassava, 'Britain May 'Own' the Elgin Marbles but Greece Wants a Loan' *New York Times* (24 January 2002).

41. Venizelos called it 'counterproductive' in an interview with me, May 2018.

42. Letter from Chairman John Boyd to Minister Venizelos of 14 November 2002. I am grateful to Matthew Taylor for sharing a copy of the letter.

43. As quoted in Yannis Hamilakis, *The Nation and its Ruins: Antiquity, Archaeology, and National Imagination in Greece* (Oxford, Oxford University Press, 2007) 277, fn 46.

44. Venizelos had earlier stated that the longstanding proposal was 'to create a common, joint exhibition of the Parthenon Marbles. The Marbles may thus come to Athens for the 2004 Olympic Games … We are prepared to sign all necessary treaties … In any case, both countries are EU members': 'Deal on the Marbles?' (*Kathimerini*, 8 April 2003).

45. In May 2007 a meeting did take place between UK and Greek representatives at the British Museum, alongside representatives from the Museum and UNESCO. A press release thereafter from the Museum on 4 May 2007 reiterated the Trustees' position that they could not accept that all the Marbles be returned, even temporarily. Later, in 2010, the founder of EasyJet, Sir Stelios Haji-Ioannou, tried to orchestrate a resolution by suggesting an exchange of some of the Marbles for choice pieces from Greece. This ended when an arranged meeting with the Greek Prime Minister fell through, after which events such as the financial crisis intervened. I am grateful to Matthew Taylor for this information.

46. Voudouri (n 2) 554.

47. See the comprehensive list provided in the Epilogue to Alexandros Mantis, 'Disjecta Membra: The dismemberment and dispersal of the Acropolis Antiquities' in *200 Years – The Parthenon Sculptures in the British Museum: New Contributions to the Issue* (Athens, Society of Friends of the Acropolis, 2016) 35–50. The original number of metopes was 92 and of frieze blocks was 115.

48. The west frieze blocks were removed from the building by the Acropolis Antiquities Service in the early 1990s and placed in care. Many of these had been damaged over the years, including during the War of Independence and also by the pollution in Athens. See Mantis (n 46) 39.

49. From 'Prime Minister Costas Karamanlis visits Ancient Agora in Athens', Press Release of the Hellenic Ministry for Culture, 8 May 2007.

50. See British Museum Director Robert Anderson's piece in *The Times*, 15 January 2002: 'There is urgent need in Athens of a proper building for displaying the many sculptures of the Parthenon and other treasures that are currently lumbered in store-rooms … If symbolic gestures for 2004 [the year of the Olympics] are called for, there could be none better than Greece making sure that it properly displays what it already has.'

51. Beard (n 4) 168.

52. For other geographical and positional links between certain sculptures and the environment, see pp 14-16).

53. See Neil MacGregor's interview with Richard Morrison in *The Times*, 'The Marbles are not Greek. They don't need reuniting. The acquisition was legal. We do the same deals today', 7 November 2014. Note, however, that this argument had long been used by the Museum, even if it became more forceful during MacGregor's tenure: see Memorandum submitted by the British Museum to the House of Commons Select Committee for Culture, Media and Sport (2000), Annex IV, 9.11.2, which describes restitution as 'no more than the transport of the Sculptures from one museum into another'.

54. Ian Jenkins, *The Parthenon Sculptures in the British Museum* (London, British Museum Press, 2007).

55. See Memorandum submitted by the British Museum to the House of Commons Select Committee (2000), 5.2: 'Exchange-loans, however, require both parties to accept the right of the other to own the material'. See also the examination by the Committee of British Museum representatives on 8 June 2000, notably the focus on this issue by the Chair of Trustees, Graham Greene, who worried mostly about 'legal impediments' in returning loaned items from Greece. For more on this issue see pp 98-102.

56. Interview with Matthew Taylor, 13 February 2018.

57. ibid. And see Robertson (n 1) xx–xxii.

58. I would like to thank Matthew Taylor for these details.

59. *Altmann et al v Republic of Austria*, 541 U.S. 677 (2004), US Supreme Court; Decision of Austrian Arbitral Court, Vienna, 15 January 2006.

60. For more detail on this matter see Martha Lufkin, 'A Sea-Snake at the Austrian National Gallery' (2006) XI *Art Antiquity and Law* 351 and, more generally, Anne-Marie O'Connor, *The Lady in Gold: The Extraordinary Tale of Gustav Klimt's Masterpiece* (London, Penguin, 2015).

61. The 'right to property' is protected at Art 1 of the First Protocol to the European Convention on Human Rights (Rome, 4 November 1950). The 'right to culture' is far less established, though on the topic see the European Court of Human Rights – Research Division, 'Cultural Rights in the Case-Law of the European Court of Human Rights' (2017).

62. Details from Matthew Taylor.

63. The group was the Tasmanian Aboriginal Centre. For more on that dispute, see Margaret Clegg and Sarah Long, 'The Natural History Museum and Human Remains' in Ruth Redmond-Cooper (ed), *Heritage Ancestry and Law: Dealing with Historical Human Remains* (Builth Wells, Institute of Art and Law, 2015).

64. The case before the Court of Appeal of England and Wales was *Republic of Iran v Barakat Galleries* [2007] EWCA 1374.

65. See footage released by Associated Press on 3 August 2015: www.youtube.com/watch?v= 8y0gNr3lkk8.

66. See George Vardas, 'The Empire Museum Strikes Back' *eKathimerini* (16 December 2014).

67. See British Museum website. Currently there are 1,400 objects out on long-term loan: www. britishmuseum.org/our-work/national/uk-touring-exhibitions-and-loans/long-term-loans.

68. The term 'normalise' comes from an interview by the author with Ian Jenkins, 14 March 2018.

69. Jonathan Jones, 'Defining Beauty Review – Greek Sculpture Alive and Kicking' *The Guardian* (23 March 2015).

70. Interview with Lydia Koniordou, 17 May 2018.

71. 'Parthenon Sculptures: A New Way Forward?' *Neos Kosmos* (3 September 2019).

72. Yannis Andritsopoulos, 'Revealed: Parthenon Marbles were pillaged and should be returned to Greece, Boris Johnson argued as student' *Ta Nea* (18 December 2021).

73. Boris Johnson, 'Elgin Goes to Athens: The President Marbles at the Grandeur that was (in) Greece' *Debate* (Spring 1986) 22.

74. Speech at Ouagadougou, Burkina Faso, 28 November 2017.

75. On the full history of the Benin Bronzes and claims relating thereto, see Barnaby Phillips, *Loot: Britain and the Benin Bronzes* (London, OneWorld, 2022).

76. For more on the global developments around restitution, see Alexander Herman, *Restitution – The Return of Cultural Artefacts* (London, Lund Humphries, 2021).

77. Decision 22.COM 6 of the Intergovernmental Committee for Promoting the Return of Cultural Property to its Countries of Origin or its Restitution in Case of Illicit Appropriation, Paris, 22nd Session, 27–29 September 2021.

78. Gareth Harris, 'Greece in Talks with Louvre to Borrow Parthenon Frieze as Part of "Temporary Exchange"' *The Art Newspaper* (27 August 2019).

79. See Acropolis Museum Press Release, 'The first return of a Parthenon sculpture from abroad to the new Acropolis Museum', 10 January 2022: 'The significance of this return does not lie in the long-term nature of the deposit of the fragment to the monument to which it belongs, the Parthenon frieze at the Acropolis Museum, but in the prospect of remaining here permanently (sine die), following the initiative launched by the Independent Regional Authority of Sicily towards the Italian Ministry of Culture.' Note that on 25 February 2022, the Italian Ministry of Culture indicated that it would begin the procedure for declassifying the piece from the national registry, thus providing for its permanent transfer: see Italian Ministry of Culture (MIC) statement, 25 February 2022.

80. This followed an earlier loan of the Vatican pieces to Athens in 2008–2012. Earlier, in 2006, the University of Heidelberg in Germany had permanently returned a fragment, also a foot, this one from the north frieze.

81. Greek Prime Minister Kyriakos Mitsotakis appearing on *Good Morning Britain*, 16 November 2021.

82. ibid.

83. According to a Downing Street spokesperson: Greg Heffer, 'Elgin Marbles: Boris Johnson Tells Greek PM Kyriakos Mitsotakis that Dispute over Parthenon Sculptures is "Matter for British Museum"' (*Sky News Online*, 16 November 2021).

84. Statement by Prime Minister Kostas Karamanlis, 7 May 2007.

85. Interview on *Leading Britain's Conversation* with Andrew Marr, 15 June 2022.

86. Gareth Harris, 'British Museum Proposes New "Parthenon Partnership" with Greece in Bid to End Deadlock over Marbles' *The Art Newspaper* (1 August 2022).

87. Yannis Andritsopoulos, 'Exclusive: Head of British Museum Held Secret Talks with Greek PM, Officials to Agree Deal for Parthenon Marbles' Return' (*Ta Nea* (English translation provided by the journalist), 3 December 2022).

88. Including former UK Culture Secretary Ben Bradshaw (Labour), actor Stephen Fry, journalist Sarah Baxter (*The Times*) and Members of the House of Lords Baroness Catherine Meyer (Tory) and Lord Michael Dobbs (Tory).

89. Katie Razzall, 'Parthenon Sculptures Belong in UK, Says Culture Secretary Michelle Donelan' (*BBC*, 11 January 2023); Aubrey Ellegretti, 'No Plans to Return Parthenon Marbles to Greece, says Rishi Sunak' *The Guardian* (13 March 2023).

90. Charities Act 2022, ss 15–16 (still to be brought into force by the Secretary of State).

91. Alexander Herman, 'Museums, Restitution and the New Charities Act' (2022) XXVII *Art Antiquity and Law* 193.

Chapter 6
The (un)titled Masterpiece

1. London solicitor Ed Powles of Maurice Turnor Gardner LLP in conversation, 2016.

2. Roy Goode and Ewan McKendrick, *Goode on Commercial Law*, 5th edn (London, Penguin 2016).

3. ibid 2.03.

4. Also note that a lien can be registered under the Bills of Sale Acts 1878 and 1882.

5. Sir Fredrick Pollock, 'An Essay on Possession in the Common Law' (Oxford, Clarendon Press, 1888). Thank you to barrister Luke Harris for alerting me to this passage.

6. This is done by bringing a civil action in the tort of conversion and seeking an order for delivery up: Torts (Interference with Goods) Act 1977.

7. See *Armory v Delamirie* [1722] EWHC KB J94 and *Parker v British Airways Board* [1982] 1 QB 1004.

8. See Treasure Act 1996, ss 4–6. The rules apply in Wales too. For the Duchies of Lancaster and Cornwall the vesting is in favour of the Crown's franchisee.

9. On deeds generally see *Halsbury's Laws of England*, 'Deeds and other Instruments', Vol 32 (LexisNexis Butterworths, 2012).

10. See Sale of Goods Act 1979, s 21; see also the rules around sales by 'mercantile agents' under the Factors Act 1889, sales under a voidable title and by a seller or buyer in possession to a good faith buyer: Sale of Goods Act 1979, ss 23–25.

11. For sale, see Sale of Goods Act 1979, s 21.

12. Limitation Act 1980, s 2 for actions founded on tort and s 5 for actions founded on simple contract.

13. See Lord Nicholls in *Kuwait Airways v Iraq Airways* [2002] UKHL 19.

14. Limitation Act 1980, s 3(2).

15. Limitation Act 1980, s 3(1).

16. Limitation Act 1980, s 4.

17. For a definition of good faith, see Sale of Goods Act 1979, s 61(3).

18. See Limitation Act 1939 at ss 2–3. For an example, see *RB Policies at Lloyds v Butler* [1950] 1 K.B. 76.

19. Italian Civil Code, Art 1153.

20. Japanese Civil Code, Art 192.

21. German Civil Code, Art 935(2).

22. In France, possession equals title ('*possession vaut titre*') and such title cannot be disturbed by an original owner beyond the three years counting from the loss or theft of the property: Civil Code, Art 2276.

23. *Winkworth v Christie Manson and Woods Ltd and Another* [1980] Ch 496.

24. Slade J in *Winkworth* referred to five exceptions to *lex situs*: see below at p 98.

25. See ch 5.

26. See Professor Sibel Özel, presentation to Institute of Art and Law, London, 27 June 2015.

27. This can be compared to situations that may arise today in which architectural sculptures are considered 'fixtures' and thus continually part of the building or monument to which they were originally affixed. In England this is often governed by the Planning (Listed Buildings and Conservation Areas) Act 1990, s 1(5), for listed buildings. Civil law countries may have principles like 'immovables by destination' by which integral parts of immovables (like buildings) can never become legally distinct

'movable property'. However, such principles are generally not known to operate inter-jurisdictionally, nor indeed retroactively.

28. See Ernest Lorenzen, 'Story's Commentaries on the Conflict of Law', *Harvard Law Review*, November 1934.

29. Jean-Louis de Lolme, *The Constitution of England* (1771).

30. *An Act for the Purchase of the Museum, etc*, C.A.P. XXII, GeorgII II, c. 22, at IX.

31. See examples such as the National Gallery Act 1856.

32. British Museum Act 1963, ss 3(1) and (3).

33. ibid s 3(4).

34. ibid s 5(1).

35. ibid.

36. As provided for under the British Museum Act 1963, s 3(4), in conjunction with s 6 of the Museums and Galleries Act 1992, and s 9.

37. Human Tissue Act 2004, s 47.

38. Holocaust (Return of Cultural Objects) Act 2009, ss 1–2.

39. See pp 71-73, 77.

40. See Explanatory Memorandum of the Museum Secretary, 1963, as well as the Parliamentary Debates, House of Commons, 9 April 1963, vol 248, col 958 (Lord Shackleton), as quoted in Elizabeth Pearson, 'Old Wounds and New Endeavours: The Case for Repatriating the Gweagal Shield from the British Museum' (XXI) *Art Antiquity and Law* 201 (Oct 2016).

41. British Museum De-accession Policy (29 September 2018) 3.5.

42. Alexander Herman, 'British Museum must Recognise its own Powers in Matters of Restitution' *The Art Newspaper* (29 May 2019); a legal opinion to this effect was provided by Samantha Knights QC in August 2021 for the Scheherazade Foundation, as reported in *The Guardian* (11 October 2021).

43. Included in the response of the Secretary of State Kim Howells to a question in Parliament on 24 May 2002: HC Deb 24 May 2002 c646W.

44. See in this respect the statement by the Director of the British Museum before the House of Commons Select Committee on Culture, Media and Sport, Minutes of Evidence, 8 June 2000: 'If the object had been acquired within the statute of limitations, we would certainly consider the possibility of returning that object. We have returned objects, not from abroad, but objects which have been stolen from this country, within that period in recent years.'

45. Memorandum submitted by the British Museum to the House of Commons Select Committee on Culture, Media and Sport (2000) 3.2. These items later re-entered the Museum's collection through the Acceptance in Lieu tax scheme in 1998.

46. See recommendations for the 'legal assessment' of a claim in the recent *Restitution and Repatriation: A Practical Guide for Museums in England* published by Arts Council England (2022) 16–17.

47. British Museum, 'Acquisition of Objects for the Collection' (6 December 2018) 2.1.

48. ibid 2.2.

49. *Combating Illicit Trade: Due Diligence Guidelines for Museums, Libraries and Archives on Collecting and Borrowing Cultural Material*, s 3, setting out the basic principles and the '1970 threshold'.

50. Museums Association, *Code of Ethics* (2015) 2.5, and ICOM, *Code of Ethics* (2004/2017) 2.3.

51. See, as an example, the Metropolitan Museum in New York returning the golden Nedjemakh sarcophagus to Egypt in February 2019: Nancy Kenney, 'Looted Coffin Acquired by Metropolitan Museum is Headed Back to Egypt' *The Art Newspaper* (26 September 2019).

52. Limitation Act 1980, ss 3(2), 4.

53. See ch 3.

54. *Re Snowden* [1970] Ch 700.

55. *Attorney General v Trustees of the British Museum* [2005] EWHC 1089 Ch.

56. In the end the Trustees agreed to offer an ex gratia payment of money, which was approved by the Spoliation Advisory Panel, as it could be ordered under the Panel's Terms of Reference, s 16(c) [now s 17(c)]: see *Report of the Spoliation Advisory Panel in Respect of Four Drawings Now in the Possession of the British Museum*, HC 1052, 27 April 2006.

57. See *Attorney General v Trustees of the British Museum* [2005] EWHC 1089 (Ch) para 43. Though note that, as a general principle of procedure before the English courts, a limitation argument must always be raised by the defendant in a case, so the court's statement here might be questioned.

58. ibid para 8.

59. See Law Commission, *Technical Issues in Charity Law – Analysis of Responses* (2017) 11.68–11.71.

60. Law Commission, *Technical Issues in Charity Law* (May 2017) 11.48–11.50, recommendation 30. Note that national institutions, including the British Museum, are charities under the Charities Act 2011, though they fall within a group of 'exempt charities', as listed in Sch 3: this means their 'principal regulator' is not the Charity Commission but the Department for Culture, Media and Sport. They can nevertheless avail themselves of the Charity Commission's support powers. The details of this are set out in *Memorandum of Understanding between the Charity Commission for England and Wales and the Department for Culture, Media and Sport* (18 November 2010) 3.5.8–3.5.10.

61. Charities Act 2022, s 16. Also included in the legislation was a provision that would allow trustees to make ex gratia applications of charity property without authorisation from the Charity Commission, Attorney General or the court, but only if under a certain value threshold, which would depend on the gross income of the charity: Charities Act 2022, s 15. For more on the changes, see Alexander Herman, 'Museums, Restitution and the New Charities Act' (October 2022) *Art Antiquity and Law* 27.

62. Charity Commission, *Ex Gratia Payments by Charities*, Guidance CC7, 9, quoting *Snowden* [1970].

63. ibid.

64. Arts Council England, *Restitution and Repatriation* (n 46) 14–17. See also Herman (n 61) 27, 215–16.

65. Charity Commission decisions regarding the 72 Benin Bronzes to be returned to Nigeria by the Horniman Museum and Gardens (August 2022) and the 116 Benin Bronzes to be returned to Nigeria by Cambridge University (December 2022). For more on these, see Herman (n 61) ibid 209–13.

66. This came as a result of a blog post of mine on the Institute of Art and Law Blog and a subsequent report on the matter by Dalya Alberge in *The Guardian* (25 September 2022).

67. *R v Secretary of State for the Home Department, ex parte Fire Brigades Union and others* [1995] 2 AC 513 (House of Lords, *per* Lord Browne-Wilkinson, Lord Lloyd and Lord Nicholls); *RM (AP) v The Scottish Ministers (Scotland)* [2012] UKSC 58 (Supreme Court, *per* Lord Reid). I am indebted to solicitor Hugh Johnson-Gilbert for bringing these cases to my attention.

68. *Winkworth v Christie Manson and Woods* [1980] Ch 496, 5.

69. Moses J in *City of Gotha v Sotheby's and Cobert Finance SA* [1998] EWHC, Case No 1993 C 3428, 1997 G 185.

70. *Kuwait Airways v Iraq Airways* [2002] UKHL 19.

71. See eg *US v Portrait of Wally*, 2009 US Dist Ct, 663 F. Supp. 2d 232 (Southern District Court of New York), *per* Judge Preska, where it was found that the US criminal legislation (the National Stolen Property Act) could apply, despite the fact that title to the painting had been acquired by the Leopold Foundation under the laws of Austria; and *Reif and Frankel v Nagy*, Supreme Court of New York, County of New York, Commercial Decision, Index no. 161799/2-15, 4 April 2018, affirmed by Appellate Division, 9 July 2019, where title to two artworks was ordered vested in the plaintiffs despite defendant art dealer having acquired, and held, title to the property under English law: on this, see Alexander Herman, 'New York Court's Affirmation of Holocaust Expropriated Art Recovery Act Brings Added Challenges to Art Dealers' (April 2018) *Art Antiquity and Law* 23.

72. Alexander Herman, 'What's in a Title? It's Time to Reframe the Parthenon Marbles Debate' *The Art Newspaper* (22 March 2019).

73. 'The Parthenon Sculptures: The Trustees' Statement', British Museum website: www.britishmuseum.org/about-us/british-museum-story/contested-objects-collection/parthenon-sculptures/parthenon.

74. British Museum Act 1963, s 4.

75. British Museum Loans Policy (7 November 2019) 2.4.

76. British Museum, Master Loan-Out Form, 18 July 2018.

77. As an example close at hand, see the British Museum Loans Policy in relation to the Museum requesting loans from lenders, 2.8.

78. Yannis Andritsopoulos, 'Experts Sense Major Shift in British Museum's Stance on Allowing Parthenon Marbles' Return to Greece' (*Ta Nea*, 12 February 2022) [English translation provided by journalist].

79. Tom Seymour, 'British Museum's Chairman Suggests Hybrid Deal with Greece over Parthenon Marbles' *The Art Newspaper* (17 February 2023).

80. Graham Greene, Chairman of the British Museum Trustees before the House of Commons Select Committee on Culture, Media and Sport, Minutes of Evidence, 8 June 2000, 601. This refrain has been taken up more recently by Sir Noel Malcolm in 'The Elgin Marbles: Keep, Lend or Return? An Analysis' (2023) *Policy Exchange* 51–56.

81. Alex Marshall, 'After 220 Years, the Fate of the Parthenon Marbles Rests in Secret Talks' *New York Times* (17 January 2023); George Parker, Eleni Varvitsioti and James Pickford, 'Acropolis Now' *Financial Times* (11 February 2023).

82. Charles Moore, 'What is George Osborne's Game of Marbles?' *The Telegraph* (10 January 2023); Parker, Varvitsioti and Pickford (n 81).

83. British Museum Loans Policy (7 November 2019) 2.4: 'the Trustees will normally expect the borrower to provide assurance of immunity from judicial seizure or comparable assurance from a government body or representative of appropriate authority.'

84. According to its website, the British Museum has lent to the National Archaeological Museum, the Museum of Cycladic Art and even to the Acropolis Museum: British Museum website, *The Parthenon Sculptures* ('Status of Discussions'): www.britishmuseum.org/about-us/british-museum-story/contested-objects-collection/parthenon-sculptures. For more on this, see the discussion at pp 141-42.

85. The list includes Australia, Austria, Belgium, the Czech Republic, Canada, Finland, Germany, Israel, Japan, Lichtenstein, the United Arab Emirates and the US.

86. See *Museums Board of Victoria v Carter* [2005] FCA 645 (Federal Court of Australia).

87. Paul Daley, 'Battle for Bark Art: Indigenous Leaders Hail Breakthrough in Talks with British Museum' *The Guardian* (9 February 2016).

88. *Trade and Cooperation Agreement between the European Union and the European Atomic Energy Community, of the one part, and the United Kingdom of Great Britain and Northern Ireland, of the other part*, Part Two, Title 1 (GOODS), Art 21(1) requiring cooperation to facilitate return, and Art 21(3)(ii) defining 'illicitly removed' to include goods 'not returned at the end of a period of lawful temporary removal'. Note that such an agreement would not apply to cultural property removed from its country of origin before 1993, so it could never be used by Greece as a basis to claim the Marbles.

89. Art 5(1) permits the request to be made for illegally exported cultural objects, while Art 5(2) defines 'illegally exported' so as to include objects temporarily exported for purposes such as exhibition under a permit and not returned in accordance with the terms of that permit. For more on the Convention, see Lyndel V Prott, *Commentary on the 1995 Unidroit Convention*, 2nd edn (Builth Wells, Institute of Art and Law, 2021).

90. Greece acceded in 2007 (2008 entry into force), with a declaration under Art 16: were a request for return of an illegally exported cultural object to be made by a Contracting State, it would have to be submitted first to the Hellenic Ministry of Culture-Directorate General of Antiquities and Cultural Heritage which would forward the request to the competent court in Greece: see Unidroit Convention, 'Declarations made by States at the time of ratification/accession under Article 16'.

91. See p 74. The British Museum had publicly supported the adoption by the UK of the Unidroit Convention in 2000, along with the UNESCO Convention, as seen in a statement made by its then Director to the House of Commons Select Committee on Culture, Media and Sport, Minutes of Evidence (8 June 2000) 642.

92. See the British Museum's *Art in Crisis* programme run by curator St John Simpson and its impressive work in helping to restore some 2,345 illegally trafficked objects to Afghanistan, Iraq and Uzbekistan: www.britishmuseum.org/blog/art-crisis-identifying-and-returning-looted-objects. Sadly such projects tend to be overlooked in the media, largely at the expense of the unresolved Parthenon Marbles dispute.

93. Marshall (n 81); Parker, Varvitsioti and Pickford (n 81).

94. See Victoria & Albert Museum press release, 1 July 2022.

95. Norman Palmer, *Palmer on Bailment*, 3rd edn (Sweet and Maxwell, 2009). Note a bailee cannot 'deviate' from the terms of a bailment and doing so makes the bailee an insurer of the goods.

96. See *Coggs v Bernard* [1703] 2 Ld Raym 909, 915–16.

97. I would like to thank Katerina Vagia for her and her colleagues' assistance with Greek legal terms.

98. Acropolis Museum Press Release, 'The first return of a Parthenon sculpture from abroad to the new Acropolis Museum', 10 January 2022. See ch 5. The Greek term for this is Κατάθεση με σκοπό την επ' 'αόριστον παραμονή (translating as 'deposit for the purpose of an indefinite stay').

99. For example, in France, the Louvre Museum received Francisco Goya's *Portrait of the Marquise de la Solana* (1794–95) from Carlos de Beistegui in 1942 and the Orsay Museum received Paul Cézanne's *Portrait of Gustave Geffroy* from the granddaughter of Auguste Pellerin in 1969, both works given under reserve of a usufruct ('sous réserve d'usufruit'). This means title would have transferred to the institutions, but the donors would have kept the works until their death, reserving all 'fruits' derived

from the goods. The author would like to thank French lawyer Anne-Sophie Nardon for her clarification of this point.

100. For more on this, see ch 10.

Chapter 7
Wellington and International Law

1. David Gilks, 'Attitudes to the Displacement of Cultural Property in the Wars of the French Revolution and Napoleon' (2013) *The Historical Journal* 56, 113.

2. See Treaty of Campo Formio, 1797, between France and Austria, and the Treaty of Tolentino, 1797, between France and the Vatican.

3. Margaret Miles, *Art as Plunder: The Ancient Origins of Debate About Cultural Property* (Cambridge, Cambridge University Press, 2010) 341; Dorothy Mackay Quynn, 'The Art Confiscations of the Napoleonic Wars' (1945) 50 *The American Historical Review* 437, 444–59. Though note the difficulty in obtaining an exact figure, especially in relation to the other objects confiscated, such as manuscripts and jewels.

4. See Quynn (n 3) 459.

5. Wellington letter to Viscount Castlereagh of 23 September 1815, published in *The Times* (14 October 1815) and laid before Parliament on 2 February 1816.

6. ibid. In his letter, Wellington also responded categorically to any claims that, by doing so, he had violated the Military Convention between the French Army and the Allied Armies of 3 July 1815 (the 'Convention of Saint-Cloud'), Art 11 of which protected public property. According to Wellington, at the time of the Convention's signing he had purposely omitted a provision requested by the French Commissioners to protect 'the Museum, or galleries of pictures' and so Art 11 must not be interpreted so as to include such property.

7. For more on Canova's mission, see Tullio Scovazzi, 'Evolutionary Trends as regards the Return of Removed Cultural Property' in Luis Durbán and Antonio Lazari (eds), *El tráfico de bienes culturales* (Valencia, Tirant lo Blanch, 2015) 26. See also Giancarlo Cunial, *Canova. Le molte vite* (Veneto, Acelum 2022).

8. British Foreign Secretary Viscount Castlereagh, note of 11 September 1815 to the Allied Ministers assembled at Paris. Castlereagh added, in relation to the newly restored French King, Louis XVIII, that 'If we are really to return to peace and ancient maxims, it cannot be wise to preserve just so much of the abuses of the past; nor can the king desire … to perpetuate in his house this odious monopoly of the arts'.

9. ibid.

10. The only noteworthy exception to this came before Castlereagh's statement when Prussian agents had in July 1815 seized two paintings from French palaces to be used as 'guarantees' in response to protests by the French: Quynn (n 3) 450.

11. See Quynn (n 3).

12. Provided for by the Chaptal Decree of 1801. Note that today many works remain at provincial museums, such as those in Lyon, Bordeaux and Dijon.

13. See Cynthia Saltzman, *Plunder: Napoleon's Theft of Veronese's Feast* (London, Thames & Hudson, 2021) 216–20; Bénédicte Savoy, '1815. Année zéro. L'Europe à l'heure des restitutions d'oeuvres d'art', Lecture series, Collège de France, Session 9 (Paris, 19 April 2019): www.college-de-france.fr/agenda/cours/1815-annee-zero-europe-heure-des-restitutions-oeuvres-art.

14. Miles (n 3) 341; Quynn (n 3) 459.

15. Alexander Herman, *Restitution – The Return of Cultural Artefacts* (London, Lund Humphries, 2021) 9–16. Though do note that Gilks situates the returns within a wider cultural context, which was by no means uniform: Gilks (n 1) 141–43.

16. For a view into international law on the eve of the French Revolution, see GF von Martens' writings on the laws of war, in which the author explains that the practice of taking art as spoils of war had fallen out of use in the eighteenth century. If the right to spoils had not been proscribed by positive law, it appeared to be limited only to extreme situations (against a State that had itself violated the rules of war, against a town taken by assault or for the purposes of reprisals): Georges Friedrich von Martens,

Précis du droit des gens moderne de l'Europe (1789); see also Xavier Perrot, 'La restitution internationale des biens culturels aux XIXe et XXe siècles' (thesis) (Limoges, Université de Limoges, 2005) 23.

17. Viscount Castlereagh, Note to the Allied Ministers, 11 September 1815.

18. *The Marquis de Somerueles* [1813] Stewart's Vice Admiralty Reports 482 (Nova Scotia).

19. ibid.

20. William Richard Hamilton's letter to the Earl of Bathurst, Secretary of State for War, 1815, quoted in Quynn (n 3). Interestingly, in his letter to Talleyrand of 16 September, Denon (wrongly) assumes that Britain's interest was in depleting the Louvre in order to enrich itself, citing as justification the acquisition of the Parthenon Marbles: Quynn (n 3) 451.

21. Savoy (n 13). Though also note Savoy's reference to the Greek writer (Andrea Mustoxidi) who at the time compared the four bronze horses returned to Venice with the Parthenon Marbles.

22. James Crawford, 'Napoleon 1814–1815: A Small Issue of Status' in *International Law in the Long Nineteenth Century* (Boston/Leiden, Brill, 2019) 18, citing Andrzej Jakubowski, *State Succession in Cultural Property* (Oxford, Oxford University Press, 2015) and, elsewhere on this point, Wayne Sandholtz, *Prohibiting Plunder: How Norms Change* (Oxford, Oxford University Press, 2008).

23. As set out in the Statute of the International Court of Justice, Art 38.

24. See *North Sea Continental Shelf Cases [Germany v Denmark and the Netherlands]* (1969) ICJ 1.

25. See *Nicaragua v United States* (1986) ICJ 14. And see also the International Committee for the Red Cross, *Study on Customary International Humanitarian Law* (Cambridge, Cambridge University Press, 2005).

26. Emer de Vattel, *Droit des gens* (1758), translated as '*Law of Nations*'.

27. Yue Zhang, 'The Right to Restitution of Cultural Property Removed as Spoils of War during Nineteenth-century International Warfare' *University of Pennsylvania Journal of International Law* [2021] 1097, 1112–22.

28. See eg Hugo Grotius, *De Iure Belli ac Pacis* (The Law of War and Peace), Book III (1625), in which the author sets out the right of States to prizes in war under the law of nations, only to then call on States to moderate their actions in the name of reason and moderation: see Book III, Ch 12, V and VI.

29. Grotius (n 28) and de Vattel (n 26), Book III, Ch 9.

30. See Savoy (n 13) on how, apart from the Veronese, it was predominantly the lesser valued works that were left behind, considered not to be worth the cost and effort of transport (eg the Florentine commissioners focused on the great works from the Palazzo Pitti and left behind others that 'were not worth the cost of travel'): Session 9, Paris, 19 April 2019.

31. Zhang (n 27) 1112–25.

32. Ana Filipa Vrdoljak, *International Law, Museums and the Return of Cultural Objects* (Cambridge, Cambridge University Press, 2008) 26.

33. Wayne Sandholtz, 'Plunder, Restitution, and International Law' (2010) 17 *International Journal of Cultural Property* 152; Zhang (n 27) 1127–32.

34. Johann Ludwig Klüber, *Droit des gens moderne de l'Europe* (Stuttgart, 1819) Vol II, Sect II, Ch I, § 253.

35. Travers Twiss, *The Law of Nations Considered as Independent Political Communities* (1863): General Halleck of the Union Army in the American Civil War, for example, did not think that a principle of international law prevented the victors from retaining works of art from conquered territories. For the other side, Twiss quoted at length the letters of Castlereagh and Wellington, 759–60.

36. Henry Wheaton, *Elements of International Law*, 8th edn, Richard Henry Dana (ed) (1866) IV – 2–6. See also Perrot (n 16) 30, citing Calvo and Pradier-Fodéré as scholars from the late nineteenth century who supported this view.

37. Note that in the Treaty of Versailles of 1919, the Allies had required the German Government to restore to the French Government 'trophies, archives, historical souvenirs or works of art carried away from France' in the course of the Franco-Prussian War of 1870–71: Art 245, Treaty of Versailles. Though it is possible that this may have been inserted into the Treaty as a result of anti-German sentiment, rather than as a remedy for any genuine looting in the earlier conflict.

38. See the Project of an International Declaration Concerning the Laws and Customs of War ('Brussels Declaration') (Brussels, 27 August 1874): Art 39 prohibits pillage, Art 8 treats property of institutions dedicated to, inter alia, arts and sciences as private property, and Art 38 prohibits confiscation of private property (including ipso facto property listed in Art 8). Under Art 8, if there is any seizure, destruction or wilful damage of 'works of art and science' inter alia this should be made the subject of legal proceedings (perpetrators presumably to be punished and restitution ordered).

39. Institute of International Law, 'The Laws of War on Land' (Oxford Manual) (Oxford, 9 September 1880): Arts 32, 53 and 85. Note that the earlier 'Brussels Declaration' had been silent on reprisals.

40. Regulations to Convention (II) with Respect to the Laws and Customs of War on Land (The Hague, 29 July 1899), Arts 47 and 56.

41. They would be replicated in Regulations to the second Hague Convention: Convention (IV) Respecting the Laws and Customs of War on Land (The Hague, 18 October 1907).

42. See pp 56-58.

43. See p 39. The language comes from the Italian translation. In addition, the permission granted by the signatory Kaimacam was said to be in conformity with 'what is due to the friendship, sincerity, alliance and good will subsisting ab antiquo between the Sublime and ever durable Ottoman Court and that of England'.

44. This included 44 cases of marble on the *HMS Braakel* in February 1803 and the final shipment of five cases of marble on the *HMS Hydra* in April 1811. In March 1810, 48 cases were taken by a chartered ship with escort from the *HMS Pylades*: William St Clair, *Lord Elgin and his Marbles* (Oxford University Press, Oxford, 1998) 113, 158 and 160. See also Geoffrey Robertson, *Who Owns History?* (London, Biteback, 2019) 80–81.

45. Reflected in the International Law Commission's Draft Articles on the Responsibility of States for Internationally Wrongful Acts (2001), Arts 4(2) and 7, generally accepted as a codification of prior customary rules on State responsibility.

46. International Law Commission, *Draft Articles on the Responsibility of States for Internationally Wrongful Acts* (2001) Art 11. Note also that UNESCO's Intergovernmental Committee for Promoting the Return of Cultural Property to its Countries of Origin or its Restitution in Case of Illicit Appropriation issued a decision in September 2021 stating that 'the obligation to return the Parthenon Sculptures lies squarely on the United Kingdom Government', indicating that this was a matter for the State and not simply for the Museum's Trustees. See p 83.

47. See the authors Grotius, de Vattel and Twiss on the rights and duties of nations in times of peace: Grotius (n 28), Book II; de Vattel (n 26), Books I and II; Travers Twiss, *On the Law of Nations Considered as Independent Political Communities: On the Right and Duties of Nations in Time of Peace* (Oxford, University of Oxford Press, 1861).

48. Statute of the International Court of Justice (San Francisco, 26 June 1945), Art 38.

49. See Geoffrey Robertson's elaboration of these points in *Who Owns History?* (n 44) ch 6 ('International law to the rescue'). See also Catharine Titi, *The Parthenon Marbles and International Law* (Springer, 2023).

50. See Charles de Visscher, 'International Protection of Works of Art and Historic Monuments', quoted in Jeanette Greenfield, *The Return of Cultural Treasures*, 3rd edn (Cambridge, Cambridge University Press, 2007) 82.

51. World Heritage Convention, Arts 4 and 5.

52. UNESCO, Operational Guidelines for the Implementation of the World Heritage Convention, WHC 21/01 (31 July 2021) 87–89.

53. World Heritage Convention, Art 6(1).

54. World Heritage Convention, Art 6(2).

55. The Athens Charter for the Restoration of Historic Monuments, 1931.

56. The Venice Charter for the Conservation and Restoration of Monuments and Sites, 1964, Arts 4 and 8.

57. ibid Art 15.

58. See, in particular, support from ICOMOS for UNESCO mediation between Greece and the UK: Resolution 18GA 2014/40.

59. See Valetta Convention for the Protection of the Archaeological Heritage of Europe, 1992, Art 1.

60. See ch 5.

61. See Law 3028 of 2002 on the Protection of Antiquities and Cultural Heritage in General, as well as the Greek Constitution of 1975 at Art 24: Daphne Voudouri, 'Law and the Politics of the Past: Legal Protection of Cultural Heritage in Greece' (2010) 17 *International Journal of Cultural Property* 547–68, 554.

62. See Ancient Monuments and Archaeological Areas Act 1979, s 2.

63. See the reporting of legislative and administrative provisions in the World Heritage Convention, Art 29. Note also that States with civil law legal systems have principles of 'immovables by destination' whereby integral parts of buildings cannot be considered legally distinct. Similarly, integral parts of buildings are usually considered 'fixtures' under English law, and thus not freely removable: see the Planning (Listed Buildings and Conservation Areas) Act 1990, s 1(5).

64. See above note 45, and Statute of the ICJ, Art 38.

65. Statute of the ICJ, Art 36. Also included in this jurisdiction are matters specially provided for in the Charter of the United Nations, of less relevance for present purposes. Art 36(2) provides the so-called 'optional clause' whereby States can choose to accept the compulsory jurisdiction of the ICJ.

66. 1970 UNESCO Convention, Art 7(b).

67. 1970 UNESCO Convention, Art 13.

68. See generally Patrick O'Keefe, *Protecting Cultural Objects: Before and After 1970* (Builth Wells, Institute of Art and Law, 2017).

69. 1970 UNESCO Convention, Art 15. Note that UNESCO has provided Operational Guidelines to assist States in agreeing to voluntary returns of such cultural property, but they are non-binding: Operational Guidelines for the Implementation of the Convention on the Means of Prohibiting and Preventing the Illicit Import, Export and Transfer of Ownership of Cultural Property (UNESCO, Paris, 1970) 2015.

70. In ch 6, I suggested that the UK ratify this Convention. For more on it, see Lyndel V Prott, *Commentary on the 1995 Unidroit Convention*, 2nd edn (Builth Wells, Institute of Art and Law, 2021).

71. UNIDROIT Convention on Stolen or Illegally Exported Cultural Objects (Rome, 24 June 1995), Arts 3–4 for the restitution of stolen cultural objects and Arts 5–7 for the return of illegally exported cultural objects.

72. See 1954 Protocol to the Convention for the Protection of Cultural Property in the Event of Armed Conflict; see also Kevin Chamberlain, *War and Cultural Heritage*, 2nd edn (Builth Wells, Institute of Art and Law, 2015).

73. Trade and Cooperation Agreement Between the European Union and the United Kingdom, Title I, Chapter 1, Article GOODS.21: the agreement to cooperate in facilitating the return of cultural property reflects the spirit of the earlier EU Directive 2014/60/EU on the Return of Cultural Objects Unlawfully Removed from the Territory of a Member State (formerly applicable in the UK), a recast of Council Directive 93/7/EEC.

74. See also the recent work of Titi (n 49).

75. Robertson (n 44) 162.

76. ibid 162–66.

77. See the UK's Declaration Recognising the Jurisdiction of the Court as Compulsory of 22 February 2017, pursuant to Art 36(2) of the Statute of the ICJ.

78. Under Art 65 of the Statute of the ICJ and Art 96 of the Charter of the United Nations: see Robertson (n 44) 163–64.

79. Resolution adopted by the UN General Assembly on 6 December 2021 on Return or Restitution of Cultural Property to the Countries of Origin, A/RES/76/16.

80. ibid at R22; And see the Operational Guidelines for the Implementation of the Convention on the Means of Prohibiting and Preventing the Illicit Import, Export and Transfer of Ownership of Cultural Property (UNESCO, Paris, 1970) 2015.

81. See p 83. Decisions 22.COM 6 and 6g of the Intergovernmental Committee for Promoting the Return of Cultural Property to its Countries of Origin or its Restitution in Case of Illicit Appropriation, Paris, 22nd Session, 27–29 September 2021.

82. Robertson (n 44) 162–66.

Chapter 8
How to Think Like a Greek

1. The discussion took place on 14 May 2018. In addition to separately interviewing public officials in Greece for this book, my intention with this discussion was to seek out a local view on the Parthenon Marbles dispute from well-informed individuals who had no ties to either the political establishment or the museum sector. With this in mind, the group was assembled by Katerina Vagia, to whom I am most grateful. The conversation was free flowing and, unlike the other interviews I conducted for the book, it was not recorded. However, I did take shorthand notes throughout, which I have on file, and have since verified statements with the relevant speakers.

2. See the Annual Report of the Organisation for Economic Co-operation and Development (OECD), *Education at a Glance*, 2021, Chapter D, Annex 3, p 150 ('Greece').

3. See the guidelines for Year 1 Upper, Γυμνάσιο ('gymnasio') provided by the Hellenic Ministry of Education and Religious Affairs: 'Instructions for the Teaching of Modern Greek Language and Writing and Ancient Greek Language and Writing in High School for the 2018–2019 School Year': www.minedu.gov.gr/gymnasio-m-2/didaktea-yli-gymn. My thanks to Katerina Vagia and Stratos Lampousis for providing further information.

4. Ancient Greek remains compulsory only in certain classically-oriented high schools in Europe, notably the *liceo classico* in Italy (curriculum provided in Annex C of the Presidential Decree (DPR) n 89 of 15 March 2010) and at certain *gymnasia* in the Netherlands and Germany, as well as certain public schools in Britain, but nowhere else is it part of the universally compulsory education system.

5. James Knowles, 'The Joke About the Elgin Marbles' (*The Nineteenth Century*, March 1891).

6. Dorothy King, 'Elgin Marbles: Fact or Fiction' *The Guardian* (21 July 2004).

7. See Tiffany Jenkins, *Keeping Their Marbles* (Oxford, Oxford University Press, 2018) 213–19; and Sir Noel Malcolm, 'The Elgin Marbles: Keep, Lend or Return? An Analysis' (*Policy Exchange*, 2023) 36–40.

8. Ann Gibbons, 'The Greeks Really do have Near-Mythical Origins, Ancient DNA Reveals' (*Science Magazine*, 2 August 2017): from a study conducted by Harvard University and the University of Washington published in *Nature*, DNA tests have shown that the Greeks have significant genetic overlap with Ancient Mycenaeans. Another report shows that populations throughout the Mediterranean share DNA, except for mainland Greece (who appear to share more with Albanians): Elizabeth Sloane and Ruth Schuster, 'Mainland Greeks Genetically Diverged from Islanders in the Middle Ages' (*Haaretz*, 29 June 2017).

9. My interview with Elena Korka, Director of Antiquities at the Greek Ministry of Culture and Sports, 14 May 2018.

10. Quoted in George Tolias, 'National Heritage and Greek Revival: Ioannis Gennadios on the Expatriated Antiquities' in D Damaskos and D Plantzos, *A Singular Antiquity: Archaeology and Hellenic Identity in Twentieth-Century Greece* (Athens, Benaki Museum Publications, 2008) 60.

11. The Koukidis story is well known, but unconfirmed. See Bruce Clark's riveting account of the very real story of Manolis Glezos: *Athens: City of Wisdom* (London, Head of Zeus, 2022) 431–39.

12. See pp 69-73.

13. ibid.

14. Ministers Venizelos, Pangalos and Tsanetakis each became Deputy Prime Minister. Ministers Bokayanni, Venizelos and Pangalos each became Foreign Minister. And Ministers Tsanetakis, Karamanlis and Samaras were each Prime Minister at one point.

15. Lydia Korniodou, Minister of Culture and Sport, interview with the author, 17 May 2018.

16. See list on Ministry of Culture and Sport website: www.culture.gov.gr/en/parthenonas/SitePages/view.aspx?iID=13.

17. See pp 73-75.

18. See for example Ely Symons, 'Dr Lina Mendoni: Greece's Culture Minister and a Champion for the Reunification of the Parthenon sculptures' (*Neos Kosmos*, 22 April 2022) and Nick Kampouris, 'Greek Culture Minister Mendoni Slams British Museum over Parthenon Gallery's Condition' (*Greek Reporter* 11 September 2019).

19. Helena Smith, 'Greece Rebuts British Museum Claim Parthenon Marbles were "Removed from Rubble"' *The Guardian* (23 May 2022).

20. Harrison Jacobs and Tessa Solomon, 'Greece Rejects Possibility of Parthenon Marbles "Loan" in New Statement' (*ArtNEWS*, 6 January 2023).

21. See website of the Ministry of Culture and Sports, *The Restitution of the Parthenon Marbles*, and in particular the page entitled 'Sculptures removed from the Parthenon': www.culture.gov.gr/en/parthenonas/SitePages/Home.aspx.

22. See pp 16-18.

23. See pp 91-92.

24. See eg former Secretary of State Oliver Dowden's 'Letter from Culture Secretary on HM Government Position on Contested Heritage' (22 September 2020); Museums Association, 'Our Response to Oliver Dowden's Letter on Contested Heritage' (September 2020): 'We feel that this contravenes the long-established principle that national museums and other bodies operate at arm's length from government and are responsible primarily to their trustees.'

25. See pp 71-73.

26. See p 81.

27. *The Telegraph* (8 December 2014). Further, he wrote: 'The idea of sending a piece of the Elgin Marbles to the Hermitage did not need to be cleared by government. The British Museum did not obtain prior government approval … This is not a tyranny. We do not have power located in one place.'

28. Yannis Andritsopoulos, 'Exclusive: Head of British Museum held Secret Talks with Greek PM, Officials to Agree Deal for Parthenon Marbles' Return' (*Ta Nea*, 3 December 2022) [translation provided by journalist].

29. The closest would be the National Gallery of Art in Athens, which has works by Caravaggio, Delacroix, Picasso and others, but this is limited to works of fine art.

30. See pp 48-51.

31. See eg the current Sixth Grade History textbook for students in Greece: Ioannis Koliopoulos, Iakovos Michaelidis, Athanasios Kallianiotis and Charalambos Minaoglou, Ιστορία ΣΤ΄ Δημοτικού Ιστορία του νεότερου και σύγχρονου κόσμου – Βιβλίο μαθητή ('Sixth Grade History: *History of the Newer and Modern World – Student's Book*') (Diofantos Institute of Computer Technology and Publications / University Studio Press) Sect B, Ch 2: 'The living conditions of slaves – Inside the Ottoman Empire, the enslaved Greeks lived a difficult life, as they faced many discriminations, especially during the first centuries of the Turkish rule. Many of them related to taxation.' My thanks to Katerina Vagia and Stratos Lampousis for drawing this to my attention.

32. By email from Stratos Lampousis on 10 March 2023. He also indicated the famous Greek painting *The Secret School* (1885–86) by Nikolaos Gyzis, depicting a group of Greek youths being taught their language by a priest in secret during the Ottoman period.

33. See Alexander Herman, *Restitution – The Return of Cultural Artefacts* (London, Lund Humphries, 2021) 50–51.

34. See p 82-83. The Universities of Oxford, Cambridge and Aberdeen have returned (or are in the process of returning) Benin Bronzes, as has the Horniman Museum and Gardens in South London.

35. Madeleine Speed, 'The Battle to Build a Mosque in Athens' *Financial Times* (1 February 2019).

36. Demetrios Ioannou, 'Athens's First Mosque since the Nineteenth Century is a "Dream Come True"' (*Middle East Eye*, 8 November 2020).

37. Dimitrios Pandermalis, 'The Odyssey of a Museum' in *200 Years – The Parthenon Sculptures in the British Museum: New Contributions to the Issue* (Athens, Society of Friends of the Acropolis, 2016) 14.

38. See p 2.

39. Yannis Hamilakis, *The Nation and Its Ruins: Antiquity, Archaeology, and National Imagination in Greece* (Oxford, Oxford University Press, 2007) 281–82.

40. See p 67.

41. John Marshall Carter, 'The Bayeux Tapestry Across the Curriculum' (1986) 60(4) *The Clearing House* 166.

42. Communiqué from the Elysée Palace (18 January 2018) 75.

43. Nicola Slawson and Mark Brown, 'Emmanuel Macron Agrees to Loan Bayeux Tapestry to Britain' *The Guardian* (17 January 2018).

44. See Jack Maidment and Hannah Furness, 'Emmanuel Macron's Decision to let Britain borrow Bayeux Tapestry Prompts calls for UK to Loan Rosetta Stone to France' *Telegraph* (17 January 2018).

45. See Roger Fisher and William Ury, *Getting to Yes: Negotiating Agreement without Giving In* (New York, Houghton Mifflin, 1981).

Chapter 9
The Ins and Outs of the British Museum

1. This particular training took place on 24 and 26 September 2019.

2. Heritage Lottery Fund, 'British Museum Unveils the World Conservation and Exhibitions Centre', 11 July 2014: www.heritagefund.org.uk/news/british-museum-unveils-world-conservation-and-exhibitions-centre.

3. See British Museum, *Report and Accounts for the Year Ended 31 March 2022* (HC 362) 27, setting out the median remuneration of the workforce at approximately £28,100 per year, whereas the British Museum Director earned a base salary of just under £200,000, noted in the report as 7.1 times the

median remuneration (this does not include the Director's pension benefits). Meanwhile, according to the Office for National Statistics, the median annual pay for full-time employees across the UK in 2021 was £31,285: Office for National Statistics, *Census 2021 – Employee earnings in the UK: 2021*.

4. One example showing the persistence of this stance is a letter written by British Museum Deputy Director Jonathan Williams to *The Telegraph* on 21 May 2022, which states that there will 'never be a magical moment when all of the sculptures are reunited.'

5. See Cristina Ruiz, 'How the British Museum's Maintenance Woes have kept Parthenon Marbles off View for a Full Year' *The Art Newspaper* (2 November 2021); and Cristina Ruiz, 'Demonstrators Descend on the British Museum to Make the Case for Athens as the Rightful – and Safer – Home for the Parthenon Marbles' (*ArtNET News*, 20 June 2022).

6. See photographs reproduced in Ruiz, 'How the British Museum's Maintenance Woes' (n 5).

7. Quoted in Cristina Ruiz, 'Is it Raining again in the Parthenon Galleries?' *The Art Newspaper* (21 August 2021), referring to discolouration and leaks in early 2020. Note also previous leaks noted in the Greek newspaper *Ta Nea* on 11 November 1989.

8. Ruiz, 'How the British Museum's Maintenance Woes' (n 5).

9. National Audit Office, Report of the Comptroller and Auditor General, *Investigation into Maintenance of the Museum Estate*, 27 March 2020, covering the 15 museums sponsored by DCMS: the British Museum requested £48.4m for the 2016/17 to 2020/21 period and received £21.3m, Figure 5, 23. See also Ruiz, 'How the British Museum's Maintenance Woes' (n 5), reporting on this.

10. DCMS then allocated additional funding of £12m in April 2019; £5m was given in March 2020 and £9.8m in July 2021 for essential maintenance delayed by the pandemic (£2.7m for fabric and roofs of galleries): see Ruiz, 'How the British Museum's Maintenance Woes' (n 5).

11. The British Museum had operating revenue of £88.2m for 2021/22, £51.5m of which came as revenue grant-in-aid from DCMS and £2.8m from admissions income, the rest as donations/ legacies, charitable activities and trading activities: British Museum, Annual Report 2021/22, July 2022, 13 ('Grant-in-Aid'), 25 (Admissions income) and 38 (Financial statement). (It also had £20.5m in capital funds, £15.1m of which was capital grant-in-aid from DCMS, so together it had £108m.) By way of comparison, the Louvre had revenues in 2021 of €270m (equivalent to £230m), €200m of which was received from the French State as a subsidy (equivalent to £170m), an increase from the usual annual amount of €100m received in order to account for the significant loss in ticket revenue due to the pandemic (which pre-pandemic ranged between €80m and €95m): see Musée du Louvre, *Rapport d'activité* 2021, pp 188 and 251. The Metropolitan Museum in New York has an operating revenue of $252m (equivalent to £207m): Metropolitan Museum of Art, *Annual Report for the Year 2020–2021*.

12. Having reviewed the British Museum Annual Reports from 2010/11 to 2021/22, the only significant purchase of a Greek or Roman antiquity was that of a Cycladic figure in 2011/12.

13. Sam Merriman, 'George Osborne Seeks £1billion for British Museum's Radical Modernisation Project' *Daily Mail* (5 February 2022); Simon Jenkins, 'The British Museum Says it Needs £1bn to Refurbish Itself – First it Must Prove it Deserves It' *The Art Newspaper* (22 March 2022). See also Director Hartwig Fischer's statements to Martin Bailey in his interview for *The Art Newspaper* (1 September 2017), notably about how the project will make the collections on display less Eurocentric. See also the British Museum Annual Report 2020/21, at 2 ('Rosetta Project Committee') and 24 (chaired by Lord Sassoon).

14. Merriman (n 14).

15. The British Museum Fact Sheet explains that 80,000 objects are on public display at any one time, therefore 1% of the entire collection of 8 million objects: British Museum, *Fact Sheet*.

16. 'British Museum to open new £64 million research centre', *The Telegraph* (20 August 2019).

17. In the 2003/04 Financial Year, the British Museum received £37.3 million in revenue grant-in-aid from DCMS, while in 2021/22, it received £51 million in revenue grant-in-aid from DCMS, which is a slightly lesser amount when accounting for inflation (however, for 2021/22 the Museum also received £15.1 million in capital grant-in-aid for specific capital projects, such as the Archaeological Research Centre referred to above and other maintenance works, much higher than the capital grant-in-aid of 2003/04 which was £2.6m): British Museum Annual Report 2004/05 (reporting on two previous years), British Museum Annual Report 2021/22. National Audit Office, Report of the Comptroller and Auditor General, *Investigation into maintenance of the museum estate*, 27 March 2020, showed that grant-in-aid subsidises across all DCMS-sponsored museums fell by 20% when adjusted for inflation between 2010/11 and 2018/19. However, during the COVID-19 pandemic, this was significantly increased by government to account for the decline in ticket sales.

18. British Museum Act 1753, s XX.

19. See the review of this policy 10 years after being introduced: Department for Culture, Media and Sport, 'Ten Years of Free Museums: DCMS-sponsored Institutions Mark 10 years since Introduction of Universal Free Access' (1 December 2011).

20. The problem was admitted recently by one Trustee, though under cover of anonymity: see Barnaby Phillips, *Loot: Britain and the Benin Bronzes* (London, OneWorld, 2022) 266.

21. This calls to mind a scene in James Joyce's *Ulysses*, in which one character explains to another that the proudest boast of the Englishman was, 'I paid my way. I never borrowed a shilling in my life … I owe nothing.' James Joyce, *Ulysses* (1922) Episode 2.

22. Though note ss 15–16 of the Charities Act 2022, which appeared to have been passed without the Government being aware of their potential impact on the trustees of national institutions: see pp 85-86.

23. See William G. Stewart, Institute of Art and Law annual lecture, December 2000, setting out how support for the British Museum's position on the Marbles became Labour policy, seemingly by accident, following the election of 1997: published in VI *Art Antiquity and Law* 37 (March 2001).

24. See pp 84-85.

25. Statements have been made supporting the Greek position by Bill Clinton, Xi Jinping and Vladimir Putin, as well as by numerous celebrities such as George Clooney, Bill Murray, Judi Dench, Stephen Fry and scholars such as Anthony Snodgrass and Paul Cartledge (University of Cambridge). See p 153 for regulations made by foreign and international bodies.

26. See p 83.

27. This can be seen in the stated priorities of the Secretary of State for Culture, Media and Sport for the British Museum for the period 2016 to 2020 (so far unrenewed), which include ensuring free entry and protecting the collections/front-line services, but do not mention improving general maintenance of the buildings or increasing remuneration or promotional opportunities for staff: *British Museum Management Agreement 2016–2020*.

28. *Archaeologists and Aesthetes in the Sculpture Galleries of the British Museum* (London, British Museum Press, 1992), *The Parthenon Frieze* (London, British Museum Press, 2002, as updated), *The Parthenon Sculptures* (London, British Museum Press, 2007), with C Bouras and M Ioannidou (eds), *Acropolis Restored* (London, British Museum Press, 2011), *The Greek Body* (London, British Museum Press, 2009), *Defining Beauty* (London, British Museum Press, 2014).

29. He has also written about it: see, for example, 'The Parthenon and its Sculptures' in Ian Jenkins, *The Parthenon Sculptures* (British Museum Press, 2007) 30–35.

30. My interview with Jenkins took place at the British Museum on 14 March 2018; all quotes come from that interview.

31. For more on the important role of the Museum as a creature of the Enlightenment, see Tiffany Jenkins, *Keeping Their Marbles* (Oxford, Oxford University Press, 2018) 37–65; 165–69 (no apparent relation).

32. See his reference to this in *The Parthenon Sculptures* (British Museum Press, 2007) 30–31. However, he did write there that: 'The tendency of Stuart and Pars to restore the sculptures as they drew them means that their work cannot always be relied upon to give an accurate rendering of what was then extant. In some instances, however, when compared with the sculpture itself, their drawings provide clear evidence of wilful damage that took place after the sculptures were drawn and before Lord Elgin's agents rescued them at the beginning of the nineteenth century.' (p 30).

33. See p 32.

34. John Henry Merryman, 'Thinking about the Elgin Marbles' (1991) 83 *Michigan Law Review* 1984–85; see also John Henry Merryman, 'Two Ways of Thinking About Cultural Property' (1986) 80(4) *American Journal of International Law* 831–53.

35. ibid.

36. See p 20.

37. Now it is called the British Committee for the Reunification of the Parthenon Marbles, chaired by Dame Janet Suzman.

38. The results came from a seminar bringing together experts from the Acropolis and the British Museum at the British School at Athens in 2005. The British Museum provided the imaging technology that would allow archaeologists to study the polychromy at the upper reaches of the Erechtheion.

39. See p 32.

40. See British Museum, *Fact Sheet – British Museum collection*: an average of 3,823 objects are lent every year (1,982 to UK borrowers; 1,841 to international borrowers).

41. This includes a group of vases to be lent in 2023.

42. For a contrary view, see Ana Filipa Vrdoljak, *International Law, Museums and the Return of Cultural Objects* (Cambridge, Cambridge University Press, 2008) 31: 'Britain, like Napoleonic France, was not reticent in projecting its imperial ambitions through a universal survey museum befitting an imperial capital of an ever-expanding colonial empire.'

43. ibid 32.

44. As Jenkins mentioned in the interview, 'the morality of Elgin's actions was scrutinised by a Parliamentary Committee in 1816 that sat to deliberate whether the Parthenon sculptures were a suitable ornament to the nation, whether they were worthy of the national museum … just as they would be by any contemporary parliamentary select Committee'.

45. See pp 59-60.

46. Planning (Listed Building and Conservation Areas) Act 1990, s 1.

47. The phrase appears three times in the statements by the Secretary of State for Digital, Culture, Media and Sport (Michelle Donelan) and the Chair of the Reviewing Committee (Sir Hayden Phillips) accompanying the Report of the Reviewing Committee on the Export of Works of Art and Objects of Cultural Interest (2021–22), December 2022. The export control system is governed by the Export Control Act 2002 and the Export of Objects of Cultural Interest (Control) Order 2003, along with statutory guidance presented by the DCMS to Parliament from time to time according to the Export Control Act 2002, s 9(6).

48. Works that have been 'saved for the nation' include JMW Turner's *The Blue Rigi* (2007), Joshua Reynolds's *The Archers* (2005) and John Constable's *Fen Lane* (2002), as well as Raphael's *Madonna of the Pinks* (2004), Antonio Canova's *Three Graces* (1993) and Edouard Manet's *Portrait of Mademoiselle Claus* (2012).

Chapter 10
Resolving the Dispute

1. See p 102.

2. Lecture given to LLM students at the Centre for Commercial Law Studies at Queen Mary University of London in a module entitled 'Art Disputes and their Resolutions', 31 March 2023 (forming part of the LLM in Art, Business and Law run by the Centre with the Institute of Art and Law).

3. Christopher Moore, *The Mediation Process: Practical Strategies for Resolving Conflict* (New York, Wiley, 1986); 2nd edn (1996), 3rd edn (2003), 4th edn (2014).

4. For present purposes, the most useful iteration of the Circle of Conflict is to be found in the 2nd edition of Moore's book (1996). In the later fourth edition (2014), Moore has expanded the circle to include a total of eight factors that lead to conflict: history and relationships, information, structural, beliefs and values, emotions, communications, procedures, and power and influence: see Moore, *The Mediation Process*, 4th edn (n 3) 130–63. While this offers new insight into the multi-faceted causes of disputes, the earlier version of Moore's typology remains the most succinct and compelling for the purposes of the present analysis.

5. My understanding of Christopher Moore's typology and the Circle of Conflict is in large part thanks to insights provided by Dr Debbie De Girolamo, Reader in Law at the Centre for Commercial Law Studies at Queen Mary University of London and to the students of the LLM in Art, Business and Law over the past six years who have adeptly applied Moore's typology to cases in the art world, including the dispute over the Parthenon Marbles. While there are other theories of disputes, Moore's is the most complete and useful for present purposes: his work as a mediator means that he has been able to study disputes with a practical methodology that allows him to consider how they are most effectively resolved. The use of his work as a core text in the above-mentioned LLM programme also demonstrates the effectiveness of his approach in fostering a better understanding of disputes over works of art. Other theories of disputes worthy of mention can be found in William Felstiner, Richard Abel and Austin Sarat, 'The Emergence and Transformation of Disputes: Naming, Blaming and Claiming' (1980–1981) 15 *Law and Society Review* 631, and Michael Palmer and Simon Roberts, *Dispute Processes: ADR and the Primary Forms of Decision-making* (3rd edn) (Cambridge, Cambridge University Press, 2020).

6. In the fourth edition his book (2014), Moore has separated out 'procedures' as a standalone cause of conflict in the typology: Moore, *The Mediation Process*, 4th edn (n 3) 146–49.

7. See p 23.

8. See pp 73-75.

9. See pp 98-104.

10. See pp 74, 124-25.

11. See pp 119-25.

12. See pp 138-44.

13. From Prime Ministers Boris Johnson in March 2021, Liz Truss in October 2022 and Rishi Sunak in March 2023; and from former Secretary of State for Digital, Culture, Media and Sport Michelle Donelan in January 2023: see p 85.

14. Harrison Jacobs and Tessa Solomon, 'Greece Rejects Possibility of Parthenon Marbles 'Loan'' in New Statement' (*ArtNEWS*, 6 January 2023).

15. See Moore, *The Mediation Process*, 4th edn (n 3) 106-68.

16. See Robert Fisher and William Ury, *Getting to Yes: Negotiating Agreement without Giving In* (New York, Houghton Mifflin, 1981).

17. See Moore, *The Mediation Process*, 2nd edn (n 3) 60.

18. One theory of dispute resolution explains how each party needs to cast aside its preferred narrative and together construct a *third* narrative: John Winslade and Gerald Monk, *Narrative Mediation: A New Approach to Conflict Resolution* (New Jersey, Jossey-Bass, 2000). My thanks to Debbie De Girolamo for bringing this theory to my attention.

19. For an example of this, see the 2010 agreement reached by the parties in the dispute over Egon Schiele's *Portrait of Wally* (see p 98 (n 71)), as approved by the US District Court for the Southern District of New York, which includes neutral text recounting the history of the work, agreed to by the parties in the dispute, and which would henceforth be placed next to the painting: Stipulation and Order of Settlement and Discontinuance, *US v Portrait of Wally*, 99 Civ 9940 (LAP), filed 20 July 2010.

20. See pp 84-85, 102.

21. See pp 98-104.

22. As an example of this sort of agreement relating to cultural property, see the Metropolitan Museum of Art–Republic of Italy Agreement of 21 February 2006 relating to the return to Italy of the Euphronios Krater and certain other artefacts, in exchange for a rotating series of loans provisioned by Italy for the Metropolitan Museum: *International Journal of Cultural Property* (2006) 13. In the UK context, the periodic loan agreements reached between the National Gallery and the Dublin City Council around the Hugh Lane Bequest (a once disputed collection of 39 paintings that is now the subject of a longstanding arrangement between the parties) may prove instructive.

23. Arts Council England, *Restitution and Repatriation: A Practical Guide for Museums in England* (5 August 2022) 2–3, 13–14.

24. See pp 74-75; 124-25.

25. See the ICOM Code of Ethics (2017) I, IV and VI. The British Museum also abides by the UK's Museums Association Code of Ethics (2015), which upholds the same principles at 1.1–1.3 and 2.1–2.7 and in Additional Guidance (2015) at 2.2 and 2.4–2.5.

26. See pp 142-44.

27. Dominic Spenser Underhill, lecture given to LLM students at the Centre for Commercial Law Studies at Queen Mary University of London in a module entitled 'Art Disputes and their Resolutions', 31 March 2023 (forming part of the LLM in Art, Business and Law run by the Centre with the Institute of Art and Law). On the need to try to understand the other party's position, see also Fisher and Ury (n 16) 'Effective Negotiation'.

28. For an example where two parties, seemingly opposed, were able to recognise the validity of the opposing position in a written agreement, see the Metropolitan Museum of Art–Republic of Italy Agreement of 21 February 2006 relating to the return to Italy of the Euphronios Krater and certain other artefacts to Italy, in exchange for a rotating series of loans provided by Italy for the Metropolitan Museum: see *International Journal of Cultural Property* (n 22).

29. See p 141.

30. See p 71-72.

31. These related to the Phra Narai lintel in 1988 (involving the United States and Thailand), the Makonde Mask in 2010 (Switzerland and Tanzania) and the Bogazkoy Sphinx in 2011 (Turkey and Germany). These are listed on the UNESCO webpage entitled 'Cases of returns and restitutions under the aegis of the ICPRCP': en.unesco.org/fighttrafficking/Cases_of_Return_and_Restitution_ICPRCP. The other three listed cases were resolved outside the procedures of the Intergovernmental Committee.

32. Niklas Luhmann, *Legitimacy Through Procedure* (Suhrkamp Verlag GmbH, 1969) and Matthias Weller, 'Key Elements of Just and Fair Solutions' in Evelien Campfens (ed), *Just and Fair Solutions* (The Hague, Eleven International Publishing, 2015) 207.

33. For instance, the UK's Spoliation Advisory Panel for artwork lost or taken during the Nazi period or the UK's Reviewing Committee on the Export of Works of Art and Objects of Cultural Interest. See Matthias Weller's assessment, above (n 32).

34. Such as those set out in the ICOM Code of Ethics: see pp 51-53.

35. See UNESCO General Assembly Resolutions starting with Resolution No 55 of July-August 1982; UNESCO Intergovernmental Committee Decision 22.COM 6 of 27-29 September 2021; ICOM Resolution No 5 of August 1983; ICOMOS Resolution 186A 2014/40 of November 2014; European Parliament Declaration 8/98 of January 1999; New Zealand Parliament Motion of 24 May 2007; Legislative Council of the South Australian Parliament Resolution of October 2022; World Hellenic Inter-Parliamentary Association call for return of 30 July 2021; letter from the Archbishop of Great Britain to Prime Minister Rishi Sunak of 22 March 2023.

36. See YouGov polls cited at p 3.

37. For a useful study on the role played by third-party actors in disputes see Lynn Mather and Barbara Yngvesson, 'Language, Audience and the Transformation of Disputes' (1980–81) 15 *Law & Society Review* 775.

38. See p 78.

39. I thank Matthew Taylor for this information.

40. Gordon Rayner, 'Are We About to Lose 'Our' Marbles?' *The Telegraph* (19 November 2021).

41. Law 3028 on the Protection of Antiquities and Cultural Heritage in General of 2002 which allows the lending, under certain conditions, of up to five years: see art 25. See on this law Daphne Voudouri, 'Law and the Politics of the Past: Legal Protection of Cultural Heritage in Greece' (2010) *International Journal of Cultural Property* 17, 556. And note the recent emphasis of the ability for long-term loans under the new museums law of 2023.

42. See p 137.

43. See pp 100-04.

44. See p 139.

45. From the Hellenic Ministry of Culture and Sports/Acropolis Museum/Acropolis Restoration Service, *The Parthenon Frieze* (2022): parthenonfrieze.gr/en/explore-the-frieze/west-frieze/?b=12.

46. See p 44.

47. Charalambos Bouras, Maria Ioannidou and Ian Jenkins (eds), *Acropolis Restored* (London, British Museum Press, 2011) 59–62.

48. Ian Jenkins, *The Parthenon Frieze* (London, British Museum Press, 2002) 31.

BIBLIOGRAPHY

Arts Council England, *Restitution and Repatriation: A Practical Guide for Museums in England* (August 2022).

Bantekas, I, 'Land Rights in Nineteenth Century Ottoman State Succession Treaties' (2015) 26 *European Journal of International Law* 375–90.

Beard, M, *The Parthenon* (London, Profile Books, 2002).

Beard, M, 'The Latest Scheme for the Parthenon', *The New York Review of Books*, March 2014.

Benvenisti, E, *The International Law of Occupation* (Oxford, Oxford University Press, 2012).

Blackburn, S. *Ethics: A Very Short Introduction*, 2nd edn (Oxford, Oxford University Press, 2021).

Bouras, Ioannidou, Jenkins (eds), *Acropolis Restored*, British Museum Research Publication no 187 (London, British Museum Press, 2015).

Brewer, D, *The Greek War of Independence* (New York, Overlook Duckworth, 2011).

Brommer, F, *The Sculptures of the Parthenon* (London, Thames & Hudson, 1979).

Byron, Lord, *English Bards and Scotch Reviewers: A Satire* (1809).

Caygill, M, *The Story of the British Museum* (London, British Museum Press, 2002).

Chamberlain, K, *War and Cultural Heritage*, 2nd edn (Builth Wells, Institute of Art and Law, 2015).

Clark, B, *Athens: City of Wisdom* (London, Head of Zeus, 2022).

Clogg, R, *The Movement for Greek Independence 1770–1821* (New York, Barnes & Noble, 1976).

Crawford, J, 'Napoleon 1814–1815: A Small Issue of Status' in *International Law in the Long Nineteenth Century* (Boston/Leiden, Brill, 2019).

Connelly, JB, *The Parthenon Enigma* (New York, Vintage Books, 2014).

Cook, BF, *The Elgin Marbles* (London, British Museum Press, 1984).

de Lolme, JL, *The Constitution of England* (1771).

de Vattel, E, *Droit des gens* (1758).

de Visscher, C, 'International Protection of Works of Art and Historic Monuments' (1937).

Demetriades, V, 'Was the Removal of the Marbles Illegal?', Submission of the British Committee for the Restitution of the Parthenon Marbles, Appendix A, House of Commons Select Committee on the Illicit Trade (2000).

Eldem, E, 'From Blissful Indifference to Anguished Concern: Ottoman Perceptions of Antiquities, 1799–1869' in Bahrani, Z, Çelik, Z, and Eldem, E (eds), *Scramble for the Past: A Story of Archaeology in the Ottoman Empire, 1753–1914* (Istanbul, SALT, 2011) 285.

Fincham, D, 'The Parthenon Sculptures and Cultural Justice' (2013) 23 *Fordham Intellectual Property, Media & Entertainment Law Journal* 943.

Fisher R and Ury, W, *Getting to Yes: Negotiating Agreement without Giving In* (New York, Houghton Mifflin, 1981).

Gennadios, I, *Lord Elgin and Earlier Antiquarian Invaders in Greece, 1440–1837* (1930).

Gilks, D, 'Attitudes to the Displacement of Cultural Property in the Wars of the French Revolution and Napoleon' (2013) 56 *The Historical Journal* 113.

Goode R and McKendrick E, *Goode on Commercial Law*, 5th edn (London, Penguin 2016).

Greenfield, J, *The Return of Cultural Treasures*, 3rd edn (Cambridge, Cambridge University Press, 2007).

Grotius, H, *De Iure Belli ac Pacis* (1625).

Guthrie, T, 'The Elgin Marbles' in *Treasures of the British Museum*, (London, Collins, 1971).

Halsbury's Laws of England, 'Deeds and other Instruments', Vol 32 (LexisNexis Butterworths, 2012).

Hamilakis, Y (ed), *The Nation and its Ruins: Antiquity, Archaeology and National Imagination in Greece* (Oxford University Press, 2007).

Harrison, F, 'Give Back the Elgin Marbles', *The Nineteenth Century* (March 1890) 495–506.

Herman, A, 'Museums, Restitution and the New Charities Act' (October 2022) *Art Antiquity and Law* 27.

Herman, A, 'New York Court's Affirmation of Holocaust Expropriated Art Recovery Act Brings Added Challenges to Art Dealers' (April 2018) *Art Antiquity and Law* 23.

Herman, A, *Restitution: The Return of Cultural Artefacts* (London, Lund Humphries, 2021).

Hitchens, C, *The Elgin Marbles: Should they be Returned to Greece?* (London, Chatto & Windos, 1987).

Jakubowski, A, *State Succession in Cultural Property* (Oxford, Oxford University Press, 2015).

Jenkins, I, 'Acquisition and Supply of Casts of the Parthenon Sculptures by the British Museum, 1835–1939' (1990) in *Annual of British School at Athens* 85.

Jenkins, I, *The Parthenon Frieze* (London, British Museum Press, 2019).

Jenkins, I, *The Parthenon Sculptures in the British Museum* (London, British Museum Press, 2019).

Jenkins, T, *Keeping Their Marbles* (Oxford, Oxford University Press, 2018).

Keats, K, 'On Seeing the Elgin Marbles' (1817).

Klüber, JL, *Droit des gens moderne de l'Europe* (Stuttgart, 1819).

Korka, E, 'New Archival Evidence for the Chronicle of the Removal of the Parthenon Marbles by Lord Elgin' in *200 Years – The Parthenon Sculptures in the British Museum: New Contributions to the Issue* (Athens, Society of Friends of the Acropolis, 2016).

Korka, E, *Fragments of the Parthenon Sculptures Displayed in Museums Across Europe* (Athens, Greek Ministry of Culture and Sports publication, 2017).

Korres, M, *Stones of the Parthenon* (Los Angeles, Getty Publications, 2001).

Korres, M, *From Pentelicon to the Parthenon* (Athens, Melissa Publishing, 1995).

Latour, B, *Reassembling the Social: An Introduction to Actor-Network Theory* (Oxford, Oxford University Press, 2005).

Law Commission, *Technical Issues in Charity Law – Analysis of Responses* (2017).

Law Commission, *Technical Issues in Charity Law* (May 2017).

Lawrence, AW, *Greek Architecture*, 3rd edn (London, Penguin, 1973).

Lewis, B, Pellat C and Schacht J (eds), *Encyclopaedia of Islam* (London, Brill, 1965).

Lorenzen, E, 'Story's Commentaries on the Conflict of Law', *Harvard Law Review*, November 1934.

Luhmann, N, *Legitimacy Through Procedure* (Suhrkamp Verlag GmbH, 1969).

Mackenzie, M, *Turkish Athens* (Reading, Ithaca Press, 1992).

Malcolm, N, 'The Elgin Marbles: Keep, Lend or Return? An Analysis', *Policy Exchange*, 2023.

Manidaki, V, 'The Fragmentation of the Parthenon Frieze' in *200 Years: The Parthenon Marbles in the British Museum* (Athens, Society of the Friends of the Acropolis, 2016).

Mantis, A 'Disjecta Membra: The dismemberment and dispersal of the Acropolis Antiquities' in *200 Years – The Parthenon Sculptures in the British Museum: New Contributions to the Issue* (Athens, Society of Friends of the Acropolis, 2016).

Mather, L and Yngvesson, B, 'Language, Audience and the Transformation of Disputes' (1980–1981) 15 *Law & Society Review* 775.

Merryman, JH, 'Thinking about the Elgin Marbles' (1984–1985) 83 *Michigan Law Review* 1881.

Merryman, JH, 'Two Ways of Thinking About Cultural Property' (1986) 80(4) *American Journal of International Law* 831–53.

Miles, M, *Art as Plunder: The Ancient Origins of the Debate About Cultural Property* (Cambridge, Cambridge University Press, 2010);

Moore, C, *The Mediation Process: Practical Strategies for Resolving Conflict* (New York, Wiley, 1986); 2nd edn (1996), 3rd edn (2003), 4th edn (2014).

O'Connor, AM, *The Lady in Gold: The Extraordinary tale of Gustav Klimt's Masterpiece* (London, Penguin, 2015).

O'Keefe, P, *Protecting Cultural Objects: Before and After 1970* (Builth Wells, Institute of Art and Law, 2017).

Palmer, N, *Palmer on Bailment*, 3rd edn (Sweet and Maxwell, 2009).

Pandermalis, D, *Acropolis Museum Guide* (Athens, Acropolis Museum, 2015).

Pausanias, *Description of Greece*.

Pearson, E, 'Old Wounds and New Endeavours: The Case for Repatriating the Gweagal Shield from the British Museum' (XXI) *Art Antiquity and Law* 201 (October 2016).

Perrot, X, 'La restitution internationale des biens culturels aux XIXe et XXe siècles' (thesis) (Limoges, Université de Limoges, 2005).

Phillips, B, *Loot: Britain and the Benin Bronzes* (London, OneWorld, 2022).

Plutarch, *The Life of Pericles*.

Pollock, F, 'An Essay on Possession in the Common Law' (Oxford, Clarendon Press, 1888)

Poulou, T, 'Giovanni Battista Lusieri, Lord Elgin's Unknown Agent and his Excavations in Athens', *200 Years: The Parthenon Sculptures in the British Museum: New Contributions to the Issue* (Athens, Society of Friends of the Acropolis, 2016).

Prott, L, *Commentary on the 1995 Unidroit Convention*, 2nd edn (Builth Wells, Institute of Art and Law, 2021).

Prott, L and O'Keefe, P, *Law and the Cultural Heritage*, Vol 1 (Abingdon, Professional Books, 1984).

Quynn, DM, 'The Art Confiscations of the Napoleonic Wars' (1945) 50 *The American Historical Review* 437.

Redmond-Cooper, R (ed), *Heritage Ancestry and Law: Dealing with Historical Human Remains* (Builth Wells, Institute of Art and Law, 2015).

Report from the Select Committee of the House of Commons on the Earl of Elgin's Collection of Sculpted Marbles; &c, Minutes of Evidence (29 February 1816).

Robertson, G, *Who Owns History?* (London, Biteback Publishing, 2019).

Rudenstine, D, 'A Tale of Three Documents: Lord Elgin and the Missing Historic 1801 Ottoman Document' (2001) 22 *Cardozo Law Review* 1853.

Rudenstine, D, 'Lord Elgin and the Ottomans: the Question of Permission' (2002) 23 *Cardozo Law Review* 449.

Rudenstine, D, 'Trophies for the Empire' (2021) 39 *Cardozo Law Review* 436.

Saltzman, C, *Plunder: Napoleon's Theft of Veronese's Feast* (London, Thames & Hudson, 2021).

Sandholtz, S, 'Plunder, Restitution, and International Law' (2010) 17 *International Journal of Cultural Property* 152.

Sandholtz, W, *Prohibiting Plunder: How Norms Change* (Oxford, Oxford University Press, 2008).

Savoy, B '1815. Année zéro. L'Europe à l'heure des restitutions d'oeuvres d'art', Lecture series, Collège de France, Session 9, Paris, 19 April 2019.

Scovazzi, T, 'Evolutionary Trends as regards the Return of Removed Cultural Property' in Durban and Lazari (eds), *El tráfico de bienes culturales* (Valencia, Tirant lo Blanch, 2015) 26. See also Giancarlo Cunial, *Canova. Le molte vite* (Veneto, Acelum 2022).

Smith, AH, 'Lord Elgin and his Collection' (1916) 36 *Journal of Hellenistic Studies*.

von Martens, GF, *Précis du droit des gens moderne de l'Europe* (1789).

St Clair, W, 'Imperial Appropriations of the Parthenon' in JH Merryman (ed), *Imperialism, Art and Restitution* (Cambridge, Cambridge University Press, 2006).

St Clair, W, *Lord Elgin and the Marbles* (Oxford, Oxford University Press, 1998).

St Clair, W, 'The Elgin Marbles: Questions of Stewardship and Accountability' (1999) 8 *International Journal of Cultural Property* 391.

St Clair, W, *Who Saved the Parthenon? A New History of the Acropolis Before, During and After the Revolution* (Open Book Publishing, 2022) 670–72.

Stuart and Revett, *The Antiquities of Athens* (1762, 1789, 1794).

Stewart, WG, 'The Marbles: Elgin or Parthenon?' (2001) VI *Art Antiquity and Law* 37.

Stirk, P, *The Politics of Military Occupation* (Edinburgh, Edinburgh University Press, 2009) 44.

Swallow, C, *The Sick Man of Europe: Ottoman Empire to Turkish Republic, 1789–1923* (London, Ernest Benn, 1973).

Thucydides, *History of the Peloponnesian War*.

Titi, C, *The Parthenon Marbles and International Law* (Springer, 2023).

Tolias, G, 'National Heritage and Greek Revival: Ioannis Gennadios on the Expatriated Antiquities' in Damaskos, D, and Plantzos, D, *A Singular Antiquity: Archaeology and Hellenic Identity in Twentieth-Century Greece* (Athens, Benaki Museum Publications, 2008).

Twiss, T, *The Law of Nations Considered as Independent Political Communities* (1863).

Wheaton, H, *Elements of International Law*, 8th edn, Richard Henry Dana (ed) (1866).

Vigderman, P, *The Real Life of the Parthenon* (Athens, Ohio, Ohio State University Press, 2018).

Voudouri, D, 'Law and the Politics of the Past: Legal Protection of Cultural Heritage in Greece' (2010) 17 *International Journal of Cultural Property* 548.

Vrdoljak, AF, *International Law, Museums and the Return of Cultural Objects* (Cambridge, Cambridge University Press, 2008).

Vrettos, T, *The Elgin Affair: The True Story of the Greatest Art Theft in History* (New York, Arcade Publishing, 2011).

Weller, M, 'Key Elements of Just and Fair Solutions' in Evelien Campfens (ed), *Just and Fair Solutions* (The Hague, Eleven International Publishing, 2015).

Williams, D, 'Lord Elgin's *firman*' (2009) *Journal of the History of Collections* 1–28.

Wilson, D, *The British Museum: A History* (London, British Museum Press, 2002).

Woodhead, C, 'The Changing Tide of Title to Cultural Heritage Objects in UK Museums' (2015) 22 *International Journal of Cultural Property*, 229.

Winslade, J and Monk, G, *Narrative Mediation: A New Approach to Conflict Resolution* (New Jersey, Jossey-Bass, 2000).

Wycherley, RE, *The Stones of Athens* (Princeton, Princeton University Press, 1978).

Zambon, A, *Aux origines de l'archéologie en Grèce – Fauvel et sa méthode* (Paris, INHA, 2014).

Zhang, Y, 'The Right to Restitution of Cultural Property Removed as Spoils of War during Nineteenth-century International Warfare' *University of Pennsylvania Journal of International Law* [2021] 1097.

INDEX

Note: to avoid scattering of entries 'Ottoman' has been used rather than 'Turkish' except where 'Turkish' refers to the language or to Turkish matters going beyond the Ottomans.

impediments
  bribery and corruption: *see* bribery and
    corruption
  legality/morality of: *see* legality of permission
    to remove the Marbles; morality/
    ethics of taking the Marbles
  original plan (facsimile copies/casts of the
    artefacts), 25–6
    access to the Acropolis/loss of/recovery, 26–7
    initial steps (sketching of
      accessible sites), 26
  the team, 24–5
    absence of an archaeologist or
      antiquarian, 25–6
    Balestra, Vincenzo (architectural
      draughtsman) with his apprentice, 23–4
    Hunt, Philip: *see* Hunt, Philip
      (Elgin's chaplain and agent)
    Ivanovitch, Feodor (painter and
      monumental drinker), 24
    Lusieri: *see* Lusieri, Giovanni Battista
    mould plasterers, 25
  value of the collection, 54
Erechtheion (c430 BCE)
  see also Caryatids (Erechtheion)
  alleged triton damage, 160n20
  classical Acropolis building, 1, 67
  polychromy, 185n39
  post-independence, 67
ethics/ethics codes: *see* **morality/ethics of**
  taking of the Marbles

Fauvel, Louis-François-Sébastien (French
  antiquarian) (Acropolis enterprise)
  activity in Athens (1780–1798), 33
    access to the Acropolis/failure to achieve
      permission to remove artefacts, 33, 61
  claim that the French Ambassador had saved
    the Parthenon's west frieze in situ,
    44, 156
  imprisonment (1798–1804), 33–4
  successful attempt to get Lusieri's activities
    banned (1804/1805), 34, 44–5
Fifth Century Athens
  an empire in the making, 12
  as leader of the Delian League/peace with
    Persia (449 BCE), 12
  Marbles as link with, 2–3
  modern respect for, 2–3
  Persian sacking (480 BCE), 12
Finland
  immunity of State-owned cultural property
    from seizure while on loan, 101

firman, **definition,** 37–9
  see also Kaimacam letter (6 July 1801)
  indiscriminate use of, 38
  required elements, 38
France
  see also Napoleon Bonaparte
  access to the Acropolis/Fauvel enterprise, 26,
    33, 34, 36, 44, 62, 156
  Egypt, activity in/*égyptologistes*, 27–8
  Elgin as prisoner of war (1803–1806), 24
  relations with the Ottoman Turks, 23, 26, 44
  restitution policy (Macron's proposals), 6–7
    loan of the Bayeux tapestry to Britain, 130–1
    return of 'African heritage' to Africa, 82
    return of part of the Parthenon frieze to
      Greece, 83
Fry, Stephen (campaigner for return), 4, 78,
  85, 170 n1

Germany
  acquisition of title, 89
    a foot from the Parthenon north frieze,
      173 n79
  Greek language in, 182 n4
  immunity of State-owned cultural property
    from seizure while on loan, 101
  restitution policy
    return of the Benin Bronzes, 82, 127
    return of the Bogazkoy Sphinx to Turkey
      (2011) (ICPRCP procedure), 152
gifts: *see* **bribery and corruption in the**
  Ottoman empire
Greece: *see* **Greece under Ottoman rule/**
  as 'occupation'; Greek legisla-
  tion; Greek Ministry/Ministers
  of Culture; Greek perspective;
  Mercouri, Melina; Papandreou,
  George (Greek Foreign Minister
  (1999–2004)/PM (2009–2011))
Greece under Ottoman rule/as 'occupation',
  48–51
  see also occupation, classification as
  arrival of the Ottomans (1458), 49
  Athenians' clear dislike of Ottoman regime, 50
  attempts to throw off the Ottoman rule,
    49–50
    see also Venetian bombardment (1687)
  Battle of Navarino (1827), 167 n85
  British recognition of Greece's 'belligerent
    rights', 50
  continuation into the 20th century, 126–7
  effect on the acquisition of the Parthenon
    Marbles, 51